A Course In Miracles
Abridged Edition

WHAT IF WE ALL GO TO HEAVEN?

ABRIDGED BY STAN HERRMANN

AUTHOR HELEN SCHUCMAN

Helen Schucman (Author, Editor) and William T. Thetford (Editor)

Abridged by: Stan Herrmann

Copyright © 2016 by Stan Herrmann

All rights reserved.

No part of this book may be reproduced or transmitted in any form or by means, electronic or mechanical, including photo copying, recording, or by any information storage or retrieval system, without permission in writing from the publisher.

ISBN-13: 978-1977852458
ISBN-10: 1977852459

Library of Congress Control Number: 2017913425

CreateSpace Independent Publishing Platform, North Charleston, SC

Acknowledgments:

Interior and cover design by Rebecca Shaw (shawrh@bellsouth.net)
Content Editor and Advisor: Jessie Gunn

This book's goal is happiness and peace.

It presents a thought system intended to inspire a universal spiritual experience.

It is not a doctrinal religion, nor the only way.

◆ ◆ ◆

"No one who lives in fear is really alive."

"For a miracle is now, it stands already here, in present grace."

"There is no journey. There is only an awakening."

ACIM

◆ ◆ ◆

www.ACIM-A.org

Table of Contents

Preface vii
About this Book ix
About the Sub-title: What if we all go to Heaven? x
The Origins of A Course in Miracles xi
What is *A Course in Miracles*? xii
The Purpose of Abridging *A Course in Miracles* xiii
The Process of Abridging *A Course in Miracles* xiv
The Good News xv
Beyond Words xvi
Thoughts on Gender Terminology xvii
Important Keywords to Understand Prior to Reading this Book xix

A Course in Miracles - Introduction 1
Chapter 1 The Meaning of Miracles 3
Chapter 2 The Separation and the Atonement 7
Chapter 3 The Innocent Perception 15
Chapter 4 The Illusions of the Ego 23
Chapter 5 Healing and Wholeness 31
Chapter 6 The Lessons of Love 39
Chapter 7 The Gifts of the Kingdom 47
Chapter 8 The Journey Back 57
Chapter 9 The Acceptance of the Atonement 65
Chapter 10 The Idols of Sickness 73
Chapter 11 God or the Ego 79
Chapter 12 The Holy Spirit's Curriculum 89
Chapter 13 The Guiltless World 99
Chapter 14 Teaching for Truth 113
Chapter 15 The Holy Instant 125
Chapter 16 The Forgiveness of Illusions 137
Chapter 17 Forgiveness and the Holy Relationship 147
Chapter 18 The Passing of the Dream 155

Chapter 19	The Attainment of Peace	165
Chapter 20	The Vision of Holiness	175
Chapter 21	Reason and Perception	181
Chapter 22	Salvation and the Holy Relationship	191
Chapter 23	The War Against Yourself	199
Chapter 24	The Goal of Specialness	205
Chapter 25	The Justice of God	213
Chapter 26	The Transition	223
Chapter 27	The Healing of the Dream	233
Chapter 28	The Undoing of Fear	243
Chapter 29	The Awakening	249
Chapter 30	The New Beginning	257
Chapter 31	The Final Vision	265
Glossary		277
The Foundation for Inner Peace		285
Book Recommendations		287

PREFACE

In 2012, I became aware of a book called *A Course in Miracles* (ACIM). I read a few pages and found that it was full of heavy religious and figurative language, making it awkward and difficult to read. So I gave up and put it on my bookshelf. About a year later, ACIM was referenced in another book I was reading, which prompted me to pull it off the bookshelf and give it one more try. I then decided to make a focused commitment to understand what this book was about. As I read, it became clear that this book was my path home.

While I continued to immerse myself in it, I discovered an internal awakening that was profoundly instructive and inspiring. As I enjoyed the experience of the book I was also puzzled there weren't more people reading it. Then, I remembered my own introductory experience of how I almost dismissed it, and understood why people may not give it a chance. That day I became aware of a need to abridge the lengthy text.

The devotion behind this work was driven by the passion to offer an alternative to those who might not read the 290,000 word original textbook. I took on the responsibility of the abridgment with a very sincere intention. Throughout the process, within every chapter, every section, every page, and every sentence I sought Higher Guidance for the wisdom to discern what words to keep and what words to omit.

This abridgment is not intended to replace the original version, yet it offers plenty of incredible insights that will hopefully encourage you to embark on a life-changing internal awakening of your own.

I know that this abridgment is not for everyone, nevertheless I trust that this book will reach those who would realize it to be *their* path home too.

Blessings,

Stan Herrmann

Palo Alto, California

ABOUT THIS BOOK

This book is an abridgment of the textbook titled, *A Course in Miracles*. It has sold over 2.5 million copies and has been translated into 25 languages. While this book uses Christian vernacular, it is not fixed in Christian theology. It offers a multitude of universal truths for everyone.

The emphasis of this book is to encourage the application of practical spiritual directives, such as:

- Forgiveness as an alternative to judgment
- Joy as a substitute for confusion
- Oneness to dissolve separation
- Peace to disarm conflict
- Love to dispel fear
- God instead of the ego

Spiritual directives are meant to steer us toward connection and harmony and show us how to extend love. The directives in this book are to *train our minds* to increasingly become aware of **what we are**. Awareness of this truth in our daily lives will transform our experiences. Awareness is a redeeming tool when used on the path to peace.

Intellectual understanding of words does not bring peace. Peace comes through *perceptual miracles* that remove the obstacles to the awareness that God is within us. Through that awareness we begin to understand the role the mind plays in the escape from fear. When we know **what we are**, we are liberated to extend and receive love.

On the journey to realize God is within us, we make choices that impact our daily involvements. God allows each of us to use our free will to make those choices. This book teaches us how to decide to experience the joy of the eternal, without the reliance on the external.

About the Sub-title: *What if we all go to Heaven?*

Is there a Heaven? Is there a hell? What are they? Where are they?

No one actually knows. They remain physically indefinable. Nevertheless, many attempts have been made to explain them, whether it be from words in a religious book, someone's experiences or opinions (stories).

Heaven and hell are words that have been around for thousands of years. Each of us decides what we want these mystical words to embody. We may perceive them as fearful or joyful, or even non-existent, but it is our choice as to the amount of influence they have in our lives.

In this book, "Heaven" and "hell" have specific meaning, which if accepted, can be used to guide us "where" we want to go.

Heaven: It is a state of mind in which we see the world as a place of union, peace, joy and serenity, without the veil of fear upon it. It is an awareness of perfect unity, and the knowledge that there is nothing else; nothing outside this unity. Heaven can be experienced in the world through the channel of unified relationships; which is accomplished through the extending and receiving of love and acceptance.

hell: It is a state of mind in which we seem to be separate, vulnerable, deficient, unfulfilled, and mistreated. A feeling that someone or something is trying to control or harm us, and we have to fight or flee to be safe. It is the pursuit of the egoic thought system which leads us to selfish and destructive behaviors that are rooted in fear and guilt; which cause pain and suffering to us and others.

This book teaches us how to differentiate the truth from the false, then make the choice for truth; this is the key to our eternal awakening. As we wake up from the dream of a false reality that we are separated from God, we will escape the ravages of hell (fear) and transcend into experiencing the peace and joy of Heaven that is always available right now.

Timeless eternity is our divine home, however; while in this world of time we are confronted with choices - love or fear, guilt or innocence, oneness or separation.

Heaven or hell? We decide.

THE ORIGINS OF *A COURSE IN MIRACLES*

Helen Schucman scribed the *A Course in Miracles* between 1965 and 1972 through a process of inner dictation. Helen did not believe in God, and always leaned on scientific explanations. She was a clinical and research psychologist, and an Associate Professor of Medical Psychology at the Columbia University College of Physicians and Surgeons at the Columbia-Presbyterian Medical Center in New York City. It was an incredible shock to her when a distinct voice became present in her mind that was not her own. It made no sound, rather a rapid inner dictation.

As the divine Voice dictated, Helen wrote the messages down in a fully conscious state. The internal voice was remarkably consistent, as Helen could stop the dictation when interrupted and then continue at the next opportunity. Having written the dictations down by hand, Helen would then read them aloud to her colleague William Thetford, who transcribed them on a typewriter. They continued this process for seven years until the main textbook and two other working manuals were completed. The first edition was thereafter published in 1975.

WHAT IS *A COURSE IN MIRACLES*?

A Course in Miracles defines "miracle" as a divine healing of human perception; a change of mind that shifts perception from *fear and guilt* to *love and forgiveness*. This higher level of perception heals the mind from pain and suffering and places it in the service of spirit.

The Course was scribed as Jesus being the author, and it is full of universal spiritual directives. It is not a doctrinal religion and makes no claim of being the only way. It uses heavy figurative and poetically structured language which requires focused, thoughtful reading. Its *language* style combines spiritual inspiration with a psychological framework to help us to understand, and consider changing, our current belief systems, perceptions and assigned identities.

Personal transformation will occur if we are willing to question and examine every value we hold, and to be ready to see things differently. While reading this text, one will find his/herself undertaking the challenge of recognizing the difference between beliefs that are rooted in *fear and guilt,* and those that incorporate *love and forgiveness.*

This book teaches us how to uncover and extend the love that is already within each of us. Its collective universal themes can provide a lifetime of spiritual practice, and also can be an additional spiritual reference for those pursuing other spiritual paths.

Beyond the questions, the text provides so many answers to our doubts, fears, and misgivings. It encourages us to be mindful and attentive so we can hear the Internal Teacher, which lifts the veil of separation to allow us to experience the joy and connection of our divine oneness.

THE PURPOSE OF ABRIDGING *A COURSE IN MIRACLES*

There are some who have questioned why abridge the original textbook version of *A Course in Miracles*. This abridged book is not meant to replace or diminish the original version – it is simply an alternative. I cherish the original version, nonetheless I felt a special call to create a shorter version for those who might not want to read the lengthy original. The overarching message for awakening is present in both versions.

It is not necessary to believe every word in this book, words are only symbols. However, words can provide the mind with a context to assist in awakening. Projections and perceptions are responsible for how we interact with the world. Undesirable interactions will change when we see the world from the standpoint of truth. This transformational book will help teach how to awake to that truth. As the veil between the mind and the truth is lifted, peace and joy will spring into awareness and the fears of the world will fall away.

The Course is a signpost guiding us to a heavenly home; a finger pointing to God. I hope this book will stir up an inner experience, and an outward application that will fill your heart and provide a foundation to your awakening journey.

The Process of Abridging *A Course in Miracles*

The original text is written in two levels: the practical level and the theoretical level. This abridgment's emphasis is on the practical level, while I was extremely careful to stay true to the principles of the original.

The abridgment removed approximately 165,000 words from the original. There was no new content added, and no rearrangement of any text. The abridgment was achieved by truncating or removing sentences and paragraphs. Some words, punctuations, transitions, and conjunctions were added or removed to sustain grammatical contextual correctness.

This book is not meant to build or sustain doctrine, as doctrine can distract from spiritual simplicity and cause one to elevate concepts above love's message. The abridgment, like the original, is to increase our encounters with *perceptual miracles*, which bring clarity to confusion and peace to our purpose.

If you enjoy this abridgment, I would suggest reading the entire A Course In Miracles Combined Volume which can be purchased at www.acim.org.

The Good News

The goal of *A Course in Miracles* is to help us increase our awareness of love's presence. This brings happiness and peace. This book explains the basis for fear and guilt, and how they can transcend into love and forgiveness.

Fear is triggered by a belief in the "lack of love". The truth is that God's love is unconditional and unlimited. It is our perceptions that keep us from experiencing and expressing that love.

Our ego (a set of beliefs) was molded from years of social and behavioral experiences. Through those years, our mind became filled with false perceptions that cause fear and guilt, and now we find reasons to blame ourselves, others, and circumstances for our unhappiness.

We need a Guide to help us correct our perceptions of fear so that we can find our way back home to experience love's presence. The key to finding this healing path is by consciously being aware of "whose" voice is guiding us. Every moment we have the opportunity to choose between the voice of the ego, or the Voice for God (our heavenly Guide).

We approach greater happiness and peace when we choose to side with God. This is the fertile ground where miracles change our perceptions that lead to an awakening of the mind. We begin to assume a more authentic identity, wherein the world of fear transforms into a place filled with opportunities to learn how we can each "see" love's presence.

This book empowers us to embrace our true Identity, liberating us to receive and extend the joy of Heaven for ourselves and for others.

Beyond Words

Perceptions define how we see the world, and this book inspires us to change the very perceptions that keep us stuck in fear. The text is written in the voice of Jesus (as our brother), who poetically encourages us to be mindful of our thoughts and feelings, which in turn helps us to identify and then abandon beliefs founded on fear, guilt and separation.

As with any spiritual writing, it is not intended for every word in this book be taken literally. If we pursue God through the lens of literalism, it limits our thinking and we can become captive to rigid viewpoints. Spiritual writings are meant to be explored and questioned with the purpose of gaining more profound wisdom and insight into our Self that God created, and thereby deepening our connection to Him.

Our spiritual heart yearns to experience the love of the Creator. Words can be a useful guide, but words are not the end-point. The challenge is always to look beyond the surface of words; to hear the Internal Voice calling us to wake up to what is true. Words can reveal spiritual truth, but they are not the embodiment of truth.

Words fall short because they are only symbols, and symbols are multifaceted. How does one explain, with words, the fragrance of a rose? Words can only symbolize the reality of the rose's aroma. Ultimately, our true desire is to experience the sweet perfume of the rose; after which, any word describing its fragrance becomes inferior.

Words are a rudder; a beacon lighting the way to *experience* God's fragrance. It is divine when words transform our worldly perceptions into an internal knowing of the Christ within. Seeing others through Christ's vision changes our judgments of separation into actions of connection and allows us to practice love's unity. Christ consciousness becomes the doorway to Heaven, and our attachment to words slowly fades into the background.

> [**Note**: *Words are the method of human communication fashioned into a language consisting of one or more spoken sounds or their written representation. They are symbols used to achieve the goal of sharing meaning with others. Words are affected by factors such as culture, ethnicity, personal bias, idioms, paradigms, metaphors, analogies, semantics, syntactics, pragmatics, denotations, connotations, sarcasm, and figures of speech. Words can be powerful; however, the power is not in the words themselves, rather the power is generated within the interpreter. As we use words, we are expressing our thoughts, creating and changing our thoughts, which continually build and shape our perceptions. They can be helpful or hurtful.*]

THOUGHTS ON GENDER TERMINOLOGY

God is not a "He". God is the infinite and eternal Source of all that exists. The One who has no gender, no form, and no ego. One who is pure love, without any anger or attack, supporting our journey to find our divine Self.

A Course In Miracles teaches that the way to universal love and peace is by undoing guilt through forgiving others. ACIM is a spiritual and instructional text from Jesus to us. So, it's understandable that the text is written in the literary-style of Christianity. Judeo-Christian texts were written during a patriarchal period when masculine pronouns, such as "He, Father, Son, Mankind, Sonship, Brother, etc." were the style of the day. Those masculine terms in ACIM are not used in order to diminish the female gender, but rather to generalize all humans under these pronouns.

If ACIM used gender-neutral terms instead, it would weaken the rhythmic poetic resonance that this text possesses. Words are symbols used for communicating, and the intention of the Course's words is to be wholly inclusive to all of creation. Its major theme is unity and oneness encouraging us all to join together to awaken from separation into joining as One Creation.

If we find ourselves bothered by gender-specific words, or by any words, it's a great opportunity to ask ourselves why that is. Words, after all, are completely neutral. It is we, the perceivers of those words who assign them any value or meaning.

In a spiritual pursuit we desire a collective experience of oneness, not the words of oneness. As we challenge ourselves to see the world through the eyes of Christ, we will see everyone as the same, and great joy will fill our hearts.

Important Keywords to Understand Prior to Reading this Book

miracle	A divine healing of human perception; a change of mind that shifts perception from guilt and fear to love and forgiveness. The undoing of delusions and illusions through divine revelation. It is an awakening that heals the mind from pain and suffering.
ego	The ego is a part of the mind (a set of beliefs) that promotes fear and separation. It tenaciously seeks for validation and fulfillment in the material world. Conditions in the material world are the results of projections, perceptions, and actions involving our emotions, thoughts, and attitudes. The ego habitually involves itself in various dramas and struggles, aggrandizing the little self and its story in order to distract us from our real purpose of knowing God and His Creations. The process of *waking up* and getting beyond the ego's deceptions is the pathway to salvation, and finding peace, joy, and contentment in this world.
love	The essence of *being*; which contains the emotions of acceptance, peace and joy. Love is already within each of us, and as the blocks to love's awareness are removed (such as; guilt, shame, etc.), we become mindful that love always has and always will encircle us and everything.
God	The infinite and eternal Source of all that exists. The One Who has no gender, no form, and no ego. One Who is pure Love, without any anger or attack.
Holy Spirit	The communication link from God to us, the Voice for God, the Internal Teacher. The Holy Spirit's function is (1) to translate the fear we see in the world into the knowledge that fear is a false perception (2) to show us that separation is error and how to express love's unity through forgiveness (3) to teach us the joy of *what we are*.

Atonement	Rectifying the false belief in the separation of God and human by accepting the Truth that we are One with God. The release from guilt by complete acceptance through forgiveness; the knowledge that we are all joined together and not separate.
sin	A mistake, error, wrong decision, or imagining against God's laws or goodness. It is the lack of love. The belief that we are separated from God and this causes us to withdraw from Him into a state of folly. We think God demands punishment and the ego's goal is to make sin a permanent reality. Yet, to God, sin is simply an error and therefore easily forgiven and healed.
body	A physical instrument (device) our mind uses to communicate with the outer world. The body is neutral and has no opinions or influence of its own. Only the mind assigns meaning to things.
Christ	Our shared Identity of Oneness. The *Self* that God created by the extension of His Spirit. Our spiritual Identity.
Christ vision	Spiritual sight; seeing beyond the body and the ego. Interpreting others behaviors as (1) an act of love or (2) a calling out for love. *Seeing* both as no reason for defense or attack, and every reason for extending love. The ability to mentally *see* beyond all worldly interference and *see* the light of holiness in everything.
Jesus	One of God's Sons, and brother to us all. Jesus serves as our role model in the awakening unto Christ consciousness.
Son of God	We are all the One Son of God. Mankind is not separate from the universal Self Who encompasses all beings.
perception	The manner in which we process our understanding of the world around us, which we inherently see as entirely separate from ourselves. Perceptions define how we see the world; some perceptions are right-minded some are wrong-minded. Both influence our thoughts, beliefs, actions, and feelings. Miracles change distorted perceptions into perceptions that foster love.
mind	The expression of the self that includes awareness, choice, thought, and emotion. Mind is non-physical, not to be confused with the brain.

split-mind — A mind divided among two parts; the "right mind" or home of God, and the "wrong mind" or home of the ego. The right mind espouses love, acceptance, and peace, while the wrong mind promulgates fear, sin, and guilt. In this divided state, the mind can become confused and short-circuits, cutting off our ability to create and communicate with others and God.

special relationship — A relationship with someone that we think will contribute to our specialness and save us from the perceived lack we feel within ourselves. This love is not real and will sooner or later end in disappointment. God's answer to this mistaken endeavor is to create holy relationships joined together by His Love. Refer to holy relationship in the back of this book.

Heaven — It is a state of mind in which we see the world as a place of union, peace, joy and serenity, without the veil of fear upon it. It is an awareness of perfect unity, and the knowledge that there is nothing else; nothing outside this unity. Heaven can be experienced in the world through the channel of unified relationships; which is accomplished through the extending and receiving of love and acceptance.

hell — It is a state of mind in which we seem to be separate, vulnerable, deficient, unfulfilled, and mistreated. A feeling that someone or something is trying to control or harm us, and we have to fight or flee to be safe. It is the pursuit of the egoic thought system which lead us to selfish and destructive behaviors that are rooted in fear and guilt; which cause pain and suffering to us and others.

crucifixion — The crucifixion is the symbol of the ego, whereas the resurrection is the symbol of awakening. Each day, each hour and minute, we are deciding between the crucifixion and the resurrection; between the ego and God. The ego is the choice for guilt, and God is the choice for guiltlessness.

forgiveness — Seeing ourselves and others with the vision of Christ which shifts our perception away from blame, resentment, judgment, punishment, and differences. Being able to take ownership of our thoughts and actions without fear. In this way, we can view wrongness as a projection of separation, and understand that forgiveness is the plan for salvation.

illusion	Something that deceives by producing a false or misleading impression of reality.
content and form	All things in this world have two aspects, the *form* and the *content*. *Form* refers to "the things" in the world while *content* is the meaning behind those things. We must realize that what will bring lasting change in us is not the change of form, but a change in how we perceive the meaning (content) of things.
time and space	The "physical world" which is home to illusions of separation, where the body and mind are acting out in a linear progression. The "place" where love and fear, joy and pain, forgiveness and judgment, peace and attack, birth and death occur. It is where past, present, and future compete for our attention, with past and future dominating our thoughts, distracting us from the reality of the present. To the struggling-self, it is a prison; to the awakening-Self, it is classroom.
awaken	A shift in consciousness. An apperception of true reality which had been previously unrealized. The continuance of such realizations brings us to the recognition of our oneness with all of existence.
holy instant	Any moment when we still our minds and become centered and present. In this stillness, we have no sense of fear, and nothing stands in the way of our connection to God's acceptance. We are illuminated with true oneness and freedom. The holy instant is a learning device that can be used to teach and share love's meaning, a moment we can experience the feeling of peace, joy, and love; a release from past and future; alignment with unity and oneness. It is an opportunity to receive guidance, and identify with what we are. Ultimately, our goal is to make every instant a holy instant.

[**Note**: *See Glossary in the back of the book for more definitions.*]

A Course In Miracles
Abridged Edition

AUTHOR HELEN SCHUCMAN

ABRIDGED BY STAN HERRMANN

A Course in Miracles - Introduction

This is a course in miracles.

The course does not aim at teaching the meaning of love, for that is beyond what can be taught. It does aim, however, at removing the blocks to the awareness of love's presence, which is your natural inheritance. The opposite of love is fear, but what is all-encompassing can have no opposite.

This course can therefore be summed up very simply in this way:

Nothing real can be threatened.
Nothing unreal exists.
Herein lies the peace of God.

Chapter 1

The Meaning of Miracles

[Note: A Course in Miracles defines "miracle" as a divine healing of human perception; a change of mind that shifts perception from fear and guilt to love and forgiveness. This higher level of perception heals the mind from pain and suffering and places it in the service of spirit.]

1.1. Principles of Miracles

Miracles are a kind of exchange. Like all expressions of love, which are always miraculous in the true sense, they bring more love both to the giver and the receiver.

Prayer is the medium of miracles. It is a means of communication of the created with the Creator. Through prayer love is received, and through miracles love is expressed.

A miracle is a service. It is the maximal service you can render to another. It is a way of loving your neighbor as yourself. You recognize your own and your neighbor's worth simultaneously.

Miracles reawaken the awareness that the spirit, not the body, is the altar of truth.

Miracles are natural signs of forgiveness. Through miracles you accept God's forgiveness by extending it to others.

Miracles praise God through you. They heal because they deny body-identification and affirm spirit-identification.

Miracles honor you because you are lovable. They dispel illusions about yourself and perceive the light in you. They thus atone for your errors by freeing you from your nightmares. By releasing your mind from the imprisonment of your illusions, they restore your sanity.

Chapter 1

Miracles restore the mind to its fullness.

Miracles are examples of right thinking, aligning your perceptions with truth as God created it.

The Holy Spirit is the mechanism of miracles. He separates the true from the false by His ability to perceive totally rather than selectively.

A major contribution of miracles is their strength in releasing you from your false sense of isolation, deprivation and lack.

The miracle is an expression of an inner awareness of Christ and the acceptance of His Atonement.

1.2. Revelation and Miracles

You are free to believe what you choose, and what you do attests to what you believe.

Revelation is intensely personal and cannot be meaningfully translated. That is why any attempt to describe it in words is impossible. Revelation induces only experience. Miracles, on the other hand, induce action. In this phase of learning, working miracles is important because freedom from fear cannot be thrust upon you. Revelation is literally unspeakable because it is an experience of unspeakable love.

1.3. Atonement and Miracles

You are the work of God, and His work is wholly lovable and wholly loving. This is how a man must think of himself in his heart, because this is what he is.

I am the only one who can perform miracles indiscriminately, because I am the Atonement. You have a role in the Atonement which I will dictate to you. Ask me which miracles you should perform. This spares you needless effort, because you will be acting under direct communication. The impersonal nature of the miracle is an essential ingredient, because it enables me to direct its application, and under my guidance miracles lead to the highly personal experience of revelation. A guide does not control but he does direct, leaving it up to you to follow. "Lead us not into temptation" means "recognize your errors and choose to abandon them by following my guidance."

You respond to what you perceive, and as you perceive so shall you behave. The Golden Rule asks you to do unto others as you would have them do unto you. This means that the perception of both must be accurate. The Golden Rule is the rule for appropriate behavior. You cannot behave appropriately unless you perceive correctly. Since you and your neighbor are equal members of one family, as you perceive both so you will do to both. You should look out from the perception of your own holiness to the holiness of others.

Miracles arise from a mind that is ready for them. As an expression of what you truly are, the miracle places the mind in a state of grace. The mind then naturally welcomes the Host within and the stranger without. When you bring in the stranger, he becomes your brother.

1.4. The Escape from Darkness

The escape from darkness involves two stages: First, the recognition that darkness cannot hide. This step usually entails fear. Second, the recognition that there is nothing you want to hide even if you could. This step brings escape from fear. When you have become willing to hide nothing, you will not only be willing to enter into communion but will also understand peace and joy.

Holiness can never be really hidden in darkness, but you can deceive yourself about it. This deception makes you fearful because you realize in your heart it is a deception, and you exert enormous efforts to establish fears reality. The miracle sets reality where it belongs. Reality belongs only to spirit, and the miracle acknowledges only truth. The miracle thus dispels illusions about yourself, and puts you in communion with yourself and God. The miracle joins in the Atonement by placing the mind in the service of the Holy Spirit. This establishes the proper function of the mind and corrects its errors, which are merely lacks of love. Your mind can be possessed by illusions, but spirit is eternally free. If a mind perceives without love, it perceives an empty shell and is unaware of the spirit within. But the Atonement restores spirit to its proper place. The mind that serves spirit is invulnerable.

Those who perceive and acknowledge that they have everything have no needs of any kind. The purpose of the Atonement is to restore everything to you; or rather, to restore it to your awareness. You were given everything when you were created, just as everyone was.

1.5. Wholeness and Spirit

The miracle is much like the body, in that both are learning aids for facilitating a state in which they become unnecessary. While you believe you are in a body, however, you can choose between loveless and miraculous channels of expression. You did not create yourself.

God is not partial. All His children have His total Love, and all His gifts are freely given to everyone alike. "Except ye become as little children" means that unless you fully recognize your complete dependence on God, you cannot know the real power of the Son in his true relationship with the Father. The specialness of God's Sons does not stem from exclusion but from inclusion. All my brothers are special.

1.6. The Illusion of Needs

Lack implies that you would be better off in a state somehow different from the one you are in. You act according to the particular order of needs you establish. This, in turn, depends on your perception of what you are.

A sense of separation from God is the only lack you really need correct. This sense of separation would never have arisen if you had not distorted your perception of truth, and had thus perceived yourself as lacking.

In sorting out the false from the true, the miracle proceeds along these lines:

Perfect love casts out fear.
If fear exists, then there is not perfect love.

Believe this and you will be free. Only God can establish this solution, and this faith is His gift.

1.7. Distortions of Miracle Impulses

Your distorted perceptions produce a dense cover over miracle impulses, making it hard for them to reach your own awareness. The confusion of miracle impulses with physical impulses is a major perceptual distortion. All real pleasure comes from doing God's Will. Do not deceive yourself into believing that you can relate in peace to God or to your brothers with anything external.

Child of God, you were created to create the good, the beautiful and the holy. Do not forget this.

This is a course in mind training. All learning involves attention and study at some level.

Chapter 2

The Separation and the Atonement

2.1. The Origins of Separation

There is no emptiness in you. Because of your likeness to your Creator you are creative. No child of God can lose this ability because it is inherent in what he is, but he can use it inappropriately by projecting. The inappropriate use of projection, or extension, occurs when you believe that some emptiness or lack exists in you, and that you can fill it with your own ideas instead of truth. This process involves the following steps:

> *First, you believe that what God created can be changed by your own mind.*
> *Second, you believe that what is perfect can be rendered imperfect or lacking.*
> *Third, you believe that you can distort the creations of God, including yourself.*
> *Fourth, you believe that you can create yourself, and that the direction of your own creation is up to you.*

None of this existed before the separation. Everything God created is like Him. Extension, as undertaken by God, is similar to the inner radiance that the children of the Father inherit from Him. Its real source is internal.

The Garden of Eden, or the pre-separation condition, was a state of mind in which nothing was needed. When Adam listened to the "lies of the serpent," all he heard was untruth. You do not have to continue to believe what is not true unless you choose to do so. All that can literally disappear in the twinkling of an eye because it is merely a mis-perception.

All fear is ultimately reducible to the basic mis-perception that you have the ability to usurp the power of God. Of course, you neither can nor have been able to do this. Here is the real basis for your escape from fear.

2.2. The Atonement as Defense

You can do anything I ask. I have asked you to perform miracles, and I have made it clear that miracles are natural, corrective, healing and universal. There is nothing they cannot do, but they cannot be performed in the spirit of doubt or fear. When you are afraid of anything, you are acknowledging its power to hurt you. Remember that where your heart is, there is your treasure also. You believe in what you value. If you are afraid you will inevitably value wrongly, and by endowing all thoughts with equal power will inevitably destroy peace. That is why the Bible speaks of "the peace of God which passeth understanding." This peace is totally incapable of being shaken by errors of any kind. It denies the ability of anything not of God to affect you. This is the proper use of denial. It is not used to hide anything, but to correct error.

True denial is a powerful protective device. You can and should deny any belief that *error* can hurt you. This kind of denial is not a concealment but a correction. Your right mind depends on it. Denial of error is a strong defense of truth, but denial of truth results in mis-creation, the projections of the ego. In the service of the right mind the denial of error frees the mind, and re- establishes the freedom of the will. When the will is really free it cannot mis-create, because it recognizes only truth.

Everyone defends his treasure, and will do so automatically. The real questions are: "what do you treasure?", and "how much do you treasure it?" Once you have learned to consider these questions and to bring them into all your actions, you will have little difficulty in clarifying the means.

The Atonement is the final lesson. Learning, like the classrooms in which it occurs, is temporary. The ability to learn has no value when change is no longer necessary. The eternally creative have nothing to learn. You can learn to improve your perceptions, and can become a better and better learner. This will bring you into closer and closer accord with the Sonship, but the Sonship itself is a perfect creation and perfection is not a matter of degree. Only while there is a belief in differences is learning meaningful.

2.3. The Altar of God

The Atonement can only be accepted within you by releasing the inner light. The many body fantasies in which minds engage arise from the distorted belief that the body can be used as a means for attaining "atonement." Perceiving the body as a temple is only the first step in correcting this distortion, because it alters only part of it. It does recognize that Atonement in physical terms is impossible. The next step, however, is to realize that a temple is not a structure at all. Its true holiness lies at the inner altar around which the structure is built. The emphasis on beautiful structures is a sign of the fear of Atonement, and an unwillingness to reach the altar itself. The real beauty of the temple cannot be seen with the physical eye. Spiritual sight, on the other hand, cannot see the structure at all because it is perfect vision. It can, however, see the altar with perfect clarity.

For perfect effectiveness the Atonement belongs at the center of the inner altar, where it undoes the separation and restores the wholeness of the mind. Before the separation the mind was invulnerable to fear, because fear did not exist. Both the separation and the fear are mis-creations that must be undone for the restoration of the temple, and for the opening of the altar to receive the Atonement.

Eventually everyone begins to recognize, however dimly, that there must be a better way. As this recognition becomes more firmly established, it becomes a turning point. This ultimately reawakens spiritual vision, simultaneously weakening the investment in physical sight.

Spiritual vision literally cannot see error, and merely looks for Atonement. All solutions the physical eye seeks dissolve. Spiritual vision looks within and recognizes immediately that the altar has been defiled and needs to be repaired and protected. Perfectly aware of the right defense it passes over all others, looking past error to truth. Because of the strength of its vision, it brings the mind into its service. This re-establishes the power of the mind and makes it increasingly unable to tolerate delay, realizing that it only adds unnecessary pain. As a result, the mind becomes increasingly sensitive to what it would once have regarded as very minor intrusions of discomfort.

The children of God are entitled to the perfect comfort that comes from perfect trust. Until they achieve this, they waste themselves and their true creative powers on useless attempts to make themselves more comfortable by inappropriate means. But the real means are already provided, and do not involve any effort at all on their part. The Atonement is the only gift that is worthy of being offered at the altar of God, because of the value of the altar itself. It was created perfect.

Whenever you are afraid you are deceived, and your mind cannot serve the Holy Spirit. This starves you by denying you your daily bread. God is lonely without His Sons, and they are lonely without Him. They must learn to look upon the world as a means of healing the separation.

2.4. Healing as Release from Fear

All healing is essentially the release from fear. To undertake this you cannot be fearful yourself. You do not understand healing because of your own fear.

A major step in the Atonement plan is to undo error at all levels. Sickness or "not-right-mindedness" is the result of level confusion, because it always entails the belief that what is amiss on one level can adversely affect another. We have referred to miracles as the means of correcting level confusion, for all mistakes must be corrected at the level on which they occur. Only the mind is capable of error. The body can act wrongly only when it is responding to mis-thought.

The body is merely part of your experience in the physical world. Its abilities can be and frequently are over evaluated. However, it is almost impossible to deny its existence in this world. Those who do so are engaging in a particularly unworthy form of denial. The term "unworthy" here implies only that it is not necessary to protect the mind by denying the unmindful. If one denies this unfortunate aspect of the mind's power, one is also denying the power itself.

The whole aim of the miracle is to raise the level of communication, not to lower it by increasing fear.

2.5. The Function of the Miracle Worker

It is essential to remember that only the mind can create, and that correction belongs at the thought level. The spirit is already perfect and therefore does not require correction. The body does not exist except as a learning device for the mind. This learning device is not subject to errors of its own, because it cannot create. It is obvious, then, that inducing the mind to give up its mis-creations is the only application of creative ability that is truly meaningful.

Corrective learning always begins with the awakening of spirit, and the turning away from the belief in physical sight. This often entails fear, because you are afraid of what your spiritual sight will show you. Spirit cannot see error, and is capable only of looking beyond it to the defense of Atonement.

The fear of healing arises in the end from an unwillingness to accept unequivocally that healing is necessary. What the physical eye sees is not corrective, nor can error be corrected by any device that can be seen physically. As long as you believe in what your physical sight tells you, your attempts at correction will be misdirected. The real vision is obscured, because you cannot endure to see your own defiled altar.

This is because healing rests on charity, and charity is a way of perceiving the perfection of another even if you cannot perceive it in yourself.

2.5.a. Special Principles of Miracle Workers

In time we exist for and with each other. In timelessness we coexist with God.

You can do much on behalf of your own healing and that of others, if in a situation calling for help, you think of it this way:

> I am here only to be truly helpful.
> I am here to represent Him Who sent me.

I do not have to worry about what to say or what to do, because He Who sent me will direct me.
I am content to be wherever He wishes, knowing He goes there with me.
I will be healed as I let Him teach me to heal.

2.6. Fear and Conflict

You may believe that you are responsible for what you do, but not for what you think. The truth is that you are responsible for what you think, because it is only at this level that you can exercise choice. What you do comes from what you think. You cannot separate yourself from the truth by "giving" autonomy to behavior. Whenever you are afraid, it is a sure sign that you have allowed your mind to mis-create and have not allowed me to guide it.

It is pointless to believe that controlling the outcome of mis-thought can result in healing. When you are fearful, you have chosen wrongly. That is why you feel responsible for it. You must change your mind, not your behavior, and this is a matter of willingness. You do not need guidance except at the mind level. Correction belongs only at the level where change is possible. Change does not mean anything at the symptom level, where it cannot work.

The correction of fear is your responsibility. When you ask for release from fear, you are implying that it is not. You should ask, instead, for help in the conditions that have brought the fear about. These conditions always entail a willingness to be separate. At that level you can help it. You are much too tolerant of mind wandering, and are passively condoning your mind's mis-creations. The particular result does not matter, but the fundamental error does. The correction is always the same. Before you choose to do anything, ask me if your choice is in accord with mine. If you are sure that it is, there will be no fear.

Fear is always a sign of strain, arising whenever what you want conflicts with what you do. This situation arises in two ways:

> *First, you can choose to do conflicting things, either simultaneously or successively. This produces conflicted behavior, which is intolerable to you because the part of the mind that wants to do something else is outraged.*

> *Second, you can behave as you think you should, but without entirely wanting to do so. This produces consistent behavior, but entails great strain.*

In both cases, the mind and the behavior are out of accord, resulting in a situation in which you are doing what you do not wholly want to do. This arouses a sense of coercion that usually produces rage, and projection is likely to follow. Whenever there is fear, it is because you have not made up your mind. Your mind is therefore split, and your behavior inevitably becomes erratic.

Chapter 2

Correcting at the behavioral level can shift the error from the first to the second type, but will not obliterate the fear.

The Holy Spirit cannot ask more than you are willing to do. The strength to do comes from your undivided decision. There is no strain in doing God's Will as soon as you recognize that it is also your own. Only your mind can produce fear. It does so whenever it is conflicted in what it wants, producing inevitable strain because wanting and doing are discordant. This can be corrected only by accepting a unified goal.

The first corrective step in undoing the error is to know first that the conflict is an expression of fear. Say to yourself that you must somehow have chosen not to love, or the fear could not have arisen. Then the whole process of correction becomes nothing more than a series of pragmatic steps in the larger process of accepting the Atonement as the remedy.

These steps may be summarized in this way:

> *Know first that this is fear.*
> *Fear arises from lack of love.*
> *The only remedy for lack of love is perfect love.*
> *Perfect love is the Atonement.*

It is obvious, then, that when you are afraid, you have placed yourself in a position where you need Atonement. You have done something loveless, having chosen without love. This is precisely the situation for which the Atonement was offered. The need for the remedy inspired its establishment. As long as you recognize only the need for the remedy, you will remain fearful. However, as soon as you accept the remedy, you have abolished the fear. This is how true healing occurs.

Everyone experiences fear. Yet it would take very little right thinking to realize why fear occurs. Few appreciate the real power of the mind, and no one remains fully aware of it all the time. However, if you hope to spare yourself from fear there are some things you must realize, and realize fully. The mind is very powerful, and never loses its creative force. It never sleeps. Every instant it is creating. It is hard to recognize that thought and belief combine into a power surge that can move mountains. It appears at first glance that to believe such power about yourself is arrogant, but that is not the real reason you do not believe it. You prefer to believe that your thoughts cannot exert real influence because you are actually afraid of them. This may allay awareness of the guilt, but at the cost of perceiving the mind as impotent. If you believe that what you think is ineffectual you may cease to be afraid of it, but you are hardly likely to respect it. There are no idle thoughts. All thinking produces form at some level.

2.7. Cause and Effect

You may still complain about fear, but you nevertheless persist in making yourself fearful. I have already indicated that you cannot ask me to release you from fear. I know it does not exist, but you do not. If I intervened between your thoughts and their results, I would be tampering with a basic law of cause and effect; the most fundamental law there is. I would hardly help you if I depreciated the power of your own thinking. This would be in direct opposition to the purpose of this course. It is much more helpful to remind you that you do not guard your thoughts carefully enough. You may feel that at this point it would take a miracle to enable you to do this, which is perfectly true. You are not used to miracle-minded thinking, but you can be trained to think that way. All miracle workers need that kind of training.

I cannot let you leave your mind unguarded, or you will not be able to help me. Miracle working entails a full realization of the power of thought in order to avoid mis-creation. The miracle worker must have genuine respect for true cause and effect as a necessary condition for the miracle to occur.

Both miracles and fear come from thoughts. If you are not free to choose one, you would also not be free to choose the other. By choosing the miracle you have rejected fear, if only temporarily. You have been fearful of everyone and everything. You are afraid of God, of me and of yourself. You have misperceived or mis-created Us, and believe in what you have made. You would not have done this if you were not afraid of your own thoughts. The fearful must mis-create, because they misperceive creation. When you mis-create, you are in pain. The fundamental conflict in this world, then, is between creation and mis-creation. All fear is implicit in the second, and all love in the first. The conflict is therefore one between love and fear.

Nothing and everything cannot coexist. To believe in one is to deny the other. Fear is really nothing and love is everything. Whenever light enters darkness, the darkness is abolished. What you believe is true for you. In this sense the separation has occurred, and to deny it is merely to use denial inappropriately. However, to concentrate on error is only a further error.

It should especially be noted that God has *only one* son. If all his creations are his sons, every one *must* be an integral part of the whole Sonship. The Sonship in its oneness transcends the sum of its parts. That is why the conflict cannot ultimately be resolved until all the parts of the Sonship have returned. Only then can the meaning of wholeness in the true sense be understood. Any part of the Sonship can believe in error or incompleteness if he so chooses The correction of this error is the Atonement.

We have already attempted to correct the fundamental error that fear can be mastered, and have emphasized that the only real mastery is through love.

2.8. The Meaning of the Last Judgment

The Last Judgment is one of the most threatening ideas in your thinking. This is because you do not understand it. Judgment is not an attribute of God.

The Last Judgment is a final healing rather than a meting out of punishment, however much you may think that punishment is deserved. Punishment is a concept totally opposed to right-mindedness, and the aim of the Last Judgment is to restore right- mindedness to you. The Last Judgment might be called a process of right evaluation. It simply means that everyone will finally come to understand what is worthy and what is not. After this, the ability to choose can be directed rationally. Until this distinction is made, however, the vacillations between free and imprisoned *will* cannot but continue.

The first step toward freedom involves a sorting out of the false from the true. At this point, the mind can begin to look with love on its own creations because of their worthiness. At the same time the mind will inevitably disown its mis-creations which, without belief, will no longer exist.

The term "Last Judgment" is frightening not only because it has been projected onto God, but also because of the association of "last" with death. This is an outstanding example of upside-down perception. If the meaning of the Last Judgment is objectively examined, it is quite apparent that it is really the doorway to life. No one who lives in fear is really alive.

Chapter 3

The Innocent Perception

3.1. Atonement without Sacrifice

The crucifixion did not establish the Atonement; the resurrection did.

Persecution frequently results in an attempt to "justify" the terrible mis-perception that God Himself persecuted His Own Son on behalf of salvation.

God does not believe in retribution. His Mind does not create that way. He does not hold your "evil" deeds against you.

Sacrifice is a notion totally unknown to God. It arises solely from fear, and frightened people can be vicious. Sacrificing in any way is a violation of my injunction that you should be merciful even as your Father in Heaven is merciful. Good teachers never terrorize their students. To terrorize is to attack, and this results in rejection of what the teacher offers. The result is learning failure.

The lion and the lamb lying down together symbolize that strength and innocence are not in conflict, but naturally live in peace. "Blessed are the pure in heart for they shall see God" is another way of saying the same thing. A pure mind knows the truth and this is its strength. It does not confuse destruction with innocence because it associates innocence with strength, not with weakness.

Innocence is incapable of sacrificing anything, because the innocent mind has everything and strives only to protect its wholeness. The Atonement itself radiates nothing but truth. It therefore epitomizes harmlessness and sheds only blessing. The resurrection demonstrated that nothing can destroy truth. Good can withstand any form of evil, as light abolishes forms of darkness. The Atonement is therefore the perfect lesson.

The innocence of God is the true state of the mind of His Son. In this state your mind knows God, for God is not symbolic; He is Fact. Knowing His Son as he is, you realize that the

Atonement, not sacrifice, is the only appropriate gift for God's altar, where nothing except perfection belongs.

3.2. Miracles as True Perception

Innocent or true perception means that you never misperceive and always see truly.

The miracle perceives everything as it is. If nothing but the truth exists, right-minded seeing cannot see anything but perfection. This, then, is all the innocent can see. They do not suffer from distorted perception.

Nothing can prevail against a Son of God who commends his spirit into the Hands of his Father. By doing this the mind awakens from its sleep and remembers its Creator. All sense of separation disappears. Because their hearts are pure, the innocent defend true perception instead of defending themselves against it.

Understanding the lesson of the Atonement they are without the wish to attack, and therefore they see truly. This is what the Bible means when it says, "When he shall appear (or be perceived) we shall be like him, for we shall see him as he is."

The way to correct distortions is to withdraw your faith in them and invest it only in what is true. Truth overcomes all error, and those who live in error and emptiness can never find lasting solace. If you perceive truly you are canceling out mis-perceptions in yourself and in others simultaneously. Because you see them as they are, you offer them your acceptance of their truth so they can accept it for themselves. This is the healing that the miracle induces.

3.3. Perception versus Knowledge

We have been emphasizing perception, and have said very little about knowledge as yet. This is because perception must be straightened out before you can know anything. To know is to be certain, and certainty is strength. Perception is temporary. As an attribute of the belief in space and time, it is subject either to fear or to love. Mis-perceptions produce fear and true perceptions foster love, but neither brings certainty because all perception varies. That is why it is not knowledge. True perception is the basis for knowledge, but knowing is the affirmation of truth and beyond all perceptions.

All your difficulties stem from the fact that you do not recognize yourself, your brother or God. To recognize means to "know again," implying that you knew before. You can see in many ways because perception involves interpretation. The miracle, being a way of perceiving, is not knowledge. It is the right answer to a question, but you do not question when you know. Questioning illusions is the first step in undoing them. The miracle, or the right answer, corrects them. Since perceptions change, their dependence on time is obvious. How you perceive at any given time determines what you do, and actions must occur in time. Knowledge is timeless, because certainty is not questionable. You *know*, when you have ceased to ask questions.

The questioning mind perceives itself in time, and therefore looks for future answers. The closed mind believes the future and the present will be the same. This establishes a seemingly stable state that is usually an attempt to counteract an underlying fear that the future will be worse than the present. This fear inhibits the tendency to question at all.

The Bible tells you to know yourself, or to be certain. Certainty is always of God. When you love someone you perceive him as he is, and this makes it possible for you to know him. Until you first perceive him as he is you cannot know him. Certainty does not require action. When you say you are acting on the basis of knowledge, you are really confusing knowledge with perception. Knowledge is the result of revelation and induces only thought. Even in its most spiritualized form perception involves the body. Knowledge comes from the altar within and is timeless because it is certain. To perceive the truth is not the same as to know it.

Right perception is necessary before God can communicate directly to His altars, which He established in His Sons. There He can communicate His certainty, and His knowledge will bring peace without question. God is not a stranger to His Sons, and His Sons are not strangers to each other.

If you attack "error" in another, you will hurt yourself. You cannot know your brother when you attack him. Attack is always made upon a stranger. You are making him a stranger by mis-perceiving him, and so you cannot know him. It is because you have made him a stranger that you are afraid of him. Perceive him correctly so that you can know him. There are no strangers in God's creation. To create as He created you can create only what you know, and therefore accept as yours. God knows His children with perfect certainty. He created them by knowing them. He recognizes them perfectly. When they do not recognize each other, they do not recognize Him.

3.4. Error and the Ego

Consciousness, the level of perception, was the first split introduced into the mind after the separation, making the mind a perceiver rather than a creator. Consciousness is correctly identified as the domain of the ego. The ego is a wrong-minded attempt to perceive yourself as you wish to be, rather than as you are.

You have every reason to feel afraid as you perceive yourself. This is why you cannot escape from fear until you realize that you did not and could not create yourself. You can never make your mis-perceptions true, and your creation is beyond your own error. That is why you must eventually choose to heal the separation.

The mind returns to its proper function only when it wills to know. This places it in the service of spirit, where perception is changed.

I demonstrated both the powerlessness of the body and the power of the mind. By uniting my will with that of my Creator, I naturally remembered spirit and its real purpose. I cannot unite your will with God's for you, but I can erase all mis-perceptions from your mind if you will bring it under my guidance. Only your mis-perceptions stand in your way. Without them your choice is certain. Sane perception induces sane choosing. I cannot choose for you, but I can help you make your own right choice. "Many are called but few are chosen" should be, "All are called but few choose to listen." Therefore, they do not choose right. The "chosen ones" are merely those who choose right sooner. Right minds can do this now, and they will find rest unto their souls. God knows you only in peace, and this is your reality.

3.5. Beyond Perception

Prayer is a way of asking for something. It is the medium of miracles. But the only meaningful prayer is for forgiveness, because those who have been forgiven have everything. The prayer for forgiveness is nothing more than a request that you may be able to recognize what you already have. You have lost the knowledge that you yourself are a miracle of God. Creation is your Source and your only real function.

Perception is impossible without a belief in "more" and "less." At every level it involves selectivity. Perception is a continual process of accepting and rejecting, organizing and reorganizing, shifting and changing. Evaluation is an essential part of perception, because judgments are necessary in order to select.

Forgiveness is the healing of the perception of separation. Correct perception of your brother is necessary, because minds have chosen to see themselves as separate. Spirit knows God completely. That is its miraculous power. The fact that each one has this power completely is a condition entirely alien to the world's thinking. The world believes that if anyone has everything, there is nothing left.

Since perception rests on lack, those who perceive have not totally accepted the Atonement and given themselves over to truth. Perception is based on a separated state, so that anyone who perceives at all needs healing. Communion, not prayer, is the natural state of those who know. God and His miracle are inseparable. How beautiful indeed are the Thoughts of God who live in His light! Your worth is beyond perception because it is beyond doubt. Do not perceive yourself in different lights. Know yourself in the One Light where the miracle that is you is perfectly clear.

3.6. Judgment and the Authority Problem

Judgment is symbolic because beyond perception there is no judgment. When the Bible says "Judge not that ye be not judged," it means that if you judge the reality of others you will be unable to avoid judging your own.

The choice to judge rather than to know is the cause of the loss of peace. Judgment is the process on which perception but not knowledge rests. I have discussed this before in terms of the selectivity of perception, pointing out that evaluation is its obvious prerequisite. Judgment always involves rejection. It never emphasizes only the positive aspects of what is judged, whether in you or in others.

You have no idea of the tremendous release and deep peace that comes from meeting yourself and your brothers totally without judgment. When you recognize what you are and what your brothers are, you will realize that judging them in any way is without meaning. You do not need judgment to organize your life, and you certainly do not need it to organize yourself.

Yet if you wish to be the author of reality, you will insist on holding on to judgment. You will also regard judgment with fear, believing that it will someday be used against you. This belief can exist only to the extent that you believe in the efficacy of judgment as a weapon of defense for your own authority.

The authority problem is "the root of all evil".

When you have an authority problem, it is always because you believe you are the author of yourself and project your delusion onto others. You then perceive the situation as one in which others are literally fighting you for your authorship. This is the fundamental error of all those who believe they have usurped the power of God. This belief is very frightening to them, but hardly troubles God. He is, however, eager to undo it, not to punish His children, but only because He knows that it makes them unhappy. God's creations are given their true Authorship, but you prefer to be anonymous when you choose to separate yourself from your Author. Being uncertain of your true Authorship, you believe that your creation was anonymous. This leaves you in a position where it sounds meaningful to believe that you created yourself. The dispute over authorship has left such uncertainty in your mind that it may even doubt whether you really exist at all.

Only those who give over all desire to reject can know that their own rejection is impossible. You have not usurped the power of God, but you have lost it. Fortunately, to lose something does not mean that it has gone. It merely means that you do not remember where it is. Its existence does not depend on your ability to identify it, or even to place it. It is possible to look on reality without judgment and merely know that it is there.

Peace is a natural heritage of spirit. Everyone is free to refuse to accept his inheritance, but he is not free to establish what his inheritance is. The problem everyone must decide is the fundamental question of authorship. All fear comes ultimately, and sometimes by way of very devious routes, from the denial of Authorship. The offense is never to God, but only to those who deny Him. To deny His Authorship is to deny yourself the reason for your peace, so that you see yourself only in segments. This strange perception is the authority problem.

There is no one who does not feel that he is imprisoned in some way. If this is the result of his own free will he must regard his will as not free, or the circular reasoning in this position would be quite apparent. Free will must lead to freedom. Judgment always imprisons because it separates segments of reality by the unstable scales of desire. Wishes are not facts. To wish is to imply that willing is not sufficient. Yet no one in his right mind believes that what is wished is as real as what is willed. Instead of "Seek ye first the Kingdom of Heaven" say, "Will ye first the Kingdom of Heaven," and you have said, "I know what I am and I accept my own inheritance. "

3.7. Creating versus the Self-Image

Every system of thought must have a starting point. It begins with either a making or a creating. Their resemblance lies in their power as foundations. Their difference lies in what rests upon them. Both are cornerstones for systems of belief by which one lives. It is a mistake to believe that a thought system based on lies is weak. Nothing made by a child of God is without power. It is essential to realize this, because otherwise you will be unable to escape from the prison you have made.

You cannot resolve the authority problem by depreciating the power of your mind. To do so is to deceive yourself, and this will hurt you because you really understand the strength of the mind. You also realize that you cannot weaken it, any more than you can weaken God. The "devil" is a frightening concept because he seems to be extremely powerful and extremely active. He is perceived as a force in combat with God, battling Him for possession of His creations. The devil deceives by lies, and builds kingdoms in which everything is in direct opposition to God. Yet he attracts men rather than repels them, and they are willing to "sell" him their souls in return for gifts of no real worth. This makes absolutely no sense.

All beliefs are real to the believer.

The mind can make the belief in separation very real and very fearful, and this belief is the "devil." It is powerful, active, destructive and clearly in opposition to God, because it literally denies His Fatherhood. Look at your life and see what the devil has made. But realize that this making will surely dissolve in the light of truth, because its foundation is a lie. Your creation by God is the only Foundation that cannot be shaken, because the light is in it. Your starting point is truth, and you must return to your Beginning. Much has been seen since then, but nothing has really happened. Your Self is still in peace, even though your mind is in conflict. You have not yet gone back far enough, and that is why you become so fearful. As you approach the Beginning, you feel the fear of the destruction of your thought system upon you as if it were the fear of death. There is no death, but there is a belief in death.

Be glad! The light will shine from the true Foundation of life, and your own thought system will stand corrected. It cannot stand otherwise. You who fear salvation are choosing death. Life and death, light and darkness, knowledge and perception, are irreconcilable. To believe that they can be reconciled is to believe that God and His Son can not. Only the oneness of knowledge is free of conflict. Your Kingdom is not of this world because it was given you from beyond this world. Only in this world is the idea of an authority problem meaningful. The world is not left by death but by truth, and truth can be known by all those for whom the Kingdom was created, and for whom it waits.

CHAPTER 4

THE ILLUSIONS OF THE EGO

Introduction

The Bible says that you should go with a brother twice as far as he asks. Devotion to a brother cannot set you back, it can lead only to mutual progress. To be egocentric is to be dis-spirited, but to be Self-centered in the right sense is to be inspired or in spirit. The truly inspired are enlightened and cannot abide in darkness.

You can speak from the spirit or from the ego, as you choose. If you speak from spirit you have chosen to "Be still and know that I am God." These words are inspired because they reflect knowledge. If you speak from the ego you are disclaiming knowledge instead of affirming it, and are thus dis-spiriting yourself. Do not embark on useless journeys, because they are indeed in vain. The ego may desire them, but spirit cannot embark on them because it is forever unwilling to depart from its foundation.

The journey to the cross should be the last "useless journey." Do not dwell upon it, but dismiss it as accomplished. If you can accept it as your own last useless journey, you are also free to join my resurrection. Until you do so your life is indeed wasted. It merely re-enacts the separation, the loss of power, the futile attempts of the ego at reparation, and finally the crucifixion of the body, or death. Such repetitions are endless until they are voluntarily given up. Do not make the pathetic error of "clinging to the old rugged cross." The only message of the crucifixion is that you can overcome the cross. Until then you are free to crucify yourself as often as you choose. This is not the gospel I intended to offer you. We have another journey to undertake, and if you will read these lessons carefully they will help prepare you to undertake it.

4.1. Right Teaching and Right Learning

A good teacher must believe in the ideas he teaches, but he must meet another condition; he must believe in the students to whom he offers the ideas.

Chapter 4

Many stand guard over their ideas because they want to protect their thought systems as they are, and learning means change. Change is always fearful to the separated, because they cannot conceive of it as a move towards healing the separation.

Spirit need not be taught, but the ego must be. Learning is ultimately perceived as frightening because it leads to the relinquishment, not the destruction, of the ego to the light of spirit.

Teaching and learning are your greatest strengths now, because they enable you to change your mind and help others to change theirs. If you are willing to renounce the role of guardian of your thought system and open it to me, I will correct it very gently and lead you back to God.

Every good teacher hopes to give his students so much of his own learning that they will one day no longer need him. This is the one true goal of the teacher.

The ego tries to exploit all situations into forms of praise for itself in order to overcome its doubts. It will remain doubtful as long as you believe in its existence. You who made it cannot trust it, because in your right mind you realize it is not real. The only sane solution is not to try to change reality, which is indeed a fearful attempt, but to accept it as it is. You are part of reality, which stands unchanged beyond the reach of your ego but within easy reach of spirit. When you are afraid, be still and know that God is real, and you are His beloved Son in whom He is well pleased. Do not let your ego dispute this, because the ego cannot know what is as far beyond its reach as you are.

God is not the author of fear. You are. You have chosen to create unlike Him, and have therefore made fear for yourself. You are not at peace because you are not fulfilling your function. God gave you a very lofty function that you are not meeting. Your ego has chosen to be afraid instead of meeting it.

The ego is afraid of the spirit's joy, because once you have experienced it you will withdraw all protection from the ego, and become totally without investment in fear. Your investment is great now because fear is a witness to the separation, and your ego rejoices when you witness to it. Leave it behind! Do not listen to it and do not preserve it. Listen only to God, who is as incapable of deception as is the spirit He created. Release yourself and release others. Do not present a false and unworthy picture of yourself to others, and do not accept such a picture of them yourself.

Of your ego you can do nothing to save yourself or others, but of your spirit you can do everything for the salvation of both. Humility is a lesson for the ego, not for the spirit. Spirit is beyond humility, because it recognizes its radiance and gladly sheds its light everywhere. The meek shall inherit the earth because their egos are humble, and this gives them truer perception.

I need devoted teachers who share my aim of healing the mind. Spirit is far beyond the need of your protection or mine. Remember this:

> *In this world, you need not have tribulation, because I have overcome the world. That is why you should be of good cheer.*

4.2. The Ego and False Autonomy

Think of the love of animals for their offspring, and the need they feel to protect them. That is because they regard them as part of themselves. No one dismisses something he considers part of himself. You react to your ego much as God does to His creations . . . with love, protection and charity. Your reactions to the self you made are not surprising. In fact, they resemble in many ways how you will one day react to your real creations, which are as timeless as you are. The question is not how you respond to the ego, but what you believe you are. Belief is an ego function, and as long as your origin is open to belief you are regarding it from an ego viewpoint. When teaching is no longer necessary you will merely know God.

Only those who have a real and lasting sense of abundance can be truly charitable. This is obvious when you consider what is involved. To the ego, to give anything implies that you will have to do without it. When you associate giving with sacrifice, you give only because you believe that you are somehow getting something better, and can therefore do without the thing you give. "Giving to get" is an inescapable law of the ego, which always evaluates itself in relation to other egos. It is therefore continually preoccupied with the belief in scarcity that gave rise to it. Its whole perception of other egos as real is only an attempt to convince itself that it is real. A "self-esteem" is always vulnerable to stress, a term which refers to any perceived threat to the ego's existence.

The ego literally lives by comparisons. Equality is beyond its grasp, and charity becomes impossible. The ego never gives out of abundance, because it was made as a substitute for it. That is why the concept of "getting" arose in the ego's thought system. Appetites are "getting" mechanisms, representing the ego's need to confirm itself. This is as true of body appetites as it is of the so-called "higher ego needs." Body appetites are not physical in origin. The ego regards the body as its home, and tries to satisfy itself through the body. But the idea that this is possible is a decision of the mind, which has become completely confused about what is really possible.

The ego believes it is completely on its own, which is merely another way of describing how it thinks it originated. This is such a fearful state that it can only turn to other egos and try to unite with them in a feeble attempt at identification, or attack them in an equally feeble show of strength. It is not free, however, to open the premise to question, because the premise is its foundation. The ego is the mind's belief that it is completely on its own.

Chapter 4

Salvation is nothing more than "right-mindedness," which is not the one-mindedness of the Holy Spirit, but which must be achieved before One-mindedness is restored. Right-mindedness leads to the next step automatically, because right perception is uniformly without attack, and therefore wrong-mindedness is obliterated.

It cannot be emphasized too often that correcting perception is merely a temporary expedient. It is necessary only because mis-perception is a block to knowledge, while accurate perception is a steppingstone towards it. The whole value of right perception lies in the inevitable realization that all perception is unnecessary. This removes the block entirely. You may ask how this is possible as long as you appear to be living in this world.

4.3. Love without Conflict

It is hard to understand what "The Kingdom of Heaven is within you" really means. This is because it is not understandable to the ego, which interprets it as if something outside is inside, and this does not mean anything. The word "within" is unnecessary. The Kingdom of Heaven is you. What else but you did the Creator create, and what else but you is His Kingdom?

> *The Kingdom is perfectly united and perfectly protected, and the ego will not prevail against it. Amen.*

It is surely apparent by now why the ego regards spirit as its "enemy." The ego arose from the separation, and its continued existence depends on your continuing belief in the separation. The ego must offer you some sort of reward for maintaining this belief. All it can offer is a sense of temporary existence, which begins with its own beginning and ends with its own ending. It tells you this life is your existence because it is its own. Against this sense of temporary existence spirit offers you the knowledge of permanence and unshakable *being*. No one who has experienced the revelation of this can ever fully believe in the ego again. How can its meager offering to you prevail against the glorious gift of God?

You who identify with your ego cannot believe God loves you. You do not love what you made, and what you made does not love you. Being made out of the denial of the Father, the ego has no allegiance to its maker. You cannot conceive of the real relationship that exists between God and His creations because of your hatred for the self you made. You project onto the ego the decision to separate, and this conflicts with the love you feel for the ego because you made it. No love in this world is without this ambivalence, and since no ego has experienced love without ambivalence the concept is beyond its understanding. Love will enter immediately into any mind that truly wants it, but it must want it truly. This means that it wants it without ambivalence, and this kind of wanting is wholly without the ego's "drive to get."

No force except your own will is strong enough or worthy enough to guide you. In this you are as free as God, and must remain so forever. Let us ask the Father in my name to keep you mindful of His Love for you, and yours for Him.

It has never really entered your mind to give up every idea you ever had that opposes knowledge. You retain thousands of little scraps of fear that prevent the Holy One from entering. Light cannot penetrate through the walls you make to block it, and it is forever unwilling to destroy what you have made. No one can see through a wall, but I can step around it. Watch your mind for the scraps of fear, or you will be unable to ask me to do so.

In your own mind, though denied by the ego, is the declaration of your release. God has given you everything. This one fact means the ego does not exist, and this makes it profoundly afraid. In the ego's language, "to have" and "to be" are different, but they are identical to the Holy Spirit. The Holy Spirit knows that you both have everything and are everything. Any distinction in this respect is meaningful only when the idea of "getting," which implies a lack, has already been accepted. That is why we make no distinction between having the Kingdom of God and being the Kingdom of God.

The calm being of God's Kingdom, which in your sane mind is perfectly conscious, is ruthlessly banished from the part of the mind the ego rules. The ego is desperate because it opposes literally invincible odds, whether you are asleep or awake. Consider how much vigilance you have been willing to exert to protect your ego, and how little to protect your right mind. Who but the insane would undertake to believe what is not true, and then protect this belief at the cost of truth?

4.4. This Need Not Be

If you cannot hear the Voice for God, it is because you do not choose to listen. That you do listen to the voice of your ego is demonstrated by your attitudes, your feelings and your behavior. Yet this is what you want. This is what you are fighting to keep, and what you are vigilant to save. Your mind is filled with schemes to save the face of your ego, and you do not seek the face of Christ. The glass in which the ego seeks to see its face is dark indeed. How can it maintain the trick of its existence except with mirrors? But where you look to find yourself is up to you.

I have said that you cannot change your mind by changing your behavior, but I have also said, and many times, that you can change your mind. When your mood tells you that you have chosen wrongly, and this is so whenever you are not joyous, then know this need not be. In every case you have thought wrongly about some brother God created, and are perceiving images your ego makes in a darkened glass. Search sincerely for what you have done and left undone accordingly, and then change your mind to think with God's. This may seem hard to do, but it is much easier than trying to think against it. Your mind is one with God's. Denying this and thinking otherwise has held your ego together, but has literally split your mind. As a loving brother I am deeply concerned with your mind, and urge you to follow my example as you look at yourself and at your brother, and see in both the glorious creations of a glorious Father.

When you are sad, *know this need not be*. Depression comes from a sense of being deprived of something you want and do not have. Remember that you are deprived of nothing except by your own decisions, and then decide otherwise.

When you are anxious, realize that anxiety comes from the capriciousness of the ego, and *know this need not be*. You can be as vigilant against the ego's dictates as vigilant for them.

When you feel guilty, remember that the ego has indeed violated the laws of God, but you have not. Leave the "sins" of the ego to me. That is what Atonement is for. But until you change your mind about those whom your ego has hurt, the Atonement cannot release you. While you feel guilty your ego is in command, because only the ego can experience guilt. *This need not be.*

Watch your mind for the temptations of the ego, and do not be deceived by it. It offers you nothing. When you have given up this voluntary dis-spiriting, you will see how your mind can focus and rise above fatigue and heal.

Have you really considered how many opportunities you have had to gladden yourself, and how many of them you have refused? There is no limit to the power of a Son of God, but he can limit the expression of his power as much as he chooses. Your mind and mine can unite in shining your ego away, releasing the strength of God into everything you think and do. Do not settle for anything less than this, and refuse to accept anything but this as your goal. Watch your mind carefully for any beliefs that hinder its accomplishment, and step away from them. Judge how well you have done this by your own feelings, for this is the one right use of judgment. Judgment, like any other defense, can be used to attack or protect; to hurt or to heal. The ego should be brought to judgment and found wanting there. Without your own allegiance, protection and love, the ego cannot exist. Let it be judged truly and you must withdraw allegiance, protection and love from it.

You are a mirror of truth, in which God Himself shines in perfect light. To the ego's dark glass you need but say, "I will not look there because I know these images are not true." Then let the Holy One shine on you in peace, knowing that this and only this must be. His mind shone on you in your creation and brought your mind into being. His mind still shines on you and must shine through you. Your ego cannot prevent Him from shining on you, but it can prevent you from letting Him shine through you.

I do not attack your ego. I do work with your higher mind, the home of the Holy Spirit, whether you are asleep or awake, just as your ego does with your lower mind, which is its home. I am your vigilance in this, because you are too confused to recognize your own hope. I am not mistaken. Your mind will elect to join with mine, and together we are invincible. You and your brother will yet come together in my name, and your sanity will be restored. I raised the dead by knowing that life is an eternal attribute of everything that the living God created. Why do you believe it is harder for me to inspire the dis-spirited or to stabilize the unstable? I do not believe that there is an order of difficulty in miracles; you do. I have called and you will answer.

4.5. The Ego-Body Illusion

A major source of the ego's off-balanced state is its lack of discrimination between the body and the Thoughts of God. Thoughts of God are unacceptable to the ego, because they clearly point to the nonexistence of the ego itself. The ego therefore either distorts them or refuses to accept them. It cannot, however, make them cease to be. It therefore tries to conceal not only "unacceptable" body impulses, but also the Thoughts of God, because both are threatening to it. Being concerned primarily with its own preservation in the face of threat, the ego perceives them as the same. By perceiving them as the same, the ego attempts to save itself from being swept away, as it would surely be in the presence of knowledge.

"Seek and ye shall find" does not mean that you should seek blindly and desperately for something you would not recognize. Meaningful seeking is consciously undertaken, consciously organized and consciously directed. The goal must be formulated clearly and kept in mind. Learning and wanting to learn are inseparable. You learn best when you believe what you are trying to learn is of value to you.

Preoccupations with problems set up to be incapable of solution are favorite ego devices for impeding learning progress. In all these diversionary tactics, however, the one question that is never asked by those who pursue them is, "What for?" This is the question that you must learn to ask in connection with everything. What is the purpose? Whatever it is, it will direct your efforts automatically. When you make a decision of purpose, then, you have made a decision about your future effort; a decision that will remain in effect unless you change your mind.

4.6. The Rewards of God

The ego does not recognize the real source of "threat," and if you associate yourself with the ego, you do not understand the situation as it is. Only your allegiance to it gives the ego any power over you.

You have very little trust in me as yet, but it will increase as you turn more and more often to me instead of to your ego for guidance. The results will convince you increasingly that this choice is the only sane one you can make. No one who learns from experience that one choice brings peace and joy while another brings chaos and disaster needs additional convincing. The fact that you believe you must escape from the ego shows this; but you cannot escape from the ego by humbling it or controlling it or punishing it.

I am teaching you to associate misery with the ego and joy with the spirit. You have taught yourself the opposite. You are still free to choose, but can you really want the rewards of the ego in the presence of the rewards of God?

As you come closer to a brother you approach me, and as you withdraw from him I become distant to you. Salvation is a collaborative venture. It cannot be undertaken successfully by those who disengage themselves from the Sonship, because they are disengaging themselves from me. God will come to you only as you will give Him to your brothers. Learn first of them and you will be ready to hear God. That is because the function of love is one.

4.7. Creation and Communication

The ego is the part of the mind that believes your existence is defined by separation.

Everything the ego perceives is a separate whole, without the relationships that imply *being*. The ego is thus against communication, except insofar as it is utilized to establish separateness rather than to abolish it. The communication system of the ego is based on its own thought system, as is everything else it dictates. Its communication is controlled by its need to protect itself, and it will disrupt communication when it experiences threat.

The Bible repeatedly states that you should praise God. This hardly means that you should tell Him how wonderful He is. He has no ego with which to accept such praise, and no perception with which to judge it. But unless you take your part in the creation, His joy is not complete because yours is incomplete.

God is praised whenever any mind learns to be wholly helpful. The truly helpful are invulnerable, because they are not protecting their egos and so nothing can hurt them. Their helpfulness is their praise of God, and He will return their praise of Him because they are like Him, and they can rejoice together. The truly helpful are God's miracle workers, whom I direct until we are all united in the joy of the Kingdom. I will direct you to wherever you can be truly helpful, and to whoever can follow my guidance through you.

Chapter 5

Healing and Wholeness

Introduction

To heal is to make happy. The light that belongs to you is the light of joy.

It is impossible for a child of God to love his neighbor except as himself. That is why the healer's prayer is: *Let me know this brother as I know myself.*

5.1. The Invitation to the Holy Spirit

I have said already that I can reach up and bring the Holy Spirit down to you, but I can bring Him to you only at your own invitation. The Holy Spirit is in your right mind, as He was in mine. The Bible says, "May the mind be in you that was also in Christ Jesus," and uses this as a blessing. It is the blessing of miracle-mindedness.

The Holy Spirit is the Christ Mind, which is aware of the knowledge that lies beyond perception. The Voice of the Holy Spirit is the Call to Atonement, or the restoration of the integrity of the mind. When the Atonement is complete and the whole Sonship is healed there will be no Call to return. But what God creates is eternal. The Holy Spirit will remain with the Sons of God, to bless their creations and keep them in the light of joy.

5.2. The Voice for God

The Holy Spirit is the spirit of joy. The Holy Spirit is God's Answer to the separation.

When the ego was made, God placed in the mind the Call to joy. This Call is so strong that the ego always dissolves at Its sound. That is why you must choose to hear one of two voices within you. One, the call of the ego, you made yourself, and that one is not of God. But the other, the Call to joy, is given you by God, Who asks you only to listen to it. The Holy Spirit, the spirit of joy, is in you in a very literal sense.

You are the Kingdom of Heaven, but you have let the belief in darkness enter your mind and so you need a new light. The Holy Spirit is the radiance that you must let banish the idea of darkness.

The choice for the Holy Spirit is the choice for God.

The Voice of the Holy Spirit does not command, because It is incapable of arrogance. It does not demand, because It does not seek control. It does not overcome, because It does not attack. It merely reminds. It is compelling only because of what It reminds you of. It brings to your mind the other way, remaining quiet even in the midst of the turmoil you may make. The Voice for God is always quiet, because It speaks of peace. Peace is stronger than war because peace heals. War is division, not increase. No one gains from strife. What profiteth it a man if he gain the whole world and lose his own soul? If you listen to the wrong voice you have lost sight of your soul. You cannot lose your soul, but you can not know it. Your soul is therefore "lost" to you until you choose right.

The Holy Spirit is your Guide in choosing. He is in the part of your mind that always speaks for the right choice, because He speaks for God. He is your remaining communication with God, which you can interrupt but cannot destroy. The Holy Spirit is the way in which God's Will is done on earth as it is in heaven. Both heaven and earth are in you, because the call of both is in your mind. The Voice for God comes from your own altars to Him. These altars are not things; they are devotions. Yet you have other devotions now. Your divided devotion has given you the two voices, and you must choose at which altar you want to serve. The decision is very simple. It is made on the basis of which call is worth more to you.

The Holy Spirit is the Call to awaken and be glad. The world is very tired, because it is the idea of weariness. Our task is the joyous one of waking it to the Call for God. Everyone will answer the Call of the Holy Spirit, or the Sonship cannot be as One. What better vocation could there be for any part of the Kingdom than to restore it to the perfect integration that can make it whole? Hear only this through the Holy Spirit within you, and teach your brothers to listen as I am teaching you.

The power of our joint motivation is beyond belief, but not beyond accomplishment. What we can accomplish together has no limits, because the Call for God is the Call to the unlimited. Child of God, my message is for you, to hear and give away as you answer the Holy Spirit within you.

5.3. The Guide to Salvation

The Holy Spirit is the Bridge for the transfer of perception to knowledge. This needs clarification, not in statement but in experience.

The Holy Spirit is the idea of healing. Being the Call for God, it is also the idea of God.

The Holy Spirit is God's Answer to the ego. The Holy Spirit has the task of undoing what the ego has made.

The Holy Spirit is the Mediator between the interpretations of the ego and the knowledge of the Spirit. He can therefore perform the function of reinterpreting what the ego makes, not by destruction but by understanding. Understanding is light, but you yourself do not know this. It is therefore the task of the Holy Spirit to reinterpret you on behalf of God.

You cannot understand yourself alone. Peace is the ego's greatest enemy because, according to its interpretation of reality, war is the guarantee of its survival. The ego becomes strong in strife. If you believe there is strife you will react viciously, because the idea of danger has entered your mind. The idea itself is an appeal to the ego. The Holy Spirit is as vigilant as the ego to the call of danger, opposing it with His strength just as the ego welcomes it. The Holy Spirit counters this welcome by welcoming peace.

Perception derives meaning from relationships. Those you accept are the foundations of your beliefs. The separation is merely another term for a split mind. The ego is the symbol of separation, just as the Holy Spirit is the symbol of peace. What you perceive in others you are strengthening in yourself. You may let your mind misperceive, but the Holy Spirit lets your mind reinterpret its own mis-perceptions.

The ego made the world as it perceives it, but the Holy Spirit, the re-interpreter of what the ego made, sees the world as a teaching device for bringing you home. The Holy Spirit must perceive time, and reinterpret it into the timeless. He must work through opposites, because He must work with and for a mind that is in opposition. Correct and learn, and be open to learning. You have not made truth, but truth can still set you free. Look as the Holy Spirit looks, and understand as He understands. His understanding looks back to God in remembrance of me. He is in communion with God always, and He is part of you. He is your Guide to salvation, because He holds the remembrance of things past and to come, and brings them to the present. He holds this gladness gently in your mind, asking only that you increase it in His Name by sharing it to increase His joy in you.

5.4. Teaching and Healing

What fear has hidden still is part of you. Joining the Atonement is the way out of fear. The Holy Spirit will help you reinterpret everything that you perceive as fearful, and teach you that only what is loving is true.

The Holy Spirit atones in all of us by undoing, and thus lifts the burden you have placed in your mind. By following Him you are led back to God where you belong, and how can you find the way except by taking your brother with you? My part in the Atonement is not complete until you join it and give it away. As you teach so shall you learn. I will never leave you or forsake you, because to forsake you would be to forsake myself and God Who created me. You forsake yourself and God if you forsake any of your brothers. You must learn to see them as they are, and understand they belong to God as you do. How could you treat your brother better than by rendering unto God the things that are God's?

I place the peace of God in your heart and in your hands, to hold and share. The heart is pure to hold it, and the hands are strong to give it. We cannot lose. My judgment is as strong as the wisdom of God, in whose Heart and Hands we have our being. His quiet children are His blessed Sons. The Thoughts of God are with you.

5.5. The Ego's Use of Guilt

Perhaps some of our concepts will become clearer and more personally meaningful if the ego's use of guilt is clarified. The ego has a purpose, just as the Holy Spirit has. The ego's purpose is fear, because only the fearful can be egotistic. The ego's logic is as impeccable as that of the Holy Spirit, because your mind has the means at its disposal to side with heaven or earth, as it elects. But again, remember that both are in you.

In heaven there is no guilt, because the Kingdom is attained through the Atonement. Guilt is always disruptive. Anything that engenders fear is divisive because it obeys the law of division. If the ego is the symbol of the separation, it is also the symbol of guilt. Guilt is more than merely not of God. It is the symbol of attack on God. This is a totally meaningless concept except to the ego, but do not underestimate the power of the ego's belief in it. This is the belief from which all guilt really stems.

The ego is the part of the mind that believes in division. The ego believes that this is what you did because it believes that it is you. If you identify with the ego, you must perceive yourself as guilty. Whenever you respond to your ego you will experience guilt, and you will fear punishment. The ego is quite literally a fearful thought.

Whatever you accept into your mind has reality for you. It is your acceptance of it that makes it real. If you enthrone the ego in your mind, your allowing it to enter makes it your reality. This is because the mind is capable of creating reality or making illusions. I said before that you must learn to think with God. To think with Him is to think like Him. This engenders joy, not guilt, because it is natural. Guilt is a sure sign that your thinking is unnatural. Unnatural thinking will always be attended with guilt, because it is the belief in sin. The ego does not perceive sin as a lack of love, but as a positive act of assault.

That is why the question, "What do you want?" must be answered. You are answering it every minute and every second, and each moment of decision is a judgment that is anything but ineffectual. Its effects will follow automatically until the decision is changed. Remember, though, that the alternatives themselves are unalterable. The Holy Spirit, like the ego, is a decision. Together they constitute all the alternatives the mind can accept and obey. The Holy Spirit and the ego are the only choices open to you. God created one, and so you cannot eradicate it. You made the other, and so you can. Delusional ideas are not real thoughts, although you can believe in them. But you are wrong. The function of thought comes from God and is in God. As part of His Thought, you cannot think apart from Him.

Every disordered thought is attended by guilt at its inception, and maintained by guilt in its continuance. Guilt is inescapable by those who believe they order their own thoughts, and must therefore obey their dictates. This makes them feel responsible for their errors without recognizing that, by accepting this responsibility, they are reacting irresponsibly. If the sole responsibility of the miracle worker is to accept the Atonement for himself, and I assure you that it is, then the responsibility for what is atoned for cannot be yours. The dilemma cannot be resolved except by accepting the solution of undoing. You would be responsible for the effects of all your wrong thinking if it could not be undone. The purpose of the Atonement is to save the past in purified form only.

The continuing decision to remain separated is the only possible reason for continuing guilt feelings. We have said this before, but did not emphasize the destructive results of the decision. Any decision of the mind will affect both behavior and experience. What you want you expect. This is not delusional. Your mind does make your future, and it will turn it back to full creation at any minute if it accepts the Atonement first.

5.6. Time and Eternity

You do not belong in time. Your place is only in eternity, where God Himself placed you forever.

Guilt feelings are the preservers of time. They induce fears of retaliation or abandonment, and thus ensure that the future will be like the past. This is the ego's continuity. Ensuring that the future will be like the past gives the ego a false sense of security by believing that you cannot escape from it. But you can and must. God offers you the continuity of eternity in exchange. When you choose to make this exchange, you will simultaneously exchange guilt for joy, viciousness for love, and pain for peace. My role is only to unchain your will and set it free. Your ego cannot accept this freedom, and will oppose it at every possible moment and in every possible way. And as its maker, you recognize what it can do because you gave it the power to do it.

When I said "I have come as a light into the world," I meant that I came to share the light with you. Remember my reference to the ego's dark glass, and remember also that I said, "Do not look there." It is still true that where you look to find yourself is up to you. Your patience with your brother is your patience with yourself. Is not a child of God worth patience? I have shown you infinite patience because my will is that of our Father, from Whom I learned of infinite patience. His Voice was in me as It is in you, speaking for patience towards the Sonship in the Name of its Creator.

Now you must learn that only infinite patience produces immediate effects. This is the way in which time is exchanged for eternity. Infinite patience calls upon infinite love, and by producing results now it renders time unnecessary. We have repeatedly said that time is a learning device to be abolished when it is no longer useful. The Holy Spirit, Who speaks for God in time, also knows that time is meaningless. He reminds you of this in every passing moment of time, because it is His special function to return you to eternity and remain to bless your creations there. He is the only blessing you can truly give, because He is truly blessed. Because He has been given you freely by God, you must give Him as you received Him.

5.7. The Decision for God

Do you really believe you can make a voice that can drown out God's? Do you really believe you can devise a thought system that can separate you from Him? Do you really believe you can plan for your safety and joy better than He can? You need be neither careful nor careless; you need merely cast your cares upon Him because He careth for you. You are His care because He loves you. His Voice reminds you always that all hope is yours because of His care. You cannot choose to escape His care because that is not His will, but you can choose to accept His care and use the infinite power of His care for all those he created by it.

God commended His Spirit to you, and asks that you commend yours to Him. He wills to keep it in perfect peace, because you are of one mind and spirit with Him. Excluding yourself from the Atonement is the ego's last-ditch defense of its own existence. It reflects both the ego's need to separate, and your willingness to side with its separateness.

Whenever you are not wholly joyous, it is because you have reacted with a lack of love to one of God's creations. Perceiving this as "sin" you become defensive because you expect attack. The decision to react in this way is yours, and can therefore be undone. It cannot be undone by repentance in the usual sense, because this implies guilt. If you allow yourself to feel guilty, you will reinforce the error rather than allow it to be undone for you.

Therefore, the first step in the undoing is to recognize that you actively decided wrongly, but can as actively decide otherwise. Be very firm with yourself in this, and keep yourself fully aware that the undoing process, which does not come from you, is nevertheless within you because God placed it there. Your part is merely to return your thinking to the point at which the error was made, and give it over to the Atonement in peace. Say this to yourself as sincerely as you can, remembering that the Holy Spirit will respond fully to your slightest invitation:

I must have decided wrongly, because I am not at peace.
I made the decision myself, but I can also decide otherwise.
I want to decide otherwise, because I want to be at peace.
I do not feel guilty, because the Holy Spirit will undo all the consequences of my wrong decision if I will let Him.
I choose to let Him, by allowing Him to decide for God for me.

CHAPTER 6

THE LESSONS OF LOVE

Introduction

The relationship of anger to attack is obvious, but the relationship of anger to fear is not always so apparent. Anger always involves projection of separation, which must ultimately be accepted as one's own responsibility, rather than being blamed on others. Anger cannot occur unless you believe that you have been attacked, that your attack is justified in return, and that you are in no way responsible for it.

6.1. The Message of the Crucifixion

Projection means anger, anger fosters assault, and assault promotes fear.

The message the crucifixion was intended to teach was that it is not necessary to perceive any form of assault in persecution. If you respond with anger, you must be equating yourself with the destructible, and are therefore regarding yourself insanely.

You are free to perceive yourself as persecuted if you choose. When you do choose to react that way, however, you might remember that I was persecuted as the world judges, and did not share this evaluation for myself.

If you react as if you are persecuted, you are teaching persecution. This is not a lesson a Son of God should want to teach if he is to realize his own salvation. Rather, teach your own perfect immunity, which is the truth in you, and realize that it cannot be assailed. Do not try to protect it yourself, or you are believing that it is assailable. You are not asked to be crucified, which was part of my own teaching contribution. You are merely asked to follow my example in the face of much less extreme temptations to misperceive, and not to accept them as false justifications for anger.

Your resurrection is your reawakening. I am the model for rebirth, but rebirth itself is merely the dawning on your mind of what is already in it. God placed it there Himself, and

Chapter 6

so it is true forever. I believed in it, and therefore accepted it as true for me. Help me to teach it to our brothers in the name of the Kingdom of God, but first believe that it is true for you.

I elected, for your sake and mine, to demonstrate that the most outrageous assault, as judged by the ego, does not matter. As the world judges these things, but not as God knows them, I was betrayed, abandoned, beaten, torn, and finally killed. It was clear that this was only because of the projection of others onto me, since I had not harmed anyone and had healed many.

We are still equal as learners, although we do not need to have equal experiences. The Holy Spirit is glad when you can learn from mine, and be reawakened by them. That is their only purpose, and that is the only way in which I can be perceived as the way, the truth and the life.

The crucifixion cannot be shared because it is the symbol of projection, but the resurrection is the symbol of sharing because the reawakening of every Son of God is necessary to enable the Sonship to know its Wholeness. Only this is knowledge.

The message of the crucifixion is perfectly clear:

Teach only love, for that is what you are.

If you interpret the crucifixion in any other way, you are using it as a weapon for assault rather than as the call for peace for which it was intended. The Apostles often misunderstood it, and for the same reason that anyone misunderstands it. Their own imperfect love made them vulnerable to projection, and out of their own fear they spoke of the "wrath of God" as His retaliatory weapon.

I do not want you to allow any fear to enter into the thought system toward which I am guiding you. I do not call for martyrs but for teachers. No one is punished for sins, and the Sons of God are not sinners. Any concept of punishment involves the projection of blame, and reinforces the idea that blame is justified.

You cannot love what you do not appreciate, for fear makes appreciation impossible. When you are afraid of what you are you do not appreciate it, and will therefore reject it. As a result, you will teach rejection.

Each one must learn to teach that all forms of rejection are meaningless. The separation is the notion of rejection. This is not as God thinks, and you must think as He thinks if you are to know Him again.

Remember that the Holy Spirit is the Communication Link between God the Father and His separated Sons.

6.2. The Alternative to Projection

What you project you disown, and therefore do not believe is yours. You are excluding yourself by the very judgment that you are different from the one on whom you project. Since you have also judged against what you project, you continue to attack it because you continue to keep it separated. By doing this unconsciously, you try to keep the fact that you attacked yourself out of your awareness, and thus imagine that you have made yourself safe.

Yet projection will always hurt you. It reinforces your belief in your own split mind, and its only purpose is to keep the separation going. It is solely a device of the ego to make you feel different from your brothers and separated from them. The ego justifies this on the grounds that it makes you seem "better" than they are, thus obscuring your equality with them still further. Projection and attack are inevitably related, because projection is always a means of justifying attack. Anger without projection is impossible. The ego uses projection only to destroy your perception of both yourself and your brothers. The process begins by excluding something that exists in you but which you do not want, and leads directly to excluding you from your brothers.

The Holy Spirit begins by perceiving you as perfect. Knowing this perfection is shared He recognizes it in others, thus strengthening it in both. Instead of anger, this arouses love for both, because it establishes inclusion. Perceiving equality, the Holy Spirit perceives equal needs. This invites Atonement automatically, because Atonement is the one need in this world that is universal. To perceive yourself this way is the only way in which you can find happiness in the world. That is because it is the acknowledgment that you are not in this world, for the world is unhappy.

The Holy Spirit remains the Bridge between perception and knowledge. By enabling you to use perception in a way that reflects knowledge, you will ultimately remember it. The ego would prefer to believe that this memory is impossible, yet it is your perception the Holy Spirit guides.

The difference between the ego's projection and the Holy Spirit's extension is very simple. The ego projects to exclude, and therefore to deceive. The Holy Spirit extends by recognizing Himself in every mind, and thus perceives them as one. Nothing conflicts in this perception, because what the Holy Spirit perceives is all the same. Wherever He looks He sees Himself, and because He is united He offers the whole Kingdom always. This is the one message God gave to Him and for which He must speak, because that is what He is. The peace of God lies in that message, and so the peace of God lies in you. The great peace of the Kingdom shines in your mind forever, but it must shine outward to make you aware of it.

6.3. The Relinquishment of Attack

As we have already emphasized, every idea begins in the mind of the thinker. You have taught yourself to believe that you are not what you are. You cannot teach what you have not learned.

If you are to be conflict-free, you must learn only from the Holy Spirit and teach only by Him. You are only love, but when you deny this, you make what you are something you must learn to remember. I said before that the message of the crucifixion was, "Teach only love, for that is what you are." This is the one lesson that is perfectly unified, because it is the only lesson that is one. Only by teaching it can you learn it. "As you teach so will you learn." If that is true, and it is true indeed, do not forget that what you teach is teaching you. And what you project or extend you believe.

The only way to have peace is to teach peace. Everything you teach you are learning. Teach only love, and learn that love is yours and you are love.

6.4. The Only Answer

Remember that the Holy Spirit is the Answer, not the question.

When God created you He made you part of Him. That is why attack within the Kingdom is impossible. You made the ego without love, and so it does not love you. You could not remain within the Kingdom without love, and since the Kingdom is love, you believe that you are without it. This enables the ego to regard itself as separate and outside its maker, thus speaking for the part of your mind that believes you are separate and outside the Mind of God. The ego raised the question that it can never answer. That question, "What are you?" The most inventive activities of the ego have never done more than obscure that question.

Hear, then, the one answer of the Holy Spirit to all the questions the ego raises: You are a child of God, a priceless part of His Kingdom, which He created as part of Him. Nothing else exists and only this is real. You have chosen a sleep in which you have had bad dreams, but the sleep is not real and God calls you to awake.

6.5. The Lessons of the Holy Spirit

Like any good teacher, the Holy Spirit knows more than you do now, but He teaches only to make you equal with Him. Would God teach you that you had made a split mind, when He knows your mind only as whole? Giving His joy is an ongoing process, not in time but in eternity. So He thought, "My children sleep and must be awakened."

How can you wake children in a more kindly way than by a gentle Voice that will not frighten them, but will merely remind them that the night is over and the light has come? You merely reassure them that they are safe now. Then you train them to recognize the difference between sleeping and waking, so they will understand they need not be afraid of dreams. And so when bad dreams come, they will themselves call on the light to dispel them.

A wise teacher teaches through approach, not avoidance. He does not emphasize what you must avoid to escape from harm, but what you need to learn to have joy.

Children do confuse fantasy and reality, and they are frightened because they do not recognize the difference. The Holy Spirit makes no distinction among dreams. He merely shines them away. His light is always the Call to awaken, whatever you have been dreaming. Nothing lasting lies in dreams, and the Holy Spirit, shining with the light from God Himself, speaks only for what lasts forever.

6.5.a. To Have, Give All to All

When your body and your ego and your dreams are gone, you will know that you will last forever. Perhaps you think this is accomplished through death, but nothing is accomplished through death, because death is nothing. Everything is accomplished through life, and life is of the mind and in the mind. The body neither lives nor dies, because it cannot contain you who are life.

The Holy Spirit, Who leads to God, translates perception into knowledge. The ego uses the body for attack, for pleasure and for pride. The Holy Spirit sees the body only as a means of communication, and because communicating is sharing it becomes communion. Those who communicate fear are promoting attack and attack always breaks communication. Egos do join together in temporary allegiance, but always for what each one can get separately. The Holy Spirit communicates only what each one can give to all. He never takes anything back, because He wants you to keep it. Therefore, His teaching begins with the lesson:

> *To have, give all to all.*

This is a very preliminary step, and the only one you must take for yourself. It is not even necessary that you complete the step yourself, but it is necessary that you turn in that direction. Having chosen to go that way, you place yourself in charge of the journey.

6.5.b. To Have Peace, Teach Peace to Learn It

All who believe in separation have a basic fear of retaliation and abandonment. They believe in attack and rejection, so that is what they perceive and teach and learn. These insane ideas are clearly the result of dissociation and projection. What you teach you are, but it is quite apparent that you can teach wrongly, and can therefore teach yourself wrong. This is because everyone identifies himself with his thought system, and every thought system centers on what you believe you are. If the center of the thought system is true, only truth extends from it. But if a lie is at its center, only deception proceeds from it.

The mind of the learner projects its own conflict, and thus does not perceive consistency in the minds of others, making him suspicious of their motivation. This is the real reason why, in many respects, the first lesson is the hardest to learn. Still strongly aware of the ego in yourself, and responding primarily to the ego in others, you are being taught to react to both as if what you do believe is not true.

The way out of conflict between two opposing thought systems is clearly to choose one and relinquish the other. If you identify with your thought system, and you cannot escape this, and if you accept two thought systems which are in complete disagreement, peace of mind is impossible. If you teach both, which you will surely do as long as you accept both, you are teaching conflict and learning it. Yet you do want peace, or you would not have called upon the Voice for peace to help you. Its lesson is not insane; the conflict is.

The ego tries to persuade you that it is up to you to decide which voice is true, but the Holy Spirit teaches you that truth was created by God, and your decision cannot change it.

The Holy Spirit perceives the conflict exactly as it is. Therefore, His second lesson is:

> *To have peace, teach peace to learn it.*

6.5.c. Be Vigilant Only for God and His Kingdom

The Holy Spirit sorts out the true from the false in your mind, and teaches you to judge every thought you allow to enter it in the light of what God put there. Whatever is in accord with this light He retains, to strengthen the Kingdom in you. What is partly in accord with it He accepts and purifies. Remember, however, that what the Holy Spirit rejects the ego accepts. This is because they are in fundamental disagreement about everything, being in fundamental disagreement about what you are. The ego's beliefs on this crucial issue vary, and that is why it promotes different moods. The Holy Spirit never varies on this point, and so the one mood He engenders is joy. He protects it by rejecting everything that does not foster joy, and so He alone can keep you wholly joyous.

The Holy Spirit does not teach you to judge others, because He does not want you to teach error and learn it yourself. He would hardly be consistent if He allowed you to strengthen what you must learn to avoid. In the mind of the thinker, then, He is judgmental, but only in order to unify the mind so it can perceive without judgment. This enables the mind to teach without judgment, and therefore to learn to be without judgment. Therefore, the Holy Spirit's third lesson is:

> *Be vigilant only for God and His Kingdom.*

This is a major step toward fundamental change.

This lesson is unequivocal in that it teaches there must be no exceptions, although it does not deny that the temptation to make exceptions will occur.

Choosing through the Holy Spirit will lead you to the Kingdom. If you allow yourself to have in your mind only what God put there, you are acknowledging your mind as God created it. Therefore, you are accepting it as it is. Since it is whole, you are teaching peace because you believe in it. The final step will still be taken for you by God, but by the third step the Holy Spirit has prepared you for God. He is getting you ready for the translation of "having" into "being."

You learn first that *having* rests on giving, and not on getting. Next you learn that you learn what you teach, and that you want to learn peace. You have believed that you are without the Kingdom, and have therefore excluded yourself from it in your belief.

The third lesson is thus one of protection for your mind, allowing you to identify only with the center, where God placed the altar to Himself. As long as belief in God and His Kingdom is assailed by any doubts in your mind, His perfect accomplishment is not apparent to you. This is why you must be vigilant on God's behalf. The ego speaks against His creation, and therefore engenders doubt.

Truth is without illusions and therefore within the Kingdom. Everything outside the Kingdom is illusion. By making another kingdom that you valued, you did not keep only the Kingdom of God in your mind, and thus placed part of your mind outside it. What you made has imprisoned your will, and given you a sick mind that must be healed. Your vigilance against this sickness is the way to heal it. Once your mind is healed it radiates health, and thereby teaches healing. This establishes you as a teacher who teaches like me.

The third lesson, then, is a statement of what you want to believe, and entails a willingness to relinquish everything else. The Holy Spirit will enable you to take this step, if you follow Him. Your vigilance is the sign that you want Him to guide you.

Chapter 7

The Gifts of the Kingdom

7.1. The Last Step

God's accomplishments are not yours, but yours are like His. He created the Sonship and you increase it. You have the power to add to the Kingdom, though not to add to the Creator of the Kingdom. You claim this power when you become vigilant only for God and his Kingdom. By accepting this power as yours you have learned to remember what you are.

Your creations belong in you, as you belong in God. To create is to love. Love extends outward simply because it cannot be contained. Eternity is yours, because He created you eternal.

Eternity is the indelible stamp of creation. The eternal are in peace and joy forever.

To think like God is to share His certainty of what you are, and to create like Him is to share the perfect love He shares with you. To this the Holy Spirit leads you, that your joy may be complete because the Kingdom of God is whole. I have said that the last step in the reawakening of knowledge is taken by God. This is true, but it is hard to explain in words because words are symbols, and nothing that is true need be explained. However, the Holy Spirit has the task of translating the useless into the useful, the meaningless into the meaningful, and the temporary into the timeless. He can therefore tell you something about this last step.

7.2. The Law of the Kingdom

Sickness and separation are not of God, but the Kingdom is. If you obscure the Kingdom, you are perceiving what is not of God.

To heal, then, is to correct perception in your brother and yourself by sharing the Holy Spirit with him. This places you both within the Kingdom, and restores its wholeness in your mind. This reflects creation, because it unifies by increasing and integrates by extending. What you project or extend is real for you.

Outside the Kingdom, the law that prevails inside is adapted to "What you project you believe." This is its teaching form, because outside the Kingdom learning is essential. This form implies that you will learn what you are from what you have projected onto others, and therefore believe they are. In the Kingdom there is no teaching or learning, because there is no belief. There is only "certainty".

Laws must be communicated if they are to be helpful. In effect, they must be translated for those who speak different languages. The Holy Spirit is the Translator of the laws of God to those who do not understand them.

The meaning of his message is always the same; only the meaning matters. God's law of creation does not involve the use of truth to convince His Sons of truth. The extension of truth, which is the law of the Kingdom, rests only on the knowledge of what truth is. This is your inheritance and requires no learning at all, but when you disinherited yourself you became a learner of necessity.

No one questions the connection of learning and memory. Learning is impossible without memory since it must be consistent to be remembered. That is why the Holy Spirit's teaching is a lesson in remembering. I said before that He teaches remembering and forgetting, but the forgetting is only to make the remembering consistent. You forget in order to remember better. You will not understand His translations while you listen to two ways of interpreting them. Therefore you must forget or relinquish one to understand the other. This is the only way you can learn consistency, so that you can finally be consistent.

It is apparent that confusion interferes with meaning, and therefore prevents the learner from appreciating it. There is no confusion in the Kingdom, because there is only one meaning. This meaning comes from God and is God. Because it is also you, you share it and extend it as your Creator did.

7.3. The Reality of the Kingdom

When I said "I am with you always," I meant it literally. I am not absent to anyone in any situation. Because I am always with you, you are the way, the truth and the life. You did not make this power, any more than I did. It was created to be shared, and therefore cannot be meaningfully perceived as belonging to anyone at the expense of another.

God's meaning waits in the Kingdom, because that is where He placed it. It does not wait in time. It merely rests in the Kingdom because it belongs there, as you do. How can you who are God's meaning perceive yourself as absent from it? You can see yourself as separated from your meaning only by experiencing yourself as unreal. This is why the ego is insane; it teaches that you are not what you are.

To be in the Kingdom is merely to focus your full attention on it.

God has lit your mind Himself, and keeps your mind lit by His light because His light is what your mind is.

7.4. Healing as the Recognition of Truth

The Holy Spirit must work through you, to teach you, He is in you. This is an intermediary step toward the knowledge that you are in God because you are part of Him. The laws of God establish this, and the Holy Spirit reminds you of it. When you heal, you are remembering the laws of God and forgetting the laws of the ego. I said before that forgetting is merely a way of remembering better.

The ego does not want to teach everyone all it has learned, because that would defeat its purpose. The Holy Spirit teaches you to use what the ego has made, to teach the opposite of what the ego has "learned". All you need do is make the effort to learn, for the Holy Spirit has a unified goal for the effort.

All abilities should therefore be given over to the Holy Spirit, Who understands how to use them properly. He uses them only for healing, because He knows you only as whole. By healing you learn of wholeness, and by learning of wholeness you learn to remember God.

The ego always seeks to divide and separate. The Holy Spirit always seeks to unify and heal.

Seek ye first the Kingdom of Heaven, because that is where the laws of God operate truly, and they can operate only truly because they are the laws of truth. But seek this only, because you can find nothing else. There is nothing else. God is All in all in a very literal sense.

Healing is a way of forgetting the sense of danger the ego has induced in you, by not recognizing its existence in your brother. This strengthens the Holy Spirit in both of you, because it is a refusal to acknowledge fear. Love needs only this invitation. It comes freely to all the Sonship, being what the Sonship is. By your awakening to it, you are merely forgetting what you are not. This enables you to remember what you are.

7.5. Healing and the Changelessness of Mind

Healing is the one ability everyone can develop and must develop if he is to be healed. Healing is the Holy Spirit's form of communication in this world, and the only one He accepts. He recognizes no other, because He does not accept the ego's confusion of mind and body. Minds can communicate, but they cannot hurt. The body in the service of the ego can hurt other bodies, but this cannot occur unless the body has already been confused with the mind.

Fear does not gladden. Healing does. Fear always makes exceptions. Healing never does. Fear produces dissociation, because it induces separation. Healing always produces harmony, because it proceeds from integration. You cannot separate your Self from your Creator, Who created you by sharing His Being with you.

As you can hear two voices, so you can see in two ways. One way shows you an image, or an idol that you may worship out of fear, but will never love. The other shows you only truth, which you will love because you will understand it. Understanding is appreciation, because what you understand you can identify with, and by making it part of you, you have accepted it with love. That is how God Himself created you; in understanding, in appreciation and in love. The whole glory and perfect joy that is the Kingdom lies in you to give.

Your mind is so powerful a light that you can look into theirs and enlighten them, as I can enlighten yours.

Come therefore unto me, and learn of the truth in you. The mind we share is shared by all our brothers. Let your mind shine with mine upon their minds, and by our gratitude to them make them aware of the light in them. This light will shine back upon you and on the whole Sonship, because this is your proper gift to God.

7.6. From Vigilance to Peace

The mind that accepts attack cannot love. That is because it believes it can destroy love, and therefore does not understand what love is. If it does not understand what love is, it cannot perceive itself as loving. This loses the awareness of being, induces feelings of unreality and results in utter confusion. Your thinking has done this because of its power, but your thinking can also save you from this because its power is not of your making. Your ability to direct your thinking as you choose is part of its power. If you do not believe you can do this you have denied the power of your thought, and thus rendered it powerless in your belief.

The ingeniousness of the ego to preserve itself is enormous, but it stems from the very power of the mind the ego denies. This means that the ego attacks what is preserving it, which must result in extreme anxiety. That is why the ego never recognizes what it is doing.

Love is your power, which the ego must deny. It must also deny everything this power gives you because it gives you everything. No one who has everything wants the ego.

The ego therefore opposes all appreciation, all recognition, all sane perception and all knowledge.

The Holy Spirit does not want you to understand conflict; he wants you to realize that, because conflict is meaningless, it is not understandable. As I have already said, understanding brings appreciation and appreciation brings love. Nothing else can be understood, because nothing else is real and therefore nothing else has meaning.

If you will keep in mind what the Holy Spirit offers you, you cannot be vigilant for anything but God and His Kingdom. The only reason you may find this hard to accept is because you may still think there is something else. Belief does not require vigilance unless it is conflicted. Vigilance has no place in peace. It is necessary against beliefs that are not true. When you believe what God does not know, your thought seems to contradict His, and this makes it appear as if you are attacking Him.

I have repeatedly emphasized that the ego does believe it can attack God, and tries to persuade you that you have done this. If the mind cannot attack, the ego proceeds perfectly logically to the belief that you must be a body. By not seeing you as you are, it can see itself as it wants to be. Aware of its weakness the ego wants your allegiance, but not as you really are. The ego therefore wants to engage your mind in its own delusional system, because otherwise the light of your understanding would dispel it. It wants no part of truth, because the ego itself is not true.

You can be perceived with meaning only by the Holy Spirit because your being is the knowledge of God. Any belief you accept apart from this will obscure God's Voice in you, and will therefore obscure God to you. Unless you perceive His creation truly you cannot know the Creator, since God and His creation are not separate. The Oneness of the Creator and the creation is your wholeness, your sanity and your limitless power. This limitless power is God's gift to you, because it is what you are. If you dissociate your mind from it you are perceiving the most powerful force in the universe as if it were weak, because you do not believe you are part of it.

Perceived without your part in it, God's creation is seen as weak, and those who see themselves as weakened do attack. The attack must be blind, however, because there is nothing to attack. Therefore, they make up images, perceive them as unworthy and attack them for their unworthiness. That is all the world of the ego is. Nothing. It has no meaning. It does not exist. Do not try to understand it because, if you do, you are believing that it can be understood and is therefore capable of being appreciated and loved. That would justify its existence, which cannot be justified. You cannot make the meaningless meaningful. This can only be an insane attempt.

Allowing insanity to enter your mind means that you have not judged sanity as wholly desirable. If you want something else you will make something else, but because it is something else, it will attack your thought system and divide your allegiance. You cannot create in this divided state, and you must be vigilant against this divided state because only peace can be "extended". Your divided mind is blocking the extension of the Kingdom, and its extension is your joy. If you do not extend the Kingdom, you are not thinking with your Creator and creating as He created.

In this depressing state the Holy Spirit reminds you gently that you are sad because you are not fulfilling your function as co- creator with God, and are therefore depriving yourself of joy. This is not God's choice but yours. Creation, not separation, is your will because it is God's, and nothing that opposes this means anything at all.

7.7. The Totality of the Kingdom

Denial has no power in itself, but you can give it the power of your mind, whose power is without limit. If you use it to deny reality, reality is gone for you. Denial is a defense, and so it is as capable of being used positively as well as negatively. Used negatively it will be destructive, because it will be used for attack. But in the service of the Holy Spirit, it can help you recognize part of reality, and thus appreciate all of it.

You do not need God's blessing because that you have forever, but you do need yours. The ego's picture of you is deprived, unloving and vulnerable. You cannot love this. Yet you can very easily escape from this image by leaving it behind. You are not there and that is not you. Your brother is the mirror in which you see the image of yourself as long as perception lasts. And perception will last until the Sonship knows itself as whole. You made perception and it must last as long as you want it.

Illusions are investments. They will last as long as you value them. Values are relative, but they are powerful because they are mental judgments. The only way to dispel illusions is to withdraw all investment from them, and they will have no life for you because you will have put them out of your mind. While you include them in it, you are giving life to them.

Attack could never promote attack unless you perceived it as a means of depriving you of something you want. Yet you cannot lose anything unless you do not value it, and therefore do not want it. This makes you feel deprived of it, and by projecting your own rejection you then believe that others are taking it from you. You must be fearful if you believe that your brother is attacking you to tear the Kingdom of Heaven from you. This is the ultimate basis for all the ego's projection.

Projection always sees your wishes in others. If you choose to separate yourself from God, that is what you will think others are doing to you.

You are the Will of God. Do not accept anything else as your will, or you are denying what you are. Deny this and you will attack, believing you have been attacked. But see the Love of God in you, and you will see it everywhere because it is everywhere. See his abundance in everyone, and you will know that you are in Him with them. They are part of you, as you are part of God. You are as lonely without understanding this as God Himself is lonely when His Sons do not know Him. The peace of God is understanding this. There is only one way out of the world's thinking, just as there was only one way into it. Understand totally by understanding totality.

Perceive any part of the ego's thought system as wholly insane, wholly delusional and wholly undesirable, and you have correctly evaluated all of it. This correction enables you to perceive any part of creation as wholly real, wholly perfect and wholly desirable. The gifts you offer to the ego are always experienced as sacrifices, but the gifts you offer to the Kingdom are gifts to you. They will always be treasured by God because they belong to His beloved Sons, who belong to Him. All power and glory are yours because the Kingdom is His.

7.8. The Unbelievable Belief

We have said that without projection there can be no anger, but it is also true that without extension there can be no love. Every mind must project or extend, because that is how it lives, and every mind is life.

The ego's use of projection and anger can be finally undone. The ego always tries to preserve conflict. It is very ingenious in devising ways that seem to diminish conflict, because it does not want you to find conflict so intolerable that you will insist on giving it up. The ego therefore tries to persuade you that it can free you of conflict, lest you give the ego up and free yourself. Using its own warped version of the laws of God, the ego utilizes the power of the mind only to defeat the mind's real purpose. It projects conflict from your mind to other minds, in an attempt to persuade you that you have gotten rid of the problem.

You cannot perpetuate an illusion about another without perpetuating it about yourself. There is no way out of this, because it is impossible to fragment the mind. To fragment is to break into pieces, and mind cannot attack or be attacked. The belief that it can, an error the ego always makes, underlies its whole use of projection. It does not understand what mind is, and therefore does not understand what you are. Yet its existence is dependent on your mind, because the ego is your belief. The ego is a confusion in identification.

Do not be afraid of the ego. It depends on your mind, and as you made it by believing in it, so you can dispel it by withdrawing belief from it. Do not project the responsibility for your belief in it onto anyone else, or you will preserve the belief. When you are willing to accept sole responsibility for the ego's existence you will have laid aside all anger and all attack, because they come from an attempt to project responsibility for your own errors. But having accepted the errors as yours, do not keep them. Give them over quickly to the Holy Spirit to be undone completely, so that all their effects will vanish from your mind and from the Sonship as a whole.

The whole purpose of this course is to teach you that the ego is unbelievable and will forever be unbelievable. You who made the ego by believing the unbelievable cannot make this judgment alone. By accepting the Atonement for yourself, you are deciding against the belief that you can be alone, thus dispelling the idea of separation and affirming your true identification with the whole Kingdom as literally part of you. This identification is as beyond doubt as it is beyond belief. Your wholeness has no limits because *being* is infinity.

7.9. The Extension of the Kingdom

Selfishness is of the ego, but Self-fullness is of spirit because that is how God created it. The Holy Spirit is in the part of the mind that lies between the ego and the spirit, mediating between them always in favor of the spirit.

The extension of God's Being is spirit's only function. Its fullness cannot be contained, any more than can the fullness of its Creator. Fullness is extension. The ego's whole thought system blocks extension, and thus blocks your only function. It therefore blocks your joy, so that you perceive yourself as unfulfilled. Unless you create you are unfulfilled, but God does not know unfulfillment and therefore you must create.

The Kingdom is forever extending because it is in the Mind of God. You do not know your joy because you do not know your own Self-fullness. Exclude any part of the Kingdom from yourself and you are not whole. A split mind cannot perceive its fullness, and needs the miracle of its wholeness to dawn upon it and heal it. This reawakens the wholeness in it, and restores it to the Kingdom because of its acceptance of wholeness. The full appreciation of the mind's Self-fullness makes selfishness impossible and extension inevitable. That is why there is perfect peace in the Kingdom. Spirit is fulfilling its function, and only complete fulfillment is peace.

Be confident that you have never lost your Identity and the extensions which maintain It in wholeness and peace. Miracles are an expression of this confidence.

7.10. The Confusion of Pain and Joy

The Holy Spirit will direct you only so as to avoid pain. Surely no one would object to this goal if he recognized it. The problem is not whether what the Holy Spirit says is true, but whether you want to listen to what He says. You no more recognize what is painful than you know what is joyful, and are, in fact, very apt to confuse the two. The Holy Spirit's main function is to teach you to tell them apart. What is joyful to you is painful to the ego, and as long as you are in doubt about what you are, you will be confused about joy and pain. This confusion is the cause of the whole idea of sacrifice. Obey the Holy Spirit, and you will be giving up the ego. But you will be sacrificing nothing. On the contrary, you will be gaining everything. If you believed this, there would be no conflict.

The Holy Spirit always sides with you and with your strength. As long as you avoid His guidance in any way, you want to be weak. Yet weakness is frightening. What else, then, can this decision mean except that you want to be fearful? The Holy Spirit never asks for sacrifice, but the ego always does.

His Voice will teach you how to distinguish between pain and joy, and will lead you out of the confusion you have made.

Miracles are in accord with the Will of God, Whose Will you do not know because you are confused about what you will. The miracle is therefore a lesson in what joy is. Being a lesson in sharing it is a lesson in love, which is joy. Every miracle is thus a lesson in truth, and by offering truth you are learning the difference between pain and joy.

7.11 The State of Grace

Grace is the natural state of every Son of God. When he is not in a state of grace, he is out of his natural environment and does not function well. Everything he does becomes a strain, because he was not created for the environment that he has made. He therefore cannot adapt to it, nor can he adapt it to him. There is no point in trying. A Son of God is happy only when he knows he is with God. That is the only environment in which he will not experience strain, because that is where he belongs. It is also the only environment that is worthy of him, because his own worth is beyond anything he can make.

I call upon you to remember that I have chosen you to teach the Kingdom to the Kingdom.

Chapter 8

The Journey Back

8.1. The Direction of the Curriculum

Knowledge is not the motivation for learning this course. Peace is.

The distractions of the ego may seem to interfere with your learning, but the ego has no power to distract you unless you give it the power to do so. The ego's voice is a hallucination. You cannot expect it to say "I am not real." Yet you are not asked to dispel your hallucinations alone. You are merely asked to evaluate them in terms of their results to you. If you do not want them on the basis of loss of peace, they will be removed from your mind for you.

Every response to the ego is a call to war, and war does deprive you of peace. Yet in this war there is no opponent. This is the reinterpretation of reality that you must make to secure peace, and the only one you need ever make. Those whom you perceive as opponents are part of your peace, which you are giving up by attacking them.

Your past learning must have taught you the wrong things, simply because it has not made you happy.

The curriculum of the Atonement is the opposite of the curriculum you have established for yourself, but so is its outcome. If the outcome of yours has made you unhappy, and if you want a different one, a change in the curriculum is obviously necessary. The first change to be introduced is a change in direction.

You cannot learn simultaneously from two teachers who are in total disagreement about everything. Their joint curriculum presents an impossible learning task. They are teaching you entirely different things in entirely different ways, which might be possible except that both are teaching you about yourself. If you listen to both, your mind will be split about what your reality is.

8.2. The Difference between Imprisonment and Freedom

There is a rationale for choice. Only one Teacher knows what your reality is. If learning to remove the obstacles to that knowledge is the purpose of the curriculum, you must learn it of Him. The ego does not know what it is trying to teach. It is trying to teach you what you are without knowing what you are. It is expert only in confusion.

Learning is joyful if it leads you along your natural path, and facilitates the development of what you have.

The ego tries to teach that you want to oppose God's Will. The Holy Spirit leads you steadily along the path of freedom, teaching you how to disregard or look beyond everything that would hold you back.

We have said that the Holy Spirit teaches you the difference between pain and joy. That is the same as saying He teaches you the difference between imprisonment and freedom. You cannot make this distinction without Him because you have taught yourself that imprisonment is freedom.

The Holy Spirit's teaching takes only one direction and has only one goal. His direction is freedom and His goal is God. When you have learned that your will is God's, you could no more will to be without Him than He could will to be without you. This is freedom and this is joy.

8.3. The Holy Encounter

When you meet anyone, remember it is a holy encounter. As you see him you will see yourself. As you treat him you will treat yourself. As you think of him you will think of yourself. Never forget this, for in him you will find yourself or lose yourself. Whenever two Sons of God meet, they are given another chance at salvation. Do not leave anyone without giving salvation to him and receiving it yourself. For I am always there with you, in remembrance of you.

The goal of the curriculum, regardless of the teacher you choose, is "Know thyself." There is nothing else to seek. Everyone is looking for himself and for the power and glory he thinks he has lost. Whenever you are with anyone, you have another opportunity to find them. Your power and glory are in him because they are yours. The ego tries to find them in yourself alone, because it does not know where to look. The Holy Spirit teaches you that if you look only at yourself you cannot find yourself, because that is not what you are. Whenever you are with a brother, you are learning what you are because you are teaching what you are. He will respond either with pain or with joy, depending on which teacher you are following. He will be imprisoned or released according to your decision, and so will you. Never forget your responsibility to him, because it is your responsibility to yourself. Give him his place in the Kingdom and you will have yours.

Through His power and glory all your wrong decisions are undone completely, releasing you and your brother from every imprisoning thought any part of the Sonship holds.

8.4. The Gift of Freedom

If God's Will for you is complete peace and joy, unless you experience only this you must be refusing to acknowledge His Will. His Will does not vacillate, being changeless forever. When you are not at peace it can only be because you do not believe you are in Him. Yet He is All in all. His peace is complete, and you must be included in it. His laws govern you because they govern everything. You cannot exempt yourself from His laws, although you can disobey them. Yet if you do, and only if you do, you will feel lonely and helpless, because you are denying yourself everything.

I said that I am with you always, even unto the end of the world. That is why I am the light of the world. If I am with you in the loneliness of the world, the loneliness is gone. You cannot maintain the illusion of loneliness if you are not alone. My purpose, then, is still to overcome the world. I do not attack it, but my light must dispel it because of what it is. Light does not attack darkness, but it does shine it away. If my light goes with you everywhere, you shine it away with me. The light becomes ours, and you cannot abide in darkness any more than darkness can abide wherever you go. The remembrance of me is the remembrance of yourself, and of Him Who sent me to you.

If you will accept the fact that I am with you, you are denying the world and accepting God. My will is His, and your decision to hear me is the decision to hear His Voice and abide in His Will. As God sent me to you so will I send you to others. And I will go to them with you, so we can teach them peace and union.

Do you not think the world needs peace as much as you do? Do you not want to give it to the world as much as you want to receive it? For unless you do, you will not receive it.

Healing is the way in which the separation is overcome. Separation is overcome by union. It cannot be overcome by separating. The decision to unite must be unequivocal, or the mind itself is divided and not whole. Your mind is the means by which you determine your own condition, because mind is the mechanism of decision. It is the power by which you separate or join, and experience pain or joy accordingly. My decision cannot overcome yours, because yours is as powerful as mine.

Nothing God created can oppose your decision, as nothing God created can oppose His Will. God gave your will its power, which I can only acknowledge in honor of His. If you want to be like me I will help you, knowing that we are alike. If you want to be different, I will wait until you change your mind. I can teach you, but only you can choose to listen to my teaching. How else can it be, if God's Kingdom is freedom? Freedom cannot be learned by tyranny of any kind, and the perfect equality of all God's Sons cannot be recognized

Chapter 8

through the dominion of one mind over another. God's Sons are equal in will, all being the Will of their Father.

Freedom is the only gift you can offer to God's Sons, being an acknowledgment of what they are and what He is. Freedom is creation, because it is love. Whom you seek to imprison you do not love. Therefore, when you seek to imprison anyone, including yourself, you do not love him and you cannot identify with him. When you imprison yourself you are losing sight of your true identification with me and with the Father.

8.5. The Undivided Will of the Sonship

There is no separation of God and His creation. You will realize this when you understand that there is no separation between your will and mine. Let the Love of God shine upon you by your acceptance of me. My reality is yours and His. By joining your mind with mine you are signifying your awareness that the Will of God is One.

When you unite with me you are uniting without the ego, because I have renounced the ego in myself and therefore cannot unite with yours. Our union is therefore the way to renounce the ego in you. The truth in both of us is beyond the ego.

Whenever fear intrudes anywhere along the road to peace, it is because the ego has attempted to join the journey with us and cannot do so. Sensing defeat and angered by it, the ego regards itself as rejected and becomes retaliative. You are invulnerable to its retaliation because I am with you. On this journey you have chosen me as your companion instead of the ego. Do not attempt to hold on to both, or you will try to go in different directions and will lose the way.

Let us not love His direction through illusions, for only illusions of another direction can obscure the one for which God's Voice speaks in all of us. Never accord the ego the power to interfere with the journey. It has none, because the journey is the way to what is true. Leave all illusions behind, and reach beyond all attempts of the ego to hold you back. I go before you because I am beyond the ego. Reach, therefore, for my hand because you want to transcend the ego.

8.6. The Treasure of God

Listen to the story of the prodigal son, and learn what God's treasure is and yours: This son of a loving father left his home and thought he had squandered everything for nothing of any value, although he had not understood its worthlessness at the time. He was ashamed to return to his father, because he thought he had hurt him. Yet when he came home the father welcomed him with joy, because the son himself was his father's treasure. He wanted nothing else.

God wants only His Son because His Son is His only treasure. You made neither yourself nor your function. You made only the decision to be unworthy of both. Yet you cannot make yourself unworthy because you are the treasure of God, and what He values is valuable.

His joy lay in creating you, and He extends His Fatherhood to you so that you can extend yourself as He did. Creation is the Will of God. His Will created you to create.

There is no question but one you should ever ask of yourself; "Do I want to know my Father's Will for me?". Our function is to work together, because apart from each other we cannot function at all. The whole power of God's Son lies in all of us, but not in any of us alone.

My devotion to you is of Him, being born of my knowledge of myself and Him. We cannot be separated. Whom God has joined cannot be separated, and God has joined all His Sons with Himself. The journey to God is merely the reawakening of the knowledge of where you are always, and what you are forever. It is a journey without distance to a goal that has never changed.

8.7. The Body as a Means of Communication

Attack is always physical. When attack in any form enters your mind you are equating yourself with a body, since this is the ego's interpretation of the body. You do not have to attack physically to accept this interpretation. You are accepting it simply by the belief that attack can get you something you want. If you did not believe this, the idea of attack would have no appeal for you. When you equate yourself with a body you will always experience depression. When a child of God thinks of himself in this way he is belittling himself, and seeing his brothers as similarly belittled. Since he can find himself only in them, he has cut himself off from salvation.

If you use the body for attack, it is harmful to you. If you use it only to reach the minds of those who believe they are bodies, and teach them through the body that this is not so, you will understand the power of the mind that is in you. If you use the body for this and only for this, you cannot use it for attack. In the service of uniting it becomes a beautiful lesson in communion. The Holy Spirit does not see the body as you do, because He knows the only reality of anything is the service it renders God on behalf of the function He gives it.

Communication ends separation. Attack promotes it. The body is beautiful or ugly, peaceful or savage, helpful or harmful, according to the use to which it is put. Misuse it and you will misunderstand it. Interpret anything apart from the Holy Spirit and you will mistrust it. This will lead you to hatred and attack and loss of peace.

When you look upon a brother as a physical entity, his power and glory are "lost" to you and so are yours. You have attacked him, but you must have attacked yourself first. Do not see him this way for your own salvation, which must bring him his. Do not allow him to belittle himself in your mind, but give him freedom from his belief in littleness, and thus escape from yours. As part of you, he is holy. As part of me, you are. To communicate with part of God Himself is to reach beyond the Kingdom to its Creator, through His Voice which He has established as part of you.

There is nothing so frustrating to a learner as a curriculum he cannot learn. His sense of adequacy suffers, and he must become depressed. Being faced with an impossible learning situation is the most depressing thing in the world. In fact, it is ultimately why the world itself is depressing. The Holy Spirit's curriculum is never depressing, because it is a curriculum of joy. Whenever the reaction to learning is depression, it is because the true goal of the curriculum has been lost sight of.

Mind cannot be made physical, but it can be made manifest through the physical if it uses the body to go beyond itself. By reaching out, the mind extends itself. It does not stop at the body, for if it does it is blocked in its purpose. A mind that has been blocked has allowed itself to be vulnerable to attack, because it has turned against itself.

The removal of blocks, then, is the only way to guarantee help and healing. Help and healing are the normal expressions of a mind that is working through the body, but not in it.

To communicate is to join and to attack is to separate. To confuse a learning device with a curriculum goal is a fundamental confusion that blocks the understanding of both.

The opposite of joy is depression. When your learning promotes depression instead of joy, you cannot be listening to God's joyous Teacher and learning His lessons.

Whenever you see another as limited to or by the body, you are imposing this limit on yourself. Are you willing to accept this, when your whole purpose for learning should be to escape from limitations?

8.8. The Body as Means or End

The body exists in a world that seems to contain two voices, , the ego's and the Holy Spirit's, fighting for its possession. In this perceived constellation the body is seen as capable of shifting its allegiance from one to the other, making the concepts of both health and sickness meaningful. The ego makes a fundamental confusion between means and end as it always does. Regarding the body as an end, the ego has no real use for it because it is not an end. You must have noticed an outstanding characteristic of every end that the ego has accepted as its own. When you have achieved it, it has not satisfied you. This is why the ego is forced to shift ceaselessly from one goal to another, so that you will continue to hope it can yet offer you something.

It has been particularly difficult to overcome the ego's belief in the body as an end, because it is synonymous with the belief in attack as an end. The ego has a profound investment in sickness. If you are sick, how can you object to the ego's firm belief that you are not invulnerable? This is an appealing argument from the ego's point of view, because it obscures the obvious attack that underlies the sickness. If you recognized this and also decided against attack, you could not give this false witness to the ego's stand.

It is hard to perceive sickness as a false witness, because you do not realize that it is entirely out of keeping with what you want. This witness, then, appears to be innocent and trustworthy because you have not seriously cross-examined him. If you had, you would not consider sickness such a strong witness on behalf of the ego's views. A more honest statement would be that those who want the ego are predisposed to defend it. Therefore, their choice of witnesses should be suspect from the beginning.

Sickness is a way of demonstrating that you can be hurt. It is a witness to your frailty, your vulnerability, and your extreme need to depend on external guidance. The ego uses this as its best argument for your need for its guidance. It dictates endless prescriptions for avoiding catastrophic outcomes.

No one can doubt the ego's skill in building up false cases. Nor can anyone doubt your willingness to listen until you choose not to accept anything except truth. When you lay the ego aside, it will be gone. The Holy Spirit's Voice is as loud as your willingness to listen. It cannot be louder without violating your freedom of choice, which the Holy Spirit seeks to restore, never to undermine.

The Holy Spirit teaches you to use your body only to reach your brothers, so He can teach His message through you. This will heal them and therefore heal you. Do not allow the body to be a mirror of a split mind. Do not let it reflect your decision to attack. Health is the beginning of the proper perspective on life under the guidance of the one Teacher Who knows what life is, being the Voice for Life Itself.

8.9. Healing as Corrected Perception

I said before that the Holy Spirit is the Answer. He is the Answer to everything, because He knows what the answer to everything is. The ego does not know what a real question is, although it asks an endless number. Yet you can learn this as you learn to question the value of the ego, and thus establish your ability to evaluate its questions. When the ego tempts you to sickness do not ask the Holy Spirit to heal the body, for this would merely be to accept the ego's belief that the body is the proper aim of healing. Ask, rather, that the Holy Spirit teach you the right perception of the body, for perception alone can be distorted. Only perception can be sick, because only perception can be wrong.

Wholeness heals because it is of the mind. All forms of sickness, even unto death, are physical expressions of the fear of awakening. "Rest in peace" is a blessing for the living, not the dead, because rest comes from waking, not from sleeping. Sleep is withdrawing; waking is joining. Dreams are illusions of joining, because they reflect the ego's distorted notions about what joining is.

Healing is release from the fear of waking. The decision to wake, is the reflection of the will to love, since all healing involves replacing fear with love.

The ego, which always wants to weaken the mind, tries to separate it from the body in an attempt to destroy it. The ego despises weakness, even though it makes every effort to induce it. The ego wants only what it hates. To the ego this is perfectly sensible. Believing in the power of attack, the ego wants attack.

Sickness is not of the body, but of the mind. All forms of sickness are signs that the mind is split, and does not accept a unified purpose.

The unification of purpose, then, is the Holy Spirit's only way of healing.

Chapter 9

The Acceptance of the Atonement

9.1. The Acceptance of Reality

Fear of the Will of God is one of the strangest beliefs the human mind has ever made. It could not possibly have occurred unless the mind were already profoundly split, making it possible for it to be afraid of what it really is. Reality cannot "threaten" anything except illusions, since reality can only uphold truth. The very fact that the Will of God, which is what you are, is perceived as fearful, demonstrates that you are afraid of what you are. It is not, then, the Will of God of which you are afraid, but yours.

Your will is not the ego's, and that is why the ego is against you. What seems to be the fear of God is really the fear of your own reality. It is impossible to learn anything consistently in a state of panic. If the purpose of this course is to help you remember what you are, and if you believe that what you are is fearful, then it must follow that you will not learn this course. Yet the reason for the course is that you do not know what you are.

If you do not know what your reality is, why would you be so sure that it is fearful? You have set up this strange situation so that it is impossible to escape from it without a Guide Who does know what your reality is. The purpose of this Guide is merely to remind you of what you want. He is merely making every possible effort, within the limits you impose on Him, to re-establish your own will in your awareness.

You have imprisoned your will beyond your own awareness, where it remains, but cannot help you. When I said that the Holy Spirit's function is to sort out the true from the false in your mind, I meant that He has the power to look into what you have hidden and recognize the Will of God there. His recognition of this Will can make it real to you because He is in your mind, and therefore He is your reality. If, then, his perception of your mind brings its reality to you, he is helping you to remember what you are. The only source of fear in this process is what you think you will lose.

Chapter 9

A divided mind cannot communicate, because it speaks for different things to the same mind.

You may insist that the Holy Spirit does not answer you, but it might be wiser to consider the kind of questioner you are. Your will is your salvation because it is the same as God's. The separation is nothing more than the belief that it is different.

No right mind can believe that its will is stronger than God's. If, then, a mind believes that its will is different from His, it can only decide either that there is no God or that God's Will is fearful. The former accounts for the atheist and the latter for the martyr, who believes that God demands sacrifices. Either of these insane decisions will induce panic, because the atheist believes he is alone, and the martyr believes that God is crucifying him. Yet no one really wants either abandonment or retaliation, even though many may seek both.

Ultimately everyone must remember the Will of God, because ultimately everyone must recognize himself. This recognition is the recognition that his will and God's are one. In the presence of truth, there are no unbelievers and no sacrifices. In the security of reality, fear is totally meaningless. To deny *what is* can only seem to be fearful. Fear cannot be real without a cause, and God is the only Cause. God is Love and you do want Him. This is your will. Ask for this and you will be answered, because you will be asking only for what belongs to you.

The fact that God is Love does not require belief, but it does require acceptance. It is indeed possible for you to deny facts, although it is impossible for you to change them. If you hold your hands over your eyes, you will not see because you are interfering with the laws of seeing. If you deny love, you will not know it because your cooperation is the law of its being. You cannot change laws you did not make, and the laws of happiness were created for you, not by you.

Any attempt to deny what *is* must be fearful, and if the attempt is strong it will induce panic. Willing against reality, though impossible, can be made into a very persistent goal even though you do not want it. But consider the result of this strange decision. You are devoting your mind to what you do not want.

As long as you believe that fear is possible, you will not create.

You cannot distort reality and know what it is. And if you do distort reality you will experience anxiety, depression and ultimately panic, because you are trying to make yourself unreal. When you feel these things, do not try to look beyond yourself for truth, for truth can only be within you. Say, therefore:

Christ is in me, and where He is God must be, for Christ is part of Him.

9.2. The Answer to Prayer

Everyone who ever tried to use prayer to ask for something has experienced what appears to be failure. This is not only true in connection with specific things that might be harmful, but also in connection with requests that are strictly in line with this course. The latter in particular might be incorrectly interpreted as "proof" that the course does not mean what it says. You must remember, however, that the course states, and repeatedly, that its purpose is the escape from fear.

9.3. The Correction of Error

To the ego it is kind and right and good to point out errors and "correct" them. This makes perfect sense to the ego, which is unaware of what errors are and what correction is. Errors are of the ego, and correction of errors lies in the relinquishment of the ego. When you correct a brother, you are telling him that he is wrong. He is still right, because he is a Son of God. His ego is always wrong, no matter what it says or does.

If you point out the errors of your brother's ego you must be seeing through yours, because the Holy Spirit does not perceive his errors. The ego makes no sense, and the Holy Spirit does not attempt to understand anything that arises from it. He does not judge it, knowing that nothing the ego makes means anything.

When you react at all to errors, you are not listening to the Holy Spirit.

When a brother behaves insanely, you can heal him only by perceiving the sanity in him. If you perceive his errors and accept them, you are accepting yours. If you want to give yours over to the Holy Spirit, you must do this with his. Unless this becomes the one way in which you handle all errors, you cannot understand how all errors are undone. How is this different from telling you that what you teach you learn? Your brother is as right as you are, and if you think he is wrong you are condemning yourself.

It is not up to you to change your brother, but merely to accept him as he is. His errors do not come from the truth that is in him, and can have no effect at all on the truth in you.

The Holy Spirit in you forgives all things in you and in your brother. His errors are forgiven with yours. Atonement is no more separate than love. Atonement cannot be separate because it comes from love. Any attempt you make to correct a brother means that you believe correction by you is possible, and this can only be the arrogance of the ego. Correction is of God, Who does not know of arrogance.

9.4. The Holy Spirit's Plan of Forgiveness

Atonement is for all, because it is the way to undo the belief that anything is for you alone. To forgive is to overlook. Look, then, beyond error and do not let your perception rest upon it, for you will believe what your perception holds. Accept as true only what your brother is, if you would know yourself. Perceive what he is not and you cannot know what you are, because you see him falsely. Remember always that your Identity is shared, and that Its sharing is Its reality.

The Atonement is a lesson in sharing. The Holy Spirit merely reminds you of the natural use of your abilities. By reinterpreting the ability to attack into the ability to share, he translates what you have made into what God created.

Forgiveness through the Holy Spirit lies simply in looking beyond error from the beginning, and thus keeping it unreal for you.

Follow the Holy Spirit's teaching in forgiveness, then, because forgiveness is His function and He knows how to fulfill it perfectly. That is what I meant when I said that miracles are natural, and when they do not occur something has gone wrong. Miracles are merely the sign of your willingness to follow the Holy Spirit's plan of salvation.

The ego literally lives on borrowed time, and its days are numbered. Do not fear the Last Judgment, but welcome it and do not wait, for the ego's time is "borrowed" from your eternity. The Second Coming is merely the return of "sense". Can this possibly be fearful?

The Second Coming is the awareness of reality, not its return.

Behold, my child, reality is here. It belongs to you and me and God, and is perfectly satisfying to all of Us. Only this awareness heals, because it is the awareness of truth.

9.5. The Unhealed Healer

There is an advantage to bringing nightmares into awareness, but only to teach that they are not real, and that anything they contain is meaningless. The unhealed healer cannot do this because he does not believe it. All unhealed healers follow the ego's plan for forgiveness in one form or another. If they are theologians they are likely to condemn themselves, teach condemnation and advocate a fearful solution. Projecting condemnation onto God, they make Him appear retaliative, and fear His retribution. What they have done is merely to identify with the ego, and by perceiving what it does, condemn themselves because of this confusion.

When God said, "Let there be light," there was light. Can you find light by analyzing darkness? Nothing will change unless it is understood, since light is understanding.

The Holy Spirit makes healing clear in any situation in which He is the Guide. You can only let Him fulfill His function. He needs no help for this. Trust Him, for help is His function, and He is of God. As you awaken other minds to the Holy Spirit through Him, and not yourself, you will understand that you are not obeying the laws of this world.

By following the right Guide, you will learn the simplest of all lessons:

By their fruits ye shall know them, and they shall know themselves.

9.6. The Acceptance of Your Brother

How can you become increasingly aware of the Holy Spirit in you except by His effects? You cannot see Him with your eyes nor hear Him with your ears. How, then, can you perceive Him at all? If you inspire joy and others react to you with joy, even though you are not experiencing joy yourself there must be something in you that is capable of producing it.

If your brothers are part of you, will you accept them? Only they can teach you what you are, for your learning is the result of what you taught them. What you call upon in them you call upon in yourself. And as you call upon it in them it becomes real to you. God has but one Son, knowing them all as One. Everyone God created is part of you and shares His glory with you. His glory belongs to Him, but it is equally yours. You cannot, then, be less glorious than He is.

You are not yet awake, but you can learn how to awaken. Very simply, the Holy Spirit teaches you to awaken others. As you see them waken you will learn what waking means, and because you have chosen to wake them, their gratitude and their appreciation of what you have given them will teach you its value.

Eternity is one time, its only dimension being "always." This cannot mean anything to you until you remember God's open Arms, and finally know His open Mind. Like Him, you are "always"; in His mind and with a mind like His. In your open mind are your creations, in perfect communication born of perfect understanding. Could you but accept one of them you would not want anything the world has to offer. Everything else would be totally meaningless.

9.7. The Two Evaluations

It is perfectly obvious that if the Holy Spirit looks with love on all He perceives, He looks with love on you. His evaluation of you is based on His knowledge of what you are, and so He evaluates you truly. And this evaluation must be in your mind, because He is. The ego is also in your mind, because you have accepted it there. Its evaluation of you, however, is the exact opposite of the Holy Spirit's, because the ego does not love you. It is unaware of what you are, and wholly mistrustful of everything it perceives because its perceptions are so shifting. The ego is therefore capable of suspiciousness at best and viciousness at worst.

You have two conflicting evaluations of yourself in your mind, and they cannot both be true. You do not yet realize how completely different these evaluations are, because you do not understand how lofty the Holy Spirit's perception of you really is. He is not deceived by anything you do, because he never forgets what you are. The ego is deceived by everything you do, especially when you respond to the Holy Spirit, because at such times its confusion increases. The ego is, therefore, particularly likely to attack you when you react lovingly, because it has evaluated you as unloving and you are going against its judgment. The ego will attack your motives as soon as they become clearly out of accord with its perception of you. This is when it will shift abruptly from suspiciousness to viciousness, since its uncertainty is increased. Yet it is surely pointless to attack in return. What can this mean except that you are agreeing with the ego's evaluation of what you are?

If you choose to see yourself as unloving you will not be happy. You are condemning yourself and must therefore regard yourself as inadequate. Would you look to the ego to help you escape from a sense of inadequacy it has produced, and must maintain for its existence? Can you escape from its evaluation of you by using its methods for keeping this picture intact?

You cannot evaluate an insane belief system from within it. Its range precludes this. You can only go beyond it, look back from a point where sanity exists and see the contrast. Only by this contrast can insanity be judged as insane. With the grandeur of God in you, you have chosen to be little and to lament your littleness.

The Holy Spirit judges against the reality of the ego's thought system merely because He knows its foundation is not true. Therefore, nothing that arises from it means anything. He judges every belief you hold in terms of where it comes from. If it comes from God, He knows it to be true. If it does not, He knows that it is meaningless.

Whenever you question your value, say:

God Himself is incomplete without me.

9.8. Grandeur versus Grandiosity

Grandeur is of God, and only of Him. Therefore, it is in you. Whenever you become aware of it, however dimly, you abandon the ego automatically, because in the presence of the grandeur of God the meaninglessness of the ego becomes perfectly apparent. Self-inflation is of the ego; its alternative to the grandeur of God.

Grandiosity is always a cover for despair. The essence of grandiosity is competitiveness, because it always involves attack. It is a delusional attempt to outdo, but not to undo. We said before that the ego vacillates between suspiciousness and viciousness. It remains suspicious as long as you despair of yourself. It shifts to viciousness when you decide not to tolerate self-abasement and seek relief. Then it offers you the illusion of attack as a "solution."

The ego does not understand the difference between grandeur and grandiosity, because it sees no difference between miracle impulses and ego-alien beliefs of its own.

The ego is immobilized in the presence of God's grandeur, because His grandeur establishes your freedom. Even the faintest hint of your reality literally drives the ego from your mind, because you will give up all investment in it. Grandeur is totally without illusions, and because it is real it is compellingly convincing. The ego will make every effort to recover and mobilize its energies against your release. It will tell you that you are insane, and argue that grandeur cannot be a real part of you because of the littleness in which it believes. Yet your grandeur is not delusional because you did not make it. You made grandiosity and are afraid of it because it is a form of attack, but your grandeur is of God, Who created it out of His Love.

The ego depends solely on your willingness to tolerate it. If you are willing to look upon your grandeur you cannot despair, and therefore you cannot want the ego. Your grandeur is God's answer to the ego, because it is true.

Your grandeur will never deceive you, but your illusions always will. Illusions are deceptions.

It is easy to distinguish grandeur from grandiosity, because love is returned and pride is not. Pride will not produce miracles, and will therefore deprive you of the true witnesses to your reality. God wants you to behold what He created because it is His joy.

God is incomplete without you because His grandeur is total, and you cannot be missing from it.

You are altogether irreplaceable in the Mind of God. No one else can fill your part in it, and while you leave your part of it empty your eternal place merely waits for your return. Your value is in God's Mind, and therefore not in yours alone. To accept yourself as God created you cannot be arrogance, because it is the denial of arrogance. To accept your littleness is arrogant, because it means that you believe your evaluation of yourself is truer than God's.

He would have you replace the ego's belief in littleness with his own exalted answer to what you are, so that you can cease to question it and know it for what it is.

Chapter 10

The Idols of Sickness

Introduction

Nothing beyond yourself can make you fearful or loving, because nothing is beyond you. Time and eternity are both in your mind, and will conflict until you perceive time solely as a means to regain eternity. You cannot do this as long as you believe that anything happening to you is caused by factors outside yourself. You must learn that time is solely at your disposal, and that nothing in the world can take this responsibility from you.

Every response you make to everything you perceive is up to you, because your mind determines your perception of it.

God does not change His mind about you, for He is not uncertain of Himself. He created you for Himself, but He gave you the power to create for yourself so you would be like Him. When anything threatens your peace of mind, ask yourself, "Has God changed his mind about me?" Then accept His decision, for it is indeed changeless, and refuse to change your mind about yourself. God will never decide against you, or He would be deciding against Himself.

10.1. At Home in God

You are at home in God, dreaming of exile but perfectly capable of awakening to reality. Is it your decision to do so? You recognize from your own experience that what you see in dreams you think is real, while you are asleep. Yet the instant you waken you realize that everything that seemed to happen in the dream did not happen at all.

You do not remember being awake. And it is in this remembering that you will know it can be so again.

You will remember everything the instant you desire it wholly, for if to-desire-wholly is to create, you will have willed away the separation, returning your mind simultaneously to your Creator and your creations. Knowing Them, you will have no wish to sleep, but only the desire to waken and be glad. Dreams will be impossible because you will want only truth, and being at last your will, it will be yours.

10.2. The Decision to Forget

Unless you first know something you cannot dissociate it. Knowledge must precede dissociation, so that dissociation is nothing more than a decision to forget. You are fearful because you have forgotten.

Offer the Holy Spirit only your willingness to remember, for He retains the knowledge of God and of yourself for you, waiting for your acceptance. Give up gladly everything that would stand in the way of your remembering, for God is in your memory. His Voice will tell you that you are part of Him when you are willing to remember Him and know your own reality again. Let nothing in this world delay your remembering of Him, for in this remembering is the knowledge of yourself.

To remember is merely to restore to your mind what is already there. Nothing is beyond His Will for you. But signify your will to remember Him, and behold, He will give you everything but for the asking.

When you attack, you are denying yourself. You are specifically teaching yourself that you are not what you are. Your denial of reality precludes the acceptance of God's gift, because you have accepted something else in its place. If you understand that this is always an attack on truth, and truth is God, you will realize why it is always fearful. If you further recognize that you are part of God, you will understand why it is that you always attack yourself first.

If you realized the complete havoc this makes of your peace of mind you could not make such an insane decision. You make it only because you still believe it can get you something you want. It follows, then, that you want something other than peace of mind, but you have not considered what it must be. Yet the logical outcome of your decision is perfectly clear, if you will only look at it. By deciding against your reality, you have made yourself vigilant against God and His Kingdom. And it is this vigilance that makes you afraid to remember Him.

10.3. The God of Sickness

When you think you are attacking yourself, it is a sure sign that you hate what you think you are. And this, and only this, can be attacked by you. What you think you are can be very hateful, and what this strange image makes you do can be very destructive.

Love cannot suffer, because it cannot attack. The remembrance of love therefore brings invulnerability with it.

To believe a Son of God is sick, is to worship the same idol he does. God created love, not idolatry. Sickness is idolatry, because it is the belief that power can be taken from you. Yet this is impossible, because you are part of God, Who is all power. A sick god must be an idol, made in the image of what its maker thinks he is. And that is exactly what the ego does perceive in a Son of God; a sick god, self-created, self-sufficient, very vicious and very vulnerable. Is this the idol you would worship? Is this the image you would be vigilant to save?

Look calmly at the logical conclusion of the ego's thought system and judge whether its offering is really what you want, for this is what it offers you.

There are no idolaters in the Kingdom, but there is great appreciation for everything that God created, because of the calm knowledge that each one is part of Him.

God is not jealous of the gods you make, but you are. You would save them and serve them, because you believe that they made you. You think they are your father, because you are projecting onto them the fearful fact that you made them to replace God. Yet when they seem to speak to you, remember that nothing can replace God, and whatever replacements you have attempted are nothing.

Very simply, then, you may believe you are afraid of nothingness, but you are really afraid of nothing. And in that awareness you are healed.

If God has but one Son, there is but one God. You share reality with Him, because reality is not divided. To accept other gods before Him is to place other images before yourself. You do not realize how much you listen to your gods, and how vigilant you are on their behalf. Yet they exist only because you honor them. Place honor where it is due, and peace will be yours. It is your inheritance from your real Father.

Only at the altar of God will you find peace. And this altar is in you because God put it there. His Voice still calls you to return, and He will be heard when you place no other gods before Him.

10.4. The End of Sickness

Oneness cannot be divided. If you perceive other gods your mind is split, and you will not be able to limit the split, because it is the sign that you have removed part of your mind from God's Will. This means it is out of control. To be out of control is to be out of reason, and then the mind does become unreasonable. By defining the mind wrongly, you perceive it as functioning wrongly.

God's laws will keep your mind at peace because peace is His Will, and His laws are established to uphold it. His are the laws of freedom, but yours are the laws of bondage. Since freedom and bondage are irreconcilable, their laws cannot be understood together.

Chapter 10

The laws of God work only for your good, and there are no other laws beside His. You have "given" your peace to the gods you made, but they are not there to take it from you, and you cannot give it to them.

You are not free to give up freedom, but only to deny it. Your gods do not bring chaos; you are endowing them with chaos, and accepting it of them. What you have made is so unworthy of you that you could hardly want it, if you were willing to see it as it is. Reality cannot break through the obstructions you interpose, but it will envelop you completely when you let them go.

When you have experienced the protection of God, the making of idols becomes inconceivable. Peace is yours because God created you, and He created nothing else.

The miracle is the act of a Son of God who has laid aside all false gods, and calls on his brothers to do likewise. It is an act of faith, because it is the recognition that his brother can do it. It is a call to the Holy Spirit in his mind, a call that is strengthened by joining. Because the miracle worker has heard God's Voice, he strengthens God's Voice in a sick brother by weakening his belief in sickness, which he does not share. The power of one mind can shine into another, because all the lamps of God were lit by the same spark. It is everywhere and it is eternal.

In many, only the spark remains, for the Great Rays are obscured. Yet God has kept the spark alive so that the Rays can never be completely forgotten. If you but see the little spark you will learn of the greater light, for the Rays are there unseen. Perceiving the spark will heal, but knowing the light will create. Yet in the returning the little light must be acknowledged first, for the separation was a descent from magnitude to littleness. But the spark is still as pure as the Great Light, because it is the remaining call of creation. Put all your faith in it, and God Himself will answer you.

10.5. The Denial of God

The rituals of the god of sickness are strange and very demanding. Joy is never permitted, for depression is the sign of allegiance to the god of sickness. Depression means that you have forsworn God.

Do not forget, however, that to deny God will inevitably result in projection, and you will believe that others and not yourself have done this to you. You must receive the message you give because it is the message you want. You may believe that you judge your brothers by the messages they give you, but you have judged them by the message you give to them. Do not attribute your denial of joy to them, or you cannot see the spark in them that would bring joy to you. It is the denial of the spark that brings depression, for whenever you see your brothers without it, you are denying God.

Allegiance to the denial of God is the ego's religion.

I said before that of yourself you can do nothing, but you are not of yourself. If you were, what you have made would be true, and you could never escape. It is because you did not make yourself that you need be troubled over nothing. Your gods are nothing, because your Father did not create them.

The Love of God is in everything He created, for His Son is everywhere. Look with peace upon your brothers, and God will come rushing into your heart in gratitude for your gift to Him.

Do not look to the god of sickness for healing but only to the God of love, for healing is the acknowledgment of Him.

Only the eternal can be loved, for love does not die. What is of God is His forever, and you are of God. Would He allow Himself to suffer? And would He offer His Son anything that is not acceptable to Him? If you will accept yourself as God created you, you will be incapable of suffering. Yet to do this you must acknowledge Him as your Creator. This is not because you will be punished otherwise. It is merely because your acknowledgment of your Father is the acknowledgment of yourself as you are. Your Father created you wholly without sin, wholly without pain and wholly without suffering of any kind. If you deny Him you bring sin, pain and suffering into your own mind because of the power He gave it. Your mind is capable of creating worlds, but it can also deny what it creates because it is free.

You do not realize how much you have denied yourself, and how much God, in His Love, would not have it so. Yet He would not interfere with you, because He would not know His Son if he were not free. To interfere with you would be to attack Himself, and God is not insane. When you deny Him you are insane. Would you have Him share your insanity? God will never cease to love His Son, and His Son will never cease to love Him. That was the condition of His Son's creation, fixed forever in the Mind of God. To know that is sanity. To deny it is insanity. God gave Himself to you in your creation, and His gifts are eternal. Would you deny yourself to Him?

Do not deny yourself the joy that was created for you for the misery you have made for yourself. God has given you the means for undoing what you have made. Listen, and you will learn how to remember what you are.

If God created His Son perfect, that is how you must learn to see him to learn of his reality. And as part of the Sonship, that is how you must see yourself to learn of yours.

Time itself is your choice. If you would remember eternity, you must look only on the eternal. If you allow yourself to become preoccupied with the temporal, you are living in time. As always, your choice is determined by what you value. Time and eternity cannot both be real, because they contradict each other. If you will accept only what is timeless as real, you will begin to understand eternity and make it yours.

CHAPTER 11

GOD OR THE EGO

Introduction

Either God or the ego is insane. If you will examine the evidence on both sides fairly, you will realize this must be true. Nothing alive is fatherless, for life is creation. Therefore, your decision is always an answer to the question, "Who is my father?" And you will be faithful to the father you choose.

If you made the ego, how can the ego have made you? The authority problem is still the only source of conflict, because the ego was made out of the wish of God's Son to father him. The ego, then, is nothing more than a delusional system in which you made your own father. Make no mistake about this. It sounds insane when it is stated with perfect honesty, but the ego never looks on what it does with perfect honesty. Yet that is its insane premise, which is carefully hidden in the dark cornerstone of its thought system. And either the ego, which you made, is your father, or its whole thought system will not stand.

The cornerstone of God's creation is you, for His thought system is light. Remember the Rays that are there unseen. The more you approach the center of His thought system, the clearer the light becomes. The closer you come to the ego's thought system, the darker and more obscure becomes the way. Yet even the little spark in your mind is enough to lighten it. Bring this light fearlessly with you, and bravely hold it up to the foundation of the ego's thought system. Be willing to judge it with perfect honesty. Open the dark cornerstone of terror on which it rests, and bring it out into the light. There you will see that it rested on meaninglessness, and that everything of which you have been afraid was based on nothing.

Chapter 11

11.1. The Gifts of Fatherhood

To be alone is to be separated from infinity, but how can this be if infinity has no end? No one can be beyond the limitless, because what has no limits must be everywhere. There are no beginnings and no endings in God, whose universe is Himself. Can you exclude yourself from the universe, or from God Who is the universe? I and my Father are one with you, for you are part of Us. Do you really believe that part of God can be missing or lost to Him?

The laws of the universe do not permit contradiction. What holds for God holds for you. If you believe you are absent from God, you will believe that He is absent from you. There is no end to God and His Son, for we are the universe. God is not incomplete, and He is not childless. Because He did not will to be alone, He created a Son like Himself. The universe of love does not stop because you do not see it, nor have your closed eyes lost the ability to see. Look upon the glory of His creation, and you will learn what God has kept for you.

God has given you a place in His mind that is yours forever.

God is your heritage, because His one gift is Himself. Give, then, without limit and without end, to learn how much He has given you. Your ability to accept Him depends on your willingness to give as He gives.

God's Will is that you are His Son. By denying this you deny your own will, and therefore do not know what it is. You must ask what God's Will is in everything, because it is yours. You do not know what it is, but the Holy Spirit remembers it for you. Ask Him, therefore, what God's Will is for you, and He will tell you yours.

The projection of the ego makes it appear as if God's Will is outside yourself, and therefore not yours. In this interpretation it seems possible for God's Will and yours to conflict. God, then, may seem to demand of you what you do not want to give, and thus deprive you of what you want. Would God, Who wants only your will, be capable of this? Your will is His life, which He has given to you.

You are afraid to know God's Will, because you believe it is not yours. This belief is your whole sickness and your whole fear. Believing this you hide in darkness, denying that the light is in you.

You are asked to trust the Holy Spirit only because He speaks for you. He is the Voice for God, but never forget that God did not will to be alone. Blessed are you who learn that to hear the Will of your Father is to know your own. God's Will is that His Son be one, and united with Him in His Oneness. That is why healing is the beginning of the recognition that your will is His.

11.2. The Invitation to Healing

Every miracle that you accomplish speaks to you of the Fatherhood of God. Every healing thought that you accept, either from your brother or in your own mind, teaches you that you are God's Son. In every hurtful thought you hold, wherever you perceive it, lies the denial of God's Fatherhood and of your Sonship.

You cannot deny part of yourself, because the rest will seem to be separate and therefore without meaning. And being without meaning to you, you will not understand it. To deny meaning is to fail to understand. You can heal only yourself, for only God's Son needs healing. You need it because you do not understand yourself, and therefore know not what you do. Having forgotten your will, you do not know what you really want.

Healing is a sign that you want to make whole. And this willingness opens your ears to the Voice of the Holy Spirit, Whose message is wholeness. He will enable you to go far beyond the healing you would undertake, for beside your small willingness to make whole He will lay His Own complete Will and make yours whole. What can the Son of God not accomplish with the Fatherhood of God in him? And yet the invitation must come from you, for you have surely learned that whom you invite as your guest will abide with you.

The Holy Spirit cannot speak to an unwelcoming host, because he will not be heard. The Eternal Guest remains, but His Voice grows faint in alien company. The Holy Spirit needs your protection, only because your care is a sign that you want Him. Think like Him ever so slightly, and the little spark becomes a blazing light that fills your mind so that He becomes your only Guest. Whenever you ask the ego to enter, you lessen His welcome. Whatever journey you choose to take, He will go with you, waiting.

Your willingness need not be perfect, because His is. If you will merely offer Him a little place, He will lighten it so much that you will gladly let it be increased. And by this increase, you will begin to remember creation.

Would you be hostage to the ego or host to God? You will accept only whom you invite. You are free to determine who shall be your guest, and how long he shall remain with you. Yet this is not real freedom, for it still depends on how you see it. The Holy Spirit is there, although He cannot help you without your invitation. Real freedom depends on welcoming reality, and of your guests only the Holy Spirit is real. Know, then, who abides with you merely by recognizing what is there already, and do not be satisfied with imaginary comforters, for the Comforter of God is in you.

11.3. From Darkness to Light

God is very quiet, for there is no conflict in Him. Conflict is the root of all evil, for being blind it does not see whom it attacks. Yet it always attacks the Son of God, and the Son of God is you.

Chapter 11

God's Son is indeed in need of comfort, for he knows not what he does, believing his will is not his own. The Kingdom is his, and yet he wanders homeless.

O my child, if you knew what God wills for you, your joy would be complete! And what He wills has happened, for it was always true. When the light comes and you have said, "God's Will is mine," you will see such beauty that you will know it is not of you. Out of your joy you will create beauty in His Name, for your joy could no more be contained than His. The bleak little world will vanish into nothingness, and your heart will be so filled with joy that it will leap into Heaven, and into the Presence of God. I cannot tell you what this will be like, for your heart is not ready. Yet I can tell you, and remind you often, that what God wills for Himself He wills for you, and what He wills for you is yours.

The way is not hard, but it is very different. Yours is the way of pain, of which God knows nothing. That way is hard indeed, and very lonely. Fear and grief are your guests, and they go with you and abide with you on the way. But the dark journey is not the way of God's Son. Walk in light and do not see the dark companions, for they are not fit companions for the Son of God, who was created of light and in light. The Great Light always surrounds you and shines out from you. How can you see the dark companions in a light such as this? If you see them, it is only because you are denying the light. But deny them instead, for the light is here and the way is clear.

God hides nothing from His Son, even though His Son would hide himself. Yet the Son of God cannot hide his glory, for God wills him to be glorious, and gave him the light that shines in him. You will never lose your way, for God leads you. When you wander, you but undertake a journey that is not real. The dark companions, the dark way, are all illusions. Turn toward the light, for the little spark in you is part of a light so great that it can sweep you out of all darkness forever. For your Father is your Creator, and you are like Him.

Do not be deceived by the dark comforters, and never let them enter the mind of God's Son, for they have no place in his temple. When you are tempted to deny Him remember that there are no other gods to place before Him, and accept His Will for you in peace.

You cannot enter God's Presence with the dark companions beside you, but you also cannot enter alone. All your brothers must enter with you, for until you have accepted them you cannot enter. For you cannot understand wholeness unless you are whole, and no part of the Son can be excluded if he would know the Wholeness of his Father.

In your mind you can accept the whole Sonship and bless it with the light your Father gave it. Time cannot separate you from God if you use it on behalf of the eternal.

11.4. The Inheritance of God's Son

Glory is your inheritance, given you by your Creator that you might extend it. Yet if you hate part of your Self all your understanding is lost, because you are looking on what God created as yourself without love. And since what He created is part of Him, you are denying Him His place in His own altar.

Only you can deprive yourself of anything. Do not oppose this realization, for it is truly the beginning of the dawn of light. Remember also that the denial of this simple fact takes many forms, and these you must learn to recognize and to oppose steadfastly, without exception. This is a crucial step in the reawakening. The beginning phases of this reversal are often quite painful, for as blame is withdrawn from without, there is a strong tendency to harbor it within. It is difficult at first to realize that this is exactly the same thing, for there is no distinction between within and without.

That is why blame must be undone, not seen elsewhere. Lay blame upon yourself and you cannot know yourself, for only the ego blames at all. Self-blame is therefore ego identification, and as much an ego defense as blaming others.

But love yourself with the Love of Christ, for so does your Father love you.

11.5. The "Dynamics" of the Ego

No one can escape from illusions unless he looks at them, for not looking is the way they are protected. There is no need to shrink from illusions, for they cannot be dangerous. We are ready to look more closely at the ego's thought system because together we have the lamp that will dispel it, and since you realize you do not want it, you must be ready. The "dynamics" of the ego will be our lesson for a while, for we must look first at this to see beyond it, since you have made it real. We will undo this error quietly together, and then look beyond it to truth.

What is healing but the removal of all that stands in the way of knowledge? And how else can one dispel illusions except by looking at them directly, without protecting them? Be not afraid, therefore, for what you will be looking at is the source of fear, and you are beginning to learn that fear is not real. Do not be afraid, then, to look upon fear, for it cannot be seen. Clarity undoes confusion by definition, and to look upon darkness through light must dispel it.

Let us begin this lesson in "ego dynamics" by understanding that the term itself does not mean anything. It contains the very contradiction in terms that makes it meaningless. "Dynamics" implies the power to do something, and the whole separation fallacy lies in the belief that the ego has the power to do anything. The ego is fearful to you because you believe this. Yet the truth is very simple:

> *All power is of God.*
> *What is not of Him has no power to do anything.*

Chapter 11

When we look at the ego, then, we are not considering dynamics but delusions. You can surely regard a delusional system without fear, for it cannot have any effects if its source is not real. Fear becomes more obviously inappropriate if you recognize the ego's goal, which is so clearly senseless that any effort on its behalf is necessarily expended on nothing. The ego's goal is quite explicitly ego autonomy. From the beginning, then, its purpose is to be separate, sufficient unto itself and independent of any power except its own. This is why it is the symbol of separation.

Your whole creative function lies in your complete dependence on God, Whose function He shares with you. The belief in ego autonomy is costing you the knowledge of your dependence on God, in which your freedom lies. The ego sees all dependency as threatening, and has twisted even your longing for God into a means of establishing itself. But do not be deceived by its interpretation of your conflict.

The ego always attacks on behalf of separation. Believing it has the power to do this it does nothing else, because its goal of autonomy is nothing else. The ego is totally confused about reality, but it does not lose sight of its goal. It is much more vigilant than you are, because it is perfectly certain of its purpose. You are confused because you do not recognize yours.

You must recognize that the last thing the ego wishes you to realize is that you are afraid of it. For if the ego could give rise to fear, it would diminish your independence and weaken your power. Yet its one claim to your allegiance is that it can give power to you. Without this belief you would not listen to it at all. How, then, can its existence continue if you realize that, by accepting it, you are belittling yourself and depriving yourself of power?

The ego can and does allow you to regard yourself as supercilious, unbelieving, "lighthearted," distant, emotionally shallow, callous, uninvolved and even desperate, but not really afraid. Minimizing fear, but not its undoing, is the ego's constant effort, and is indeed a skill at which it is very ingenious. How can it preach separation without upholding it through fear, and would you listen to it if you recognized this is what it is doing?

Your recognition that whatever seems to separate you from God is only fear, regardless of the form it takes and quite apart from how the ego wants you to experience it, is therefore the basic ego threat. Its dream of autonomy is shaken to its foundation by this awareness. For though you may countenance a false idea of independence, you will not accept the cost of fear if you recognize it. Yet this is the cost, and the ego cannot minimize it. If you overlook love you are overlooking yourself, and you must fear unreality because you have denied yourself. By believing that you have successfully attacked truth, you are believing that attack has power. Very simply, then, you have become afraid of yourself. And no one wants to find what he believes would destroy him.

Only by learning what fear is can you finally learn to distinguish the possible from the impossible and the false from the true. According to the ego's teaching, its goal can be accomplished and God's purpose can not. According to the Holy Spirit's teaching, only God's purpose can be accomplished, and it is accomplished already.

For only the insane would choose fear in place of love, and only the insane could believe that love can be gained by attack. But the sane realize that only attack could produce fear, from which the Love of God completely protects them.

The ego analyzes; the Holy Spirit accepts. The appreciation of wholeness comes only through acceptance, for to analyze means to break down or to separate out. The attempt to understand totality by breaking it down is clearly the characteristically contradictory approach of the ego to everything. The ego believes that power, understanding and truth lie in separation, and to establish this belief it must attack. Unaware that the belief cannot be established, and obsessed with the conviction that separation is salvation, the ego attacks everything it perceives by breaking it into small, disconnected parts, without meaningful relationships and therefore without meaning. The ego will always substitute chaos for meaning, for if separation is salvation, harmony is threat.

The ego focuses on error and overlooks truth. It makes real every mistake it perceives, and with characteristically circular reasoning concludes that because of the mistake, consistent truth must be meaningless. The next step, then, is obvious. If consistent truth is meaningless, inconsistency must be true. Holding error clearly in mind, and protecting what it has made real, the ego proceeds to the next step in its thought system: Error is real and truth is error.

Selective perception chooses its witnesses carefully, and the ego's witnesses are consistent. The case for insanity is strong to the insane. For reasoning ends at its beginning, and no thought system transcends its source.

Every brother you meet becomes a witness for Christ or for the ego, depending on what you perceive in him. Everyone convinces you of what you want to perceive, and of the reality of the kingdom you have chosen for your vigilance. Everything you perceive is a witness to the thought system you want to be true. Every brother has the power to release you, if you choose to be free. You cannot accept false witness of him unless you have evoked false witnesses against him. If he speaks not of Christ to you, you spoke not of Christ to him. You hear but your own voice, and if Christ speaks through you, you will hear Him.

11.6. Waking to Redemption

It is impossible not to believe what you see, but it is equally impossible to see what you do not believe. Perceptions are built up on the basis of experience, and experience leads to beliefs. It is not until beliefs are fixed that perceptions stabilize. In effect, then, what you believe you do see. The resurrection is the complete triumph of Christ over the ego, not by attack but by transcendence. For Christ does rise above the ego and all its works, and ascends to the Father and His Kingdom.

This course is perfectly clear. If you do not see it clearly, it is because you are interpreting against it, and therefore do not believe it. And since belief determines perception, you do not perceive what it means and therefore do not accept it. Yet different experiences lead to different beliefs and experience does teach. I am leading you to a new kind of experience that you will become less and less willing to deny. Learning of Christ is easy, for to perceive with Him involves no strain at all. His perceptions are your natural awareness, and it is only the distortions you introduce that tire you. Let the Christ in you interpret for you, and do not try to limit what you see by narrow little beliefs that are unworthy of God's Son. For until Christ comes into His Own, the Son of God will see himself as Fatherless.

I am your resurrection and your life. You live in me because you live in God.

Resurrection must compel your allegiance gladly, because it is the symbol of joy. Its whole compelling power lies in the fact that it represents what you want to be. The freedom to leave behind everything that hurts you and humbles you and frightens you cannot be thrust upon you, but it can be offered you through the grace of God. And you can accept it by His grace, for God is gracious to His Son, accepting him without question as His Own.

You have nailed yourself to a cross, and placed a crown of thorns upon your own head. Yet you cannot crucify God's Son, for the will of God cannot die. His Son has been redeemed from his own crucifixion, and you cannot assign to death whom God has given eternal life. The dream of crucifixion still lies heavy on your eyes, but what you see in dreams is not reality. While you perceive the Son of God as crucified, you are asleep.

You will awaken to your own call, for the Call to awake is within you. If I live in you, you are awake. Yet you must see the works I do through you, or you will not perceive that I have done them unto you. Do not set limits on what you believe I can do through you, or you will not accept what I can do for you. Yet it is done already, and unless you give all that you have received you will not know that your redeemer liveth, and that you have awakened with him. Redemption is recognized only by sharing it.

11.7. The Condition of Reality

If you believe in truth and illusion, you cannot tell which is true. To establish your personal autonomy you tried to create unlike your Father, believing that what you made is capable of being unlike Him. Yet everything true is like Him. Perceiving only the real world will lead you to the real Heaven, because it will make you capable of understanding it.

You have made many ideas that you have placed between yourself and your Creator, and these beliefs are the world as you perceive it. Truth is not absent here, but it is obscure. You do not know the difference between what you have made and what you have created.

To believe that you can perceive the real world is to believe that you can know yourself. You can know God because it is His Will to be known. The real world is all that the Holy Spirit has saved for you out of what you have made, and to perceive only this is salvation, because it is the recognition that reality is only what is true.

11.8. The Problem and the Answer

The end of the world is not its destruction, but its translation into Heaven. The reinterpretation of the world is the transfer of all perception to knowledge.

Perceptions are learned, and you are not without a Teacher. Yet your willingness to learn of Him depends on your willingness to question everything you learned of yourself, for you who learned amiss should not be your own teacher.

Ask yourself, therefore, but one simple question:

> *Do I want the problem or do I want the answer?*

Only by asking will you learn that nothing of God demands anything of you. God gives; He does not take. When you refuse to ask, it is because you believe that asking is taking rather than sharing.

Little child of God, you do not understand your Father. You believe in a world that takes, because you believe that you can get by taking. And by that perception you have lost sight of the real world. You are afraid of the world as you see it, but the real world is still yours for the asking. Do not deny it to yourself, for it can only free you. Nothing of God will enslave His Son whom He created free and whose freedom is protected by His Being. Blessed are you who are willing to ask the truth of God without fear, for only thus can you learn that his answer is the release from fear.

Children perceive frightening ghosts and monsters and dragons, and they are terrified. Yet if they ask someone they trust for the meaning of what they perceive, and are willing to let their own interpretations go in favor of reality, their fear goes with them. When a child is helped to translate his "ghost" into a curtain, his "monster" into a shadow, and his "dragon" into a dream he is no longer afraid, and laughs happily at his own fear.

You, my child, are afraid of your brothers and of your Father and of yourself. But you are merely deceived in them. Ask what they are of the Teacher of reality, and hearing His answer, you too will laugh at your fears and replace them with peace. For fear lies not in reality, but in the minds of children who do not understand reality. It is only their lack of understanding that frightens them, and when they learn to perceive truly they are not afraid. And because of this they will ask for truth again when they are frightened. It is not the reality of your brothers or your Father or yourself that frightens you. You do not know what they are, and so you perceive them as ghosts and monsters and dragons. Ask what their reality is from the One Who knows it, and He will tell you what they are. For you do not understand them, and because you are deceived by what you see, you need reality to dispel your fears.

Would you not exchange your fears for truth, if the exchange is yours for the asking? For if God is not deceived in you, you can be deceived only in yourself. Yet you can learn the truth about yourself from the Holy Spirit. When you perceive yourself without deceit, you will accept the real world in place of the false one you have made. And then your Father will lean down to you and take the last step for you, by raising you unto Himself.

Chapter 12

The Holy Spirit's Curriculum

12.1. The Judgment of the Holy Spirit

Understand that you do not respond to anything directly, but to your interpretation of it. Your interpretation thus becomes the justification for the response. That is why analyzing the motives of others is hazardous to you. If you decide that someone is really trying to attack you or desert you or enslave you, you will respond as if he had actually done so, having made his error real to you. To interpret error is to give it power, and having done this you will overlook truth.

The analysis of ego motivation is very complicated, very obscuring, and never without your own ego involvement. The whole process represents a clear-cut attempt to demonstrate your own ability to understand what you perceive. This is shown by the fact that you react to your interpretations as if they were correct. You may then control your reactions behaviorally, but not emotionally.

The Holy Spirit's judgment requires no effort at all on your part. Every loving thought is true. Everything else is an appeal for healing and help, regardless of the form it takes. Can anyone be justified in responding with anger to a brother's plea for help?

To fail to recognize a call for help is to refuse help. Would you maintain that you do not need it? Yet this is what you are maintaining when you refuse to recognize a brother's appeal, for only by answering his appeal can you be helped. Deny your brother help and you will not recognize God's Answer to you. The Holy Spirit does not need your help in interpreting motivation, but you do need His.

Only appreciation is an appropriate response to your brother. Gratitude is due him for both his loving thoughts and his appeals for help, for both are capable of bringing love into your awareness if you perceive them truly. And all your sense of strain comes from your attempts not to do just this. How simple, then, is God's plan for salvation.

CHAPTER 12

Your interpretations of your brother's needs are your interpretation of yours. By giving help you are asking for it, and if you perceive but one need in yourself you will be healed. Every appeal you answer in the Name of Christ brings the remembrance of your Father closer to your awareness. For the sake of your need, then, hear every call for help as what it is, so God can answer you.

By applying the Holy Spirit's interpretation of the reactions of others more and more consistently, you will gain an increasing awareness that His criteria are equally applicable to you. For to recognize fear is not enough to escape from it, although the recognition is necessary to demonstrate the need for escape. The Holy Spirit must still translate the fear into truth. If you were left with the fear, once you had recognized it, you would have taken a step away from reality, not towards it. Yet we have repeatedly emphasized the need to recognize fear and face it without disguise as a crucial step in the undoing of the ego. Consider how well the Holy Spirit's interpretation of the motives of others will serve you then. Having taught you to accept only loving thoughts in others and to regard everything else as an appeal for help, He has taught you that fear itself is an appeal for help. This is what recognizing fear really means. That is the ultimate value in learning to perceive attack as a call for love.

Fear is a symptom of your own deep sense of loss. Fear and love are the only emotions of which you are capable. One is false, for it was made out of denial; and denial depends on the belief in what is denied for its own existence. By interpreting fear correctly as a positive affirmation of the underlying belief it masks, you are undermining its perceived usefulness by rendering it useless. You have denied its power to conceal love, which was its only purpose. The veil that you have drawn across the face of love has disappeared.

Thus does the Holy Spirit replace fear with love and translate error into truth. And thus will you learn of Him how to replace your dream of separation with the fact of unity. For the separation is only the denial of union, and correctly interpreted, attests to your eternal knowledge that union is true.

12.2. The Way to Remember God

Miracles are merely the translation of denial into truth. If to love oneself is to heal oneself, those who are sick do not love themselves. Therefore, they are asking for the love that would heal them, but which they are denying to themselves. If they knew the truth about themselves they could not be sick. The task of the miracle worker thus becomes to deny the denial of truth. The sick must heal themselves, for the truth is in them. Yet having obscured it, the light in another mind must shine into theirs because that light is theirs.

The light in them shines as brightly regardless of the density of the fog that obscures it. If you give no power to the fog to obscure the light, it has none.

Perceive in sickness but another call for love, and offer your brother what he believes he cannot offer himself. Whatever the sickness, there is but one remedy. You will be made whole as you make whole, for to perceive in sickness the appeal for health is to recognize in hatred the call for love. And to give a brother what he really wants is to offer it unto yourself, for your Father wills you to know your brother as yourself. Answer his call for love, and yours is answered. Healing is the love of Christ for His Father and for Himself.

Remember what was said about the frightening perceptions of little children, which terrify them because they do not understand them. If they ask for enlightenment and accept it, their fears vanish. But if they hide their nightmares they will keep them. it is easy to help an uncertain child, for he recognizes that he does not understand what his perceptions mean. Yet you believe that you do understand yours. Little child, you are hiding your head under the cover of the heavy blankets you have laid upon yourself. You are hiding your nightmares in the darkness of your own false certainty, and refusing to open your eyes and look at them.

Let us not save nightmares, for they are not fitting offerings for Christ, and so they are not fit gifts for you. Take off the covers and look at what you are afraid of. Only the anticipation will frighten you, for the reality of nothingness cannot be frightening. Let us not delay this, for your dream of hatred will not leave you without help, and Help is here. Learn to be quiet in the midst of turmoil, for quietness is the end of strife and this is the journey to peace. Look straight at every image that rises to delay you, for the goal is inevitable because it is eternal. The goal of love is but your right, and it belongs to you despite your dreams.

You still want what God wills, and no nightmare can defeat a child of God in his purpose. For your purpose was given you by God, and you must accomplish it because it is His Will. Awake and remember your purpose, for it is your will to do so. What has been accomplished for you must be yours. Do not let your hatred stand in the way of love, for nothing can withstand the love of Christ for His Father, or His Father's Love for Him.

A little while and you will see me, for I am not hidden because you are hiding. I will awaken you as surely as I awakened myself, for I awoke for you. In my resurrection is your release. Our mission is to escape from crucifixion, not from redemption.

12.3. The Investment in Reality

Insistence means investment, and what you invest in, is always related to your notion of salvation. The question is always twofold; first, what is to be saved? And second, how can it be saved?

CHAPTER 12

Whenever you become angry with a brother, for whatever reason, you are believing that the ego is to be saved, and to be saved by attack. If he attacks, you are agreeing with this belief; and if you attack, you are reinforcing it. Remember that those who attack are poor.

Salvation is for the mind, and it is attained through peace. This is the only thing that can be saved and the only way to save it. Any response other than love arises from a confusion about the "what" and the "how" of salvation, and this is the only answer. Never lose sight of this, and never allow yourself to believe, even for an instant, that there is another answer.

To identify with the ego is to attack yourself and make yourself poor. That is why everyone who identifies with the ego feels deprived. What he experiences then is depression or anger, because what he did was to exchange self-love for self-hate, making him afraid of himself. He does not realize this. Even if he is fully aware of anxiety he does not perceive its source as his own ego identification, and he always tries to handle it by making some sort of insane "arrangement" with the world. He always perceives this world as outside himself, for this is crucial to his adjustment. He does not realize that he makes this world, for there is no world outside of him.

Everything you perceive as the outside world is merely your attempt to maintain your ego identification, for everyone believes that identification is salvation. You have projected outward what is antagonistic to what is inward, and therefore you would have to perceive it this way. That is why you must realize that your hatred is in your mind and not outside it before you can get rid of it; and why you must get rid of it before you can perceive the world as it really is.

Do not believe it is outside of yourself, for only by recognizing where it is will you gain control over it. For you do have control over your mind, since the mind is the mechanism of decision.

If you will recognize that all the attack you perceive is in your own mind and nowhere else, you will at last have placed its source, and where it begins it must end. For in this same place also lies salvation. The altar of God where Christ abideth is there. You have defiled the altar, but not the world. Yet Christ has placed the Atonement on the altar for you. Bring your perceptions of the world to this altar, for it is the altar to truth. There you will see your vision changed, and there you will learn to see truly. From this place, where God and His Son dwell in peace and where you are welcome, you will look out in peace and behold the world truly. Yet to find the place, you must relinquish your investment in the world as you project it, allowing the Holy Spirit to extend the real world to you from the altar of God.

12.4. Seeking and Finding

The ego is certain that love is dangerous, and this is always its central teaching. It never puts it this way; on the contrary, everyone who believes that the ego is salvation seems to be intensely engaged in the search for love. Yet the ego, though encouraging the search for love very actively, makes one proviso; do not find it. Its dictates, then, can be summed up simply as: "Seek and do not find." This is the one promise the ego holds out to you, and the one promise it will keep. For the ego pursues its goal with fanatic insistence, and its judgment, though severely impaired, is completely consistent.

It is surely obvious that no one wants to find what would utterly defeat him. Being unable to love, the ego would be totally inadequate in love's presence, for it could not respond at all. Then, you would have to abandon the ego's guidance, for it would be quite apparent that it had not taught you the response you need. The ego will therefore distort love, and teach you that love really calls forth the responses the ego can teach. Follow its teaching, then, and you will search for love, but will not recognize it.

Do you realize that the ego must set you on a journey which cannot but lead to a sense of futility and depression? To seek and not to find is hardly joyous. Is this the promise you would keep? The Holy Spirit offers you another promise, and one that will lead to joy. For His promise is always, "Seek and you will find," and under His guidance you cannot be defeated. His is the journey to accomplishment, and the goal He sets before you He will give you. For He will never deceive God's Son whom He loves with the Love of the Father.

You will undertake a journey because you are not at home in this world. And you will search for your home whether you realize where it is or not. If you believe it is outside you the search will be futile, for you will be seeking it where it is not. You do not remember how to look within for you do not believe your home is there. Yet the Holy Spirit remembers it for you, and He will guide you to your home because that is His mission.

12.5. The Sane Curriculum

Only love is strong because it is undivided. The strong do not attack because they see no need to do so. Before the idea of attack can enter your mind, you must have perceived yourself as weak. Because you attacked yourself and believed that the attack was effective, you behold yourself as weakened. No longer perceiving yourself and your brothers as equal, and regarding yourself as weaker, you attempt to "equalize" the situation you made. You use attack to do so because you believe that their attack was successful in weakening you.

That is why the recognition of your own invulnerability is so important to the restoration of your sanity. For if you accept your invulnerability, you are recognizing that attack has no effect. Once you realize this you will no longer see any sense in attack, for it manifestly does not work and cannot protect you.

The Holy Spirit's Love is your strength, for yours is divided and therefore not real. You cannot trust your own love when you attack it. You cannot learn of perfect love with a split mind, because a split mind has made itself a poor learner.

You do not know the meaning of love, and that is your handicap. Do not attempt to teach yourself what you do not understand, and do not try to set up curriculum goals where yours have clearly failed.

I have said that the ego's rule is, "Seek and do not find." Translated into curricular terms this means, "Try to learn but do not succeed." Such a curriculum does not make sense. This attempt at "learning" has so weakened your mind that you cannot love, for the curriculum you have chosen is against love, and amounts to a course in how to attack yourself. But perhaps you do not realize, even yet, that there is something you want to learn, and that you can learn it because it is your choice to do so.

Resign now as your own teacher. This resignation will not lead to depression. It is merely the result of an honest appraisal of what you have taught yourself, and of the learning outcomes that have resulted. Under the proper learning conditions, which you can neither provide nor understand, you will become an excellent learner and an excellent teacher.

Your learning potential, properly understood, is limitless because it will lead you to God.

12.6. The Vision of Christ

The ego is trying to teach you how to gain the whole world and lose your own soul. The Holy Spirit teaches that you cannot lose your soul and there is no gain in the world, for of itself it profits nothing. To invest without profit is surely to impoverish yourself, and the overhead is high. Not only is there no profit in the investment, but the cost to you is enormous. For this investment costs you the world's reality by denying yours, and gives you nothing in return. You cannot sell your soul, but you can sell your awareness of it. You cannot perceive your soul, but you will not know it while you perceive something else as more valuable.

The Holy Spirit is your strength because He knows nothing but the spirit as you. He is perfectly aware that you do not know yourself, and perfectly aware of how to teach you to remember what you are. Because He loves you, He will gladly teach you what He loves, for He wills to share it. Remembering you always, He cannot let you forget your worth. For the Father never ceases to remind Him of His Son, and He never ceases to remind His Son of the Father. God is in your memory because of Him. You chose to forget your Father but you do not really want to do so, and therefore you can decide otherwise. As it was my decision, so is it yours.

You do not want the world. The only thing of value in it is whatever part of it you look upon with love. This gives it the only reality it will ever have. Its value is not in itself, but yours is in you. As self-value comes from self-extension, so does the perception of self-value come from the extension of loving thoughts outward. Make the world real unto yourself, for the real world is the gift of the Holy Spirit, and so it belongs to you.

Correction is for all who cannot see. To open the eyes of the blind is the Holy Spirit's mission, for He knows that they have not lost their vision, but merely sleep. He would awaken them from the sleep of forgetting to the remembering of God. Christ's eyes are open, and He will look upon whatever you see with love if you accept His vision as yours. The Holy Spirit keeps the vision of Christ for every Son of God who sleeps. In His sight the Son of God is perfect, and he longs to share His vision with you.

Yet you must learn the cost of sleeping, and refuse to pay it.

Heaven is your home, and being in God it must also be in you.

12.7. Looking Within

Miracles demonstrate that learning has occurred under the right guidance, for learning is invisible and what has been learned can be recognized only by its results. Its generalization is demonstrated as you use it in more and more situations. There is no situation to which miracles do not apply, and by applying them to all situations you will gain the real world. For in this holy perception you will be made whole, and the Atonement will radiate from your acceptance of it for yourself to everyone the Holy Spirit sends you for your blessing. In every child of God His blessing lies, and in your blessing of the children of God is His blessing to you.

The Holy Spirit is invisible, but you can see the results of His Presence, and through them you will learn that He is there. Perceiving His results, you will understand where He must be, and finally know what He is.

You cannot see the Holy Spirit, but you can see His manifestations. And unless you do, you will not realize He is there. Do the Holy Spirit's work, for you share in His function. As your function in Heaven is creation, so your function on earth is healing. God shares His function with you in Heaven, and the Holy Spirit shares His with you on earth. As long as you believe you have other functions, so long will you need correction. For this belief is the destruction of peace, a goal in direct opposition to the Holy Spirit's purpose.

You see what you expect, and you expect what you invite. Your perception is the result of your invitation, coming to you as you sent for it. Whose manifestations would you see? Of whose presence would you be convinced? For you will believe in what you manifest, and as you look out so will you see in. Two ways of looking at the world are in your mind, and your perception will reflect the guidance you have chosen.

CHAPTER 12

Remember always that you see what you seek, for what you seek you will find. The ego finds what it seeks, and only that. It does not find love, for that is not what it is seeking.

I said before that what you project or extend is up to you, but you must do one or the other, for that is a law of mind, and you must look in before you look out. As you look in, you choose either the ego or the Holy Spirit as the guide for seeing. And then you look out and behold your guide's witnesses.

The power of decision is your one remaining freedom as a prisoner of this world. You can decide to see it right. What you made of it is not its reality, for its reality is only what you give it. It was only this decision that determined what you found, for it was the decision for what you sought.

You are afraid of me because you looked within and are afraid of what you saw. Yet you could not have seen reality, for the reality of your mind is the loveliest of God's creations. Coming only from God, its power and grandeur could only bring you peace if you really looked upon it. If you are afraid, it is because you saw something that is not there. Yet in that same place you could have looked upon me and all your brothers, in the perfect safety of the Mind which created us. For we are there in the peace of the Father, who wills to extend His peace through you.

Through the eyes of Christ, only the real world exists and only the real world can be seen. As you decide so will you see. And all that you see but witnesses to your decision.

The ego is not a traitor to God, to Whom treachery is impossible. But it is a traitor to you who believe that you have been treacherous to your Father. That is why the undoing of guilt is an essential part of the Holy Spirit's teaching. For as long as you feel guilty you are listening to the voice of the ego, which tells you that you have been treacherous to God and therefore deserve death. You will think that death comes from God and not from the ego because, by confusing yourself with the ego, you believe that you want death. And from what you want God does not save you.

When you are tempted to yield to the desire for death, remember that I did not die. You will realize that this is true when you look within and see me. Would I have overcome death for myself alone? And would eternal life have been given me of the Father unless he had also given it to you? When you learn to make me manifest, you will never see death. For you will have looked upon the deathless in yourself, and you will see only the eternal as you look out upon a world that cannot die.

12.8. The Attraction of Love for Love

You attack the real world every day and every hour and every minute, and yet you are surprised that you cannot see it. If you seek love in order to attack it, you will never find it. For if love is sharing, how can you find it except through itself? Offer it and it will come to you, because it is drawn to itself. But offer attack and love will remain hidden, for it can live only in peace.

Because of your Father's Love you can never forget Him, for no one can forget what God Himself placed in his memory. You can deny it, but you cannot lose it. You are waiting only for Him, and do not know it. Yet His memory shines in your mind and cannot be obliterated. It is no more past than future, being forever always.

You have but to ask for this memory, and you will remember. Yet the memory of God cannot shine in a mind that has obliterated it and wants to keep it so. For the memory of God can dawn only in a mind that chooses to remember, and that has relinquished the insane desire to control reality. You who cannot even control yourself should hardly aspire to control the universe. But look upon what you have made of it, and rejoice that it is not so.

The real world was given you by God in loving exchange for the world you made and the world you see. Only take it from the hand of Christ and look upon it. Its reality will make everything else invisible, for beholding it is total perception. And as you look upon it you will remember that it was always so. Nothingness will become invisible, for you will at last have seen truly. Redeemed perception is easily translated into knowledge, for only perception is capable of error and perception has never been. Being corrected it gives place to knowledge, which is forever the only reality. The Atonement is but the way back to what was never lost. Your Father could not cease to love His Son.

Chapter 13

The Guiltless World

Introduction

If you did not feel guilty you could not attack, for condemnation is the root of attack. It is the judgment of one mind by another as unworthy of love and deserving of punishment. But herein lies the split. For the mind that judges, perceives itself as separate from the mind being judged, believing that by punishing another, it will escape punishment. All this is but the delusional attempt of the mind to deny itself, and escape the penalty of denial. It is not an attempt to relinquish denial, but to hold on to it. For it is guilt that has obscured the Father to you, and it is guilt that has driven you insane.

The acceptance of guilt into the mind of God's Son was the beginning of the separation, as the acceptance of the Atonement is separation's end. The world you see is the delusional system of those made mad by guilt. Look carefully at this world, and you will realize that this is so. For this world is the symbol of punishment, and all the laws that seem to govern it are the laws of death. Children are born into this world through pain and in pain. Their growth is attended by suffering, and they learn of sorrow and separation and death. Their minds seem to be trapped in their brain, and the mind's powers decline if their bodies are hurt. The children seem to love, yet they desert and are deserted. They appear to lose what they love, perhaps the most insane belief of all. And their bodies wither and gasp and are laid in the ground, and are no more. Not one of them but has thought that God is cruel.

If this were the real world, God would be cruel. For no Father could subject His children to this as the price of salvation and be loving. Love does not kill to save. If it did, attack would be salvation, and this is the ego's interpretation, not God's. Only the world of guilt could demand this, for only the guilty could conceive of it. Adam's "sin" could have touched no one, had he not believed it was the Father Who drove him out of Paradise. For in that belief the knowledge of the Father was lost, since only those who do not understand Him could believe it.

This world is a picture of the crucifixion of God's Son. And until you realize that God's Son cannot be crucified, this is the world you will see.

13.1. Guiltlessness and Invulnerability

Love and guilt cannot coexist, and to accept one is to deny the other. Guilt hides Christ from your sight, for it is the denial of the blamelessness of God's Son.

Without guilt the ego has no life, and God's Son is without guilt.

As you look upon yourself and judge what you do honestly, you may be tempted to wonder how you can be guiltless. Yet consider this: You are not guiltless in time, but in eternity. You have "sinned" in the past, but there is no past. Time seems to go in one direction, but when you reach its end it will roll up like a long carpet spread along the past behind you, and will disappear. As long as you believe the Son of God is guilty you will walk along this carpet, believing that it leads to death. And the journey will seem long and cruel and senseless, for so it is.

The journey the Son of God has set himself is useless indeed, but the journey on which his Father sets him is one of release and joy. The Father is not cruel, and His Son cannot hurt himself. The retaliation that he fears and that he sees will never touch him, for although he believes in it the Holy Spirit knows it is not true. The Holy Spirit stands at the end of time, where you must be because He is with you. He has already undone everything unworthy of the Son of God, for such was His mission, given Him by God. And what God gives has always been.

For the idea of guilt brings a belief in condemnation of one by another, projecting separation in place of unity. You can condemn only yourself, and by so doing you cannot know that you are God's Son. You have denied the condition of his being, which is his perfect blamelessness. Out of love he was created, and in love he abides. Goodness and mercy have always followed him, for he has always extended the Love of his Father.

As you perceive the holy companions who travel with you, you will realize that there is no journey, but only an awakening. There is no road to travel on, and no time to travel through. For God waits not for His Son in time, being forever unwilling to be without him. And so it has always been. Let the holiness of God's Son shine away the cloud of guilt that darkens your mind, and by accepting his purity as yours, learn of him that it is yours.

You are invulnerable because you are guiltless. You can hold on to the past only through guilt. For guilt establishes that you will be punished for what you have done, and thus depends on one-dimensional time, proceeding from past to future. No one who believes this can understand what "always" means, and therefore guilt must deprive you of the appreciation of eternity. You are immortal because you are eternal, and "always" must be now. Guilt, then, is a way of holding past and future in your mind to ensure the ego's continuity. For if what has been will be punished, the ego's continuity is guaranteed. Yet the guarantee of your continuity is God's, not the ego's. And immortality is the opposite of time, for time passes away, while immortality is constant.

The ego teaches you to attack yourself because you are guilty, and this must increase the guilt, for guilt is the result of attack. In the ego's teaching, then, there is no escape from guilt. For attack makes guilt real, and if it is real there is no way to overcome it. The Holy Spirit dispels it simply through the calm recognition that it has never been. As He looks upon the guiltless Son of God, He knows that this is true. And being true for you, you cannot attack yourself, for without guilt attack is impossible. You, then, are saved because God's Son is guiltless. And being wholly pure, you are invulnerable.

13.2. The Guiltless Son of God

The ultimate purpose of projection is always to get rid of guilt. Yet, characteristically, the ego attempts to get rid of guilt from its viewpoint only, for much as the ego wants to retain guilt you find it intolerable, since guilt stands in the way of your remembering God, Whose pull is so strong that you cannot resist it. On this issue, then, the deepest split of all occurs, for if you are to retain guilt, as the ego insists, you cannot be you. Only by persuading you that it is you could the ego possibly induce you to project guilt, and thereby keep it in your mind.

Yet consider how strange a solution the ego's arrangement is. You project guilt to get rid of it, but you are actually merely concealing it. You do experience the guilt, but you have no idea why. On the contrary, you associate it with a weird assortment of "ego ideals," which the ego claims you have failed. Yet you have no idea that you are failing the Son of God by seeing him as guilty. Believing you are no longer you, you do not realize that you are failing yourself.

This course has explicitly stated that its goal for you is happiness and peace. Yet you are afraid of it. You have been told again and again that it will set you free, yet you sometimes react as if it is trying to imprison you. You often dismiss it more readily than you dismiss the ego's thought system. To some extent, then, you must believe that by not learning the course you are protecting yourself. And you do not realize that it is only your guiltlessness that can protect you.

The Atonement has always been interpreted as the release from guilt, and this is correct if it is understood. Yet even when I interpret it for you, you may reject it and do not accept it for yourself. You have perhaps recognized the futility of the ego and its offerings, but though you do not want them, you may not yet look upon the alternative with gladness. In the extreme, you are afraid of redemption and you believe it will kill you. Make no mistake about the depth of this fear. For you believe that, in the presence of truth, you might turn on yourself and destroy yourself.

Little child, this is not so. Your "guilty secret" is nothing, and if you will but bring it to the light, the light will dispel it. And then no dark cloud will remain between you and the remembrance of your Father, for you will remember His guiltless Son, who did not die because he is immortal. And you will see that you were redeemed with him, and have never been separated from him. In this understanding lies your remembering, for it is the recognition of love without fear. There will be great joy in Heaven on your homecoming, and the joy will be yours. For the redeemed son of man is the guiltless Son of God, and to recognize him is your redemption.

13.3. The Fear of Redemption

We have said that no one will countenance fear if he recognizes it. Yet in your disordered state of mind you are not afraid of fear. You do not like it, but it is not your desire to attack that really frightens you. You are not seriously disturbed by your hostility. You keep it hidden because you are more afraid of what it covers. You could look even upon the ego's darkest cornerstone without fear if you did not believe that, without the ego, you would find within yourself something you fear even more. You are not really afraid of crucifixion. Your real terror is of redemption.

Under the ego's dark foundation is the memory of God, and it is of this that you are really afraid. For this memory would instantly restore you to your proper place, and it is this place that you have sought to leave. Your fear of attack is nothing compared to your fear of love. You would be willing to look even upon your savage wish to kill God's Son, if you did not believe that it saves you from love. For this wish caused the separation, and you have protected it because you do not want the separation healed. You realize that, by removing the dark cloud that obscures it, your love for your Father would impel you to answer His call and leap into Heaven. You believe that attack is salvation because it would prevent you from this. For still deeper than the ego's foundation, and much stronger than it will ever be, is your intense and burning love of God, and His for you. This is what you really want to hide.

You have built your whole insane belief system because you think you would be helpless in God's Presence, and you would save yourself from His Love because you think it would crush you into nothingness. You are afraid it would sweep you away from yourself and make you little, because you believe that magnitude lies in defiance, and that attack is grandeur. You think you have made a world God would destroy; and by loving Him, which you do, you would throw this world away, which you would. Therefore, you have used the world to cover your love, and the deeper you go into the blackness of the ego's foundation, the closer you come to the Love that is hidden there. And it is this that frightens you.

You can accept insanity because you made it, but you cannot accept love because you did not. You would rather be a slave of the crucifixion than a Son of God in redemption. Your individual death seems more valuable than your living oneness, for what is given you is not so dear as what you made. You are more afraid of God than of the ego, and love cannot enter where it is not welcome. But hatred can, for it enters of its own volition and cares not for yours.

You must look upon your illusions and not keep them hidden, because they do not rest on their own foundation. In concealment they appear to do so, and thus they seem to be self-sustained. This is the fundamental illusion on which the others rest. For beneath them, and concealed as long as they are hidden, is the loving mind that thought it made them in anger. And the pain in this mind is so apparent, when it is uncovered, that its need of healing cannot be denied. Not all the tricks and games you offer it can heal it, for here is the real crucifixion of God's Son.

And yet he is not crucified. Here is both his pain and his healing, for the Holy Spirit's vision is merciful and His remedy is quick. Do not hide suffering from His sight, but bring it gladly to Him. Lay before His eternal sanity all your hurt, and let Him heal you. Do not leave any spot of pain hidden from His light, and search your mind carefully for any thoughts you may fear to uncover. For He will heal every little thought you have kept to hurt you and cleanse it of its littleness, restoring it to the magnitude of God.

Beneath all the grandiosity you hold so dear is your real call for help. For you call for love to your Father as your Father calls you to Himself. In that place which you have hidden, you will only to unite with the Father, in loving remembrance of Him. You will find this place of truth as you see it in your brothers, for though they may deceive themselves, like you they long for the grandeur that is in them. And perceiving it you will welcome it, and it will be yours. For grandeur is the right of God's Son, and no illusions can satisfy him or save him from what he is. Only his love is real, and he will be content only with his reality.

Save God's Son from his illusions that you may accept the magnitude of your Father in peace and joy.

For a darkened mind cannot live in the light, and it must seek a place of darkness where it can believe it is where it is not.

To "single out" is to "make alone," and thus make lonely. God did not do this to you. Could He set you apart, knowing that your peace lies in His Oneness? He denied you only your request for pain, for suffering is not of His creation. Having given you creation, He could not take it from you. He could but answer your insane request with a sane answer that would abide with you in your insanity. For His answer is the reference point beyond illusions, from which you can look back on them and see them as insane. But seek this place beyond illusions and you will find it, for Love is in you and will lead you there.

Chapter 13

13.4. The Function of Time

And now the reason why you are afraid of this course should be apparent. For this is a course on love, because it is about you. You have been told that your function in this world is healing, and your function in Heaven is creating. The ego teaches that your function on earth is destruction, and you have no function at all in Heaven. It would thus destroy you here and bury you here, leaving you no inheritance except the dust out of which it thinks you were made. As long as the ego is reasonably satisfied with you, as its reasoning goes, it offers you oblivion. When the ego becomes overtly savage, it offers you hell.

The ego has a strange notion of time, and it is with this notion that your questioning might well begin. The ego invests heavily in the past, and in the end believes that the past is the only aspect of time that is meaningful. Remember that its emphasis on guilt enables it to ensure its continuity by making the future like the past, and thus avoiding the present. By the notion of paying for the past in the future, the past becomes the determiner of the future, making them continuous without an intervening present. For the ego regards the present only as a brief transition to the future, in which it brings the past to the future by interpreting the present in past terms.

"Now" has no meaning to the ego. The present merely reminds it of past hurts, and it reacts to the present as if it were the past. The ego cannot tolerate release from the past, and although the past is over, the ego tries to preserve its image by responding as if it were present. It dictates your reactions to those you meet in the present from a past reference point, obscuring their present reality. In effect, if you follow the ego's dictates you will react to your brother as though he were someone else, and this will surely prevent you from recognizing him as he is. And you will receive messages from him out of your own past because, by making it real in the present, you are forbidding yourself to let it go. You thus deny yourself the message of release that every brother offers you now.

The shadowy figures from the past are precisely what you must escape. They are not real, and have no hold over you unless you bring them with you. They carry the spots of pain in your mind, directing you to attack in the present in retaliation for a past that is no more. And this decision is one of future pain. Unless you learn that past pain is an illusion, you are choosing a future of illusions and losing the many opportunities you could find for release in the present. The ego would preserve your nightmares, and prevent you from awakening and understanding they are past.

It is evident that the Holy Spirit's perception of time is the exact opposite of the ego's. The reason is equally clear, for they perceive the goal of time as diametrically opposed. The Holy Spirit interprets time's purpose as rendering the need for time unnecessary. He regards the function of time as temporary, serving only His teaching function, which is temporary by definition. His emphasis is therefore on the only aspect of time that can extend to the infinite, for now is the closest approximation of eternity that this world offers. It is in the reality of "now," without past or future, that the beginning of the appreciation of eternity lies. For only "now" is here, and only "now" presents the opportunities for the holy encounters in which salvation can be found.

The ego, on the other hand, regards the function of time as one of extending itself (the ego) in place of eternity, for like the Holy Spirit, the ego interprets the goal of time as its own. The continuity of past and future, under its direction, is the only purpose the ego perceives in time, and it closes over the present so that no gap in its own continuity can occur. Its continuity, then, would keep you in time, while the Holy Spirit would release you from it. It is His interpretation of the means of salvation that you must learn to accept, if you would share His goal of salvation for you.

You, too, will interpret the function of time as you interpret yours. If you accept your function in the world of time as one of healing, you will emphasize only the aspect of time in which healing can occur. Healing cannot be accomplished in the past. It must be accomplished in the present to release the future. This interpretation ties the future to the present, and extends the present rather than the past. But if you interpret your function as destruction, you will lose sight of the present and hold on to the past to ensure a destructive future. And time will be as you interpret it, for of itself it is nothing.

13.5. The Two Emotions

I have said you have but two emotions, love and fear. One is changeless the other has many forms. Projection makes perception, and you cannot see beyond it. Again and again have you attacked your brother, because you saw in him a shadow figure in your private world. And thus it is you must attack yourself first, for what you attack is not in others. Its only reality is in your own mind, and by attacking others you are literally attacking what is not there.

The delusional can be very destructive, for they do not recognize they have condemned themselves. They do not wish to die, yet they will not let condemnation go. And so they separate into their private worlds, where everything is disordered, and where what is within appears to be without. Yet what is within they do not see, for the reality of their brothers they cannot recognize.

You have but two emotions, fear and love, yet in your private world you react to each of them as though it were the other. If you see your own hatred as your brother, you are not seeing him. Everyone draws nigh unto what he loves, and recoils from what he fears. And you react with fear to love, and draw away from love. Yet fear attracts you, and believing fear is love, you call it to yourself. Your private world is filled with figures of fear you have invited into it, and all the love your brothers offer you, you do not see.

Chapter 13

God calls you and you do not hear, for you are preoccupied with your own voice. And the vision of Christ is not in your sight, for you look upon yourself alone.

Do not seek vision through your eyes, for you made your way of seeing that you might see in darkness, and in this you are deceived. Beyond this darkness, and yet still within you, is the vision of Christ, Who looks on all in light. Your "vision" comes from fear, as His from love. And He sees for you, as your witness to the real world. He is the Holy Spirit's manifestation, looking always on the real world, and calling forth its witnesses and drawing them to you. He loves what He sees within you, and He would extend it. And He will not return unto the Father until He has extended your perception even unto Him. And there perception is no more, for He has returned you to the Father with Him.

You have but two emotions, and one you made and one was given you. Each is a way of seeing, and different worlds arise from their different sights. See through the vision that is given you, for through Christ's vision He beholds Himself. And seeing what He is, He knows His Father. Beyond your darkest dreams he sees God's guiltless Son within you, shining in perfect radiance that is undimmed by your dreams. And this you will see as you look with Him, for His vision is His gift of love to you, given Him of the Father for you.

13.6. Finding the Present

You consider it "natural" to use your past experience as the reference point from which to judge the present. Yet this is unnatural because it is delusional. When you have learned to look on everyone with no reference at all to the past, either his or yours as you perceived it, you will be able to learn from what you see now. For the past can cast no shadow to darken the present, unless you are afraid of light. And only if you are would you choose to bring darkness with you, and by holding it in your mind, see it as a dark cloud that shrouds your brothers and conceals their reality from your sight.

Your past was made in anger, and if you use it to attack the present, you will not see the freedom that the present holds.

There is a light that this world cannot give. Yet you can give it, as it was given you. And as you give it, it shines forth to call you from the world and follow it. For this light will attract you as nothing in this world can do. And you will lay aside the world and find another. This other world is bright with love which you have given it. And here will everything remind you of your Father and His holy Son. Light is unlimited, and spreads across this world in quiet joy. All those you brought with you will shine on you, and you will shine on them in gratitude because they brought you here. Your light will join with theirs in power so compelling, that it will draw the others out of darkness as you look on them.

Awaking unto Christ is following the laws of love of your free will, and out of quiet recognition of the truth in them. In sleep you are alone, and your awareness is narrowed to yourself. And that is why the nightmares come. You dream of isolation because your eyes are closed. You do not see your brothers, and in the darkness you cannot look upon the light you gave to them.

And yet the laws of love are not suspended because you sleep. And you have followed them through all your nightmares, and have been faithful in your giving, for you were not alone. Even in sleep has Christ protected you, ensuring the real world for you when you awake. In your name He has given for you, and given you the gifts He gave. God's Son is still as loving as his Father. Continuous with his Father, he has no past apart from Him.

13.7. Attainment of the Real World

Sit quietly and look upon the world you see, and tell yourself: "The real world is not like this. It has no buildings and there are no streets where people walk alone and separate. There are no stores where people buy an endless list of things they do not need. It is not lit with artificial light, and night comes not upon it. There is no day that brightens and grows dim. There is no loss. Nothing is there but shines, and shines forever."

The world you see must be denied, for sight of it is costing you a different kind of vision. You cannot see both worlds, for each of them involves a different kind of seeing, and depends on what you cherish. The sight of one is possible because you have denied the other. Both are not true, yet either one will seem as real to you as the amount to which you hold it dear. And yet their power is not the same, because their real attraction to you is unequal.

You do not really want the world you see, for it has disappointed you since time began. The homes you built have never sheltered you. The roads you made have led you nowhere, and no city that you built has withstood the crumbling assault of time. Nothing you made but has the mark of death upon it. Hold it not dear, for it is old and tired and ready to return to dust even as you made it. This aching world has not the power to touch the living world at all. You could not give it that, and so although you turn in sadness from it, you cannot find in it the road that leads away from it into another world.

Christ is still there, although you know Him not. His Being does not depend upon your recognition. He lives within you in the quiet present, and waits for you to leave the past behind and enter into the world He holds out to you in love.

You wait but for yourself. To give this sad world over and exchange your errors for the peace of God is but your will.

The peace of God passeth your understanding only in the past. Yet here it is, and you can understand it now. God loves His Son forever, and His Son returns his Father's Love forever. The real world is the way that leads you to remembrance of the one thing that is wholly true and wholly yours. For all else you have lent yourself in time, and it will fade. But this one thing is always yours, being the gift of God unto His Son. Your one reality was given you, and by it God created you as one with Him.

The ego wants to have things for salvation, for possession is its law. Possession for its own sake is the ego's fundamental creed, a basic cornerstone in the churches it builds to itself. And at its altar it demands you lay all of the things it bids you get, leaving you no joy in them.

Therefore ask not of yourself what you need, for you do not know, and your advice to yourself will hurt you. For what you think you need will merely serve to tighten up your world against the light, and render you unwilling to question the value that this world can really hold for you.

Only the Holy Spirit knows what you need. For He will give you all things that do not block the way to light. And what else could you need?

Leave, then, your needs to Him. He will supply them with no emphasis at all upon them. What comes to you of Him comes safely, for He will ensure it never can become a dark spot, hidden in your mind and kept to hurt you.

Whenever you are tempted to undertake a useless journey that would lead away from light, remember what you really want, and say:

> The Holy Spirit leads me unto Christ, and where else would I go?
> What need have I but to awake in Him?

Then follow Him in joy, with faith that He will lead you safely through all dangers to your peace of mind this world may set before you. Kneel not before the altars to sacrifice, and seek not what you will surely lose. Content yourself with what you will surely keep, and be not restless, for you undertake a quiet journey to the peace of God, where He would have you be in quietness.

13.8. From Perception to Knowledge

All healing is release from the past. That is why the Holy Spirit is the only Healer. He teaches that the past does not exist, a fact which belongs to the sphere of knowledge, and which therefore no one in the world can know. It would indeed be impossible to be in the world with this knowledge. For the mind that knows this unequivocally knows also it dwells in eternity, and utilizes no perception at all. It therefore does not consider where it is, because the concept "where" does not mean anything to it. It knows that it is everywhere, just as it has everything, and forever.

The very real difference between perception and knowledge becomes quite apparent if you consider this: There is nothing partial about knowledge. Every aspect is whole, and therefore no aspect is separate. You are an aspect of knowledge, being in the Mind of God,

Who knows you. All knowledge must be yours, for in you is all knowledge. Perception, at its loftiest, is never complete. Even the perception of the Holy Spirit, as perfect as perception can be, is without meaning in Heaven. Perception can reach everywhere under His guidance, for the vision of Christ beholds everything in light. Yet no perception, however holy, will last forever.

When you have seen your brothers as yourself you will be released to knowledge, having learned to free yourself through Him Who knows of freedom. Unite with me under the holy banner of His teaching, and as we grow in strength the power of God's Son will move in us, and we will leave no one untouched and no one left alone. And suddenly time will be over, and we will all unite in the eternity of God the Father.

13.9. The Cloud of Guilt

Guilt remains the only thing that hides the Father, for guilt is the attack upon His Son. The guilty always condemn, and having done so they will still condemn, linking the future to the past as is the ego's law. Between the future and the past the laws of God must intervene, if you would free yourself. Atonement stands between them, like a lamp shining so brightly that the chain of darkness in which you bound yourself will disappear.

Faith makes the power of belief, and where it is invested determines its reward. For faith is always given what is treasured, and what is treasured is returned to you.

Be faithful unto darkness and you will not see, because your faith will be rewarded as you gave it. You will accept your treasure, and if you place your faith in the past, the future will be like it. Whatever you hold dear you think is yours. The power of your valuing will make it so.

See no one as guilty, and you will affirm the truth of guiltlessness unto yourself. In every condemnation that you offer the Son of God lies the conviction of your own guilt. If you would have the Holy Spirit make you free of it, accept His offer of Atonement for all your brothers. For so you learn that it is true for you.

Guilt makes you blind, for while you see one spot of guilt within you, you will not see the light. And by projecting it, the world seems dark, and shrouded in your guilt. You throw a dark veil over it, and cannot see it because you cannot look within. You are afraid of what you would see there, but it is not there. The thing you fear is gone. If you would look within you would see only the Atonement, shining in quiet and in peace upon the altar to your Father.

Do not be afraid to look within. The ego tells you all is black with guilt within you, and bids you not to look. Instead, it bids you look upon your brothers, and see the guilt in them. Yet this you cannot do without remaining blind. For those who see their brothers in the dark, and guilty in the dark in which they shroud them, are too afraid to look upon the light within. Within you is not what you believe is there, and what you put your faith in. Within you is the holy sign of perfect faith your Father has in you. Look, then, upon the light He placed within you, and learn that what you feared was there has been replaced with love.

13.10. Release from Guilt

In any union with a brother in which you seek to lay your guilt upon him, or share it with him or perceive his own, you will feel guilty.

As long as you believe that guilt is justified in any way, in anyone, whatever he may do, you will not look within, where you would always find Atonement. The end of guilt will never come as long as you believe there is a reason for it. For you must learn that guilt is always totally insane, and has no reason.

The Holy Spirit does not keep illusions in your mind to frighten you, and show them to you fearfully to demonstrate what he has saved you from. What He has saved you from is gone. Give no reality to guilt, and see no reason for it.

Now it is given you to heal and teach, to make what will be now. As yet it is not now. The Son of God believes that he is lost in guilt, alone in a dark world where pain is pressing everywhere upon him from without. When he has looked within and seen the radiance there, he will remember how much his Father loves him. And it will seem incredible that he ever thought his Father loved him not, and looked upon him as condemned. The moment that you realize guilt is insane, wholly unjustified and wholly without reason, you will not fear to look upon the Atonement and accept it wholly.

Praise be to you who make the Father one with His Own Son. Alone we are all lowly, but together we shine with brightness so intense that none of us alone can even think of it. Before the glorious radiance of the Kingdom guilt melts away, and transformed into kindness will never more be what it was. Every reaction you experience will be so purified that it is fitting as a hymn of praise unto your Father. See only praise of Him in what He has created, for He will never cease His praise of you. United in this praise we stand before the gates of Heaven where we will surely enter in our sinlessness. God loves you.

13.11 The Peace of Heaven

Forgetfulness and sleep and even death become the ego's best advice for dealing with the perceived and harsh intrusion of guilt on peace. Yet no one sees himself in conflict and ravaged by a cruel war unless he believes that both opponents in the war are real. Believing this he must escape, for such a war would surely end his peace of mind, and so destroy him. Yet if he could but realize the war is between real and unreal powers, he could look upon himself and see his freedom. No one finds himself ravaged and torn in endless battles if he himself perceives them as wholly without meaning.

God wills you be in Heaven, and nothing can keep you from it, or it from you. Your wildest mis-perceptions, your weird imaginings, your blackest nightmares all mean nothing. They will not prevail against the peace God wills for you. The Holy Spirit will restore your sanity because insanity is not the Will of God.

God willed you Heaven, and will always will you nothing else. The Holy Spirit knows only of His Will. There is no chance that Heaven will not be yours, for God is sure, and what He wills is as sure as He is.

Can God's Son lose himself in dreams, when God has placed within him the glad Call to waken and be glad? He cannot separate himself from what is in him. His sleep will not withstand the Call to wake. The mission of redemption will be fulfilled as surely as the creation will remain unchanged throughout eternity. You do not have to know that Heaven is yours to make it so. It is so. Yet to know it, the Will of God must be accepted as your will.

Failure is of the ego, not of God. From Him you cannot wander, and there is no possibility that the plan the Holy Spirit offers to everyone, for the salvation of everyone, will not be perfectly accomplished. You will be released, and you will not remember anything you made that was not created for you and by you in return. For how can you remember what was never true, or not remember what has always been? It is this reconciliation with truth, and only truth, in which the peace of Heaven lies.

Chapter 14

Teaching for Truth

Introduction

Yes, you are blessed indeed. Yet in this world you do not know it. But you have the means for learning it and seeing it quite clearly. The Holy Spirit uses logic as easily and as well as does the ego, except that His conclusions are not insane. They take a direction exactly opposite, pointing as clearly to Heaven as the ego points to darkness and to death. We have followed much of the ego's logic, and have seen its logical conclusions. Let us now turn away from them, and follow the simple logic by which the Holy Spirit teaches the simple conclusions that speak for truth, and only truth.

14.1. The Conditions of Learning

You can learn to bless, and cannot give what you have not. If, then, you offer blessing, it must have come first to yourself. And you must also have accepted it as yours, for how else could you give it away? That is why miracles offer you the testimony that you are blessed. If what you offer is complete forgiveness you must have let guilt go, accepting the Atonement for yourself and learning you are guiltless.

14.2. The Happy Learner

The Holy Spirit needs a happy learner, in whom His mission can be happily accomplished.

The Holy Spirit, seeing where you are but knowing you are elsewhere, begins His lesson in simplicity with the fundamental teaching that truth is true. This is the hardest lesson you will ever learn, and in the end the only one. Simplicity is very difficult for twisted minds. Consider all the distortions you have made of nothing; all the strange forms and feelings and actions and reactions that you have woven out of it. The simple and the obvious are not apparent to those who would make palaces and royal robes of nothing, believing they are kings with golden crowns because of them.

Chapter 14

If you would be a happy learner, you must give everything you have learned to the Holy Spirit, to be unlearned for you. And then begin to learn the joyous lessons that come quickly on the firm foundation that truth is true. The universe of learning will open up before you in all its gracious simplicity. With truth before you, you will not look back.

All this lies in the Holy Spirit's plan to free you from the past, and open up the way to freedom for you. For truth is true. What else could ever be, or ever was? This simple lesson holds the key to the dark door that you believe is locked forever. You made this door of nothing, and behind it is nothing. The key is only the light that shines away the shapes and forms and fears of nothing. Accept this key to freedom from the hands of Christ Who gives it to you, that you may join Him in the holy task of bringing light. For, like your brothers, you do not realize the light has come and freed you from the sleep of darkness.

The quietness of its simplicity is so compelling that you will realize it is impossible to deny the simple truth. For there is nothing else. God is everywhere, and His Son is in Him with everything.

14.3. The Decision for Guiltlessness

Perhaps you are accustomed to using guiltlessness merely to offset the pain of guilt, and do not look upon it as having value in itself. You believe that guilt and guiltlessness are both of value, each representing an escape from what the other does not offer you. You do not want either alone, for without both you do not see yourself as whole and therefore happy. Yet you are whole only in your guiltlessness, and only in your guiltlessness can you be happy. There is no conflict here. To wish for guilt in any way, in any form, will lose appreciation of the value of your guiltlessness, and push it from your sight.

Whenever the pain of guilt seems to attract you, remember that if you yield to it, you are deciding against your happiness, and will not learn how to be happy. Say therefore, to yourself, gently, but with the conviction born of the Love of God and of His Son:

> *What I experience I will make manifest. If I am guiltless, I have nothing to fear.*
> *I choose to testify to my acceptance of the Atonement, not to its rejection.*
> *I would accept my guiltlessness by making it manifest and sharing it.*
> *Let me bring peace to God's Son from his Father.*

Each day, each hour and minute, even each second, you are deciding between the crucifixion and the resurrection; between the ego and the Holy Spirit. The ego is the choice for guilt; the Holy Spirit the choice for guiltlessness. The power of decision is all that is yours. What you can decide between is fixed, because there are no alternatives except truth and illusion. And there is no overlap between them, because they are opposites which cannot be reconciled and cannot both be true. You are guilty or guiltless, bound or free, unhappy or happy.

The miracle teaches you that you have chosen guiltlessness, freedom and joy. It is not a cause, but an effect. It is the natural result of choosing right, attesting to your happiness that comes from choosing to be free of guilt. Everyone you offer healing to returns it. Everyone you attack keeps it and cherishes it by holding it against you. Whether he does this or does it not will make no difference; you will think he does.

The joy of learning that darkness has no power over the Son of God is the happy lesson the Holy Spirit teaches, and would have you teach with Him. It is His joy to teach it, as it will be yours.

The way to teach this simple lesson is merely this: Guiltlessness is invulnerability. Therefore, make your invulnerability manifest to everyone. Teach your brother that whatever he may try to do to you, your perfect freedom from the belief that you can be harmed shows him that he is guiltless. He can do nothing that can hurt you, and by refusing to allow him to think he can, you teach him that the Atonement, which you have accepted for yourself, is also his. There is nothing to forgive. No one can hurt the Son of God. His guilt is wholly without cause, and being without cause, cannot exist.

God is the only Cause, and guilt is not of Him. Teach no one he has hurt you, for if you do, you teach yourself that what is not of God has power over you.

Peace abides in every mind that quietly accepts the plan God set for its Atonement, relinquishing its own. Make no decisions about what it is or where it lies, but ask the Holy Spirit everything, and leave all decisions to His gentle counsel.

Every decision you undertake alone but signifies that you would define what salvation is, and what you would be saved from. The Holy Spirit knows that all salvation is escape from guilt. You have no other "enemy," and against this strange distortion of the purity of the Son of God the Holy Spirit is your only Friend. He is the strong protector of the innocence that sets you free.

Let Him, therefore, be the only guide that you would follow to salvation. He knows the way, and leads you gladly on it. With Him you will not fail to learn that what God wills for you is your will. Without His guidance you will think you know alone, and will decide against your peace as surely as you decided that salvation lay in you alone. Salvation is of Him to Whom God gave it for you. He has not forgotten it. Forget Him not and He will make every decision for you, for your salvation and the peace of God in you.

Say to the Holy Spirit only, "Decide for me," and it is done. For His decisions are reflections of what God knows about you, and in this light, error of any kind becomes impossible. Why would you struggle so frantically to anticipate all you cannot know, when all knowledge lies behind every decision the Holy Spirit makes for you? Learn of His wisdom and His Love, and teach His answer to everyone who struggles in the dark.

Chapter 14

How gracious it is to decide all things through Him Whose equal Love is given equally to all alike! He leaves you no one outside you. In everything be led by Him, and do not reconsider. Trust Him to answer quickly, surely, and with Love for everyone who will be touched in any way by the decision. And everyone will be.

You taught yourself the most unnatural habit of not communicating with your Creator. Yet you remain in close communication with Him, and with everything that is within him, as it is within yourself. Unlearn isolation through His loving guidance, and learn of all the happy communication that you have thrown away but could not lose.

Whenever you are in doubt what you should do, think of His Presence in you, and tell yourself this, and only this:

> He leads me and knows the way, which I know not.
> Yet He will never keep from me what He would have me learn.
> And so I trust Him to communicate to me all that He knows for me.

Then let Him teach you quietly how to perceive your guiltlessness, which is already there.

14.4. Your Function in the Atonement

When you accept a brother's guiltlessness you will see the Atonement in him. For by proclaiming it in him you make it yours, and you will see what you sought. You will not see the symbol of your brother's guiltlessness shining within him while you still believe it is not there. His guiltlessness is your Atonement. Grant it to him, and you will see the truth of what you have acknowledged. Yet truth is offered first to be received, even as God gave it first to His Son.

When you have let all that obscured the truth in your most holy mind be undone for you, and therefore stand in grace before your Father, He will give Himself to you as He has always done. Giving Himself is all He knows, and so it is all knowledge. Ask not to be forgiven, for this has already been accomplished. Ask, rather, to learn how to forgive, and to restore what always was to your unforgiving mind. Atonement becomes real and visible to those who use it. On earth this is your only function, and you must learn that it is all you want to learn.

Decide that God is right and you are wrong about yourself. He created you out of Himself, but still within Him. He knows what you are. Remember that there is no second to Him. There cannot, therefore, be anyone without His Holiness, nor anyone unworthy of His perfect Love.

You who have tried to throw yourself away and valued God so little, hear me speak for Him and for yourself. You cannot understand how much your Father loves you, for there is no parallel in your experience of the world to help you understand it. There is nothing on earth with which it can compare, and nothing you have ever felt apart from Him resembles it ever so faintly.

The children of Heaven live in the light of the blessing of their Father, because they know that they are sinless. The Atonement was established as the means of restoring guiltlessness to minds that have denied it, and thus denied Heaven to itself. Atonement teaches you the true condition of the Son of God. It does not teach you what you are, or what your Father is. The Holy Spirit, Who remembers this for you, merely teaches you how to remove the blocks that stand between you and what you know.

14.5. The Circle of Atonement

Everyone has a special part to play in the Atonement, but the message given to each one is always the same; God's Son is guiltless. Each one teaches the message differently, and learns it differently. Yet until he teaches it and learns it, he will suffer the pain of dim awareness that his true function remains unfulfilled in him. The burden of guilt is heavy, but God would not have you bound by it. His plan for your awaking is as perfect as yours is fallible. You know not what you do, but He who knows is with you. His gentleness is yours, and all the love you share with God He holds in trust for you. He would teach you nothing except how to be happy.

Blessed Son of a wholly blessing Father, joy was created for you. Who can condemn whom God has blessed? There is nothing in the Mind of God that does not share His shining innocence. Creation is the natural extension of perfect purity. Your only calling here is to devote yourself, with active willingness, to the denial of guilt in all its forms. To accuse is not to understand. The happy learners of the Atonement become the teachers of the innocence that is the right of all that God created. Deny them not what is their due, for you will not withhold it from them alone.

We are all joined in the Atonement here, and nothing else can unite us in this world. So will the world of separation slip away, and full communication be restored between the Father and the Son. The miracle acknowledges the guiltlessness that must have been denied to produce the need of healing. Do not withhold this glad acknowledgment, for hope of happiness and release from suffering of every kind lie in it. Who is there but wishes to be free of pain? He may not yet have learned how to exchange guilt for innocence, nor realize that only in this exchange can freedom from pain be his. Yet those who have failed to learn need teaching, not attack. To attack those who have need of teaching is to fail to learn from them.

Peace, then, be unto everyone who becomes a teacher of peace. For peace is the acknowledgment of perfect purity, from which no one is excluded. Within its holy circle is everyone whom God created as His Son. Joy is its unifying attribute, with no one left outside to suffer guilt alone. The power of God draws everyone to its safe embrace of love and union. Stand quietly within this circle, and attract all tortured minds to join with you in the safety of its peace and holiness. Abide with me within it, as a teacher of Atonement, not of guilt.

Blessed are you who teach with me. Our power comes not of us, but of our Father. In guiltlessness we know Him, as He knows us guiltless. I stand within the circle, calling you to peace. Teach peace with me, and stand with me on holy ground. Remember for everyone your Father's power that He has given His Son. Believe not that you cannot teach His perfect peace. Stand not outside, but join with me within. Fail not the only purpose to which my teaching calls you. Restore to God His Son as He created him, by teaching him his innocence.

The Holy Spirit sees only guiltlessness, and in His gentleness He would release from fear and re-establish the reign of love. The power of love is in His gentleness, which is of God and therefore cannot crucify nor suffer crucifixion. The temple you restore becomes your altar, for it was rebuilt through you. And everything you give to God is yours. Thus He creates, and thus must you restore.

Each one you see you place within the holy circle of Atonement or leave outside, judging him fit for crucifixion or for redemption. If you bring him into the circle of purity, you will rest there with him. If you leave him without, you join him there. Judge not except in quietness which is not of you. Refuse to accept anyone as without the blessing of Atonement, and bring him into it by blessing him. Holiness must be shared, for therein lies everything that makes it holy. Come gladly to the holy circle, and look out in peace on all who think they are outside. Cast no one out, for here is what he seeks along with you. Come, let us join him in the holy place of peace which is for all of us, united as one within the Cause of peace.

14.6. The Light of Communication

The journey that we undertake together is the exchange of dark for light, of ignorance for understanding. Nothing you understand is fearful. It is only in darkness and in ignorance that you perceive the frightening, and shrink away from it to further darkness. And yet it is only the hidden that can terrify, not for what it is, but for its hiddenness. The obscure is frightening because you do not understand its meaning. If you did, it would be clear and you would be no longer in the dark. Nothing has hidden value, for what is hidden cannot be shared, and so its value is unknown. The hidden is kept apart, but value always lies in joint appreciation. What is concealed cannot be loved, and so it must be feared.

The quiet light in which the Holy Spirit dwells within you is merely perfect openness, in which nothing is hidden and therefore nothing is fearful. Attack will always yield to love if it is brought to love, not hidden from it. There is no darkness that the light of love will not dispel, unless it is concealed from love's beneficence. What is kept apart from love cannot share its healing power, because it has been separated off and kept in darkness.

The sentinels of darkness watch over it carefully, and you who made these guardians of illusion out of nothing are now afraid of them.

The light of guiltlessness shines guilt away because, when they are brought together, the truth of one must make the falsity of its opposite perfectly clear.

You have regarded the separation as a means for breaking your communication with your Father. The Holy Spirit reinterprets it as a means of re-establishing what was not broken, but has been made obscure. All things you made have use to Him, for His most holy purpose. He knows you are not separate from God, but He perceives much in your mind that lets you think you are. All this and nothing else would He separate from you. The power of decision, which you made in place of the power of creation, He would teach you how to use on your behalf. You who made it to crucify yourself must learn of Him how to apply it to the holy cause of restoration.

The Holy Spirit's function is entirely communication. He therefore must remove whatever interferes with communication in order to restore it. Therefore, keep no source of interference from His sight, for He will not attack your sentinels. But bring them to Him and let His gentleness teach you that, in the light, they are not fearful, and cannot serve to guard the dark doors behind which nothing at all is carefully concealed. We must open all doors and let the light come streaming through. There are no hidden chambers in God's temple. Its gates are open wide to greet His Son. No one can fail to come where God has called him, if he close not the door himself upon his Father's welcome.

14.7. Sharing Perception with the Holy Spirit

Perception is the medium by which ignorance is brought to knowledge. Yet the perception must be without deceit, for otherwise it becomes the messenger of ignorance rather than a helper in the search for truth.

Light cannot enter darkness when a mind believes in darkness, and will not let it go. Truth does not struggle against ignorance, and love does not attack fear.

The Holy Spirit asks of you but this; bring to Him every secret you have locked away from Him. Open every door to Him, and bid Him enter the darkness and lighten it away. At your request He enters gladly. He brings the light to darkness if you make the darkness open to Him. But what you hide He cannot look upon. He sees for you, and unless you look with Him He cannot see. The vision of Christ is not for Him alone, but for Him with you. Bring, therefore, all your dark and secret thoughts to Him, and look upon them with Him. He holds the light, and you the darkness. They cannot coexist when Both of You together look on them. His judgment must prevail, and He will give it to you as you join your perception to His.

14.8. The Holy Meeting Place

In the darkness you have obscured the glory God gave you, and the power He bestowed upon His guiltless Son. All this lies hidden in every darkened place, shrouded in guilt and in the dark denial of innocence. Behind the dark doors you have closed, lies nothing, because nothing can obscure the gift of God. It is the closing of the doors that interferes with recognition of the power of God that shines in you. Banish not power from your mind, but let all that would hide your glory be brought to the judgment of the Holy Spirit, and there undone. Whom He would save for glory is saved for it. He has promised the Father that through Him you would be released from littleness to glory. To what He promised God He is wholly faithful, for He shares with God the promise that was given Him to share with you.

Let your mind wander not through darkened corridors, away from light's center. You may choose to lead yourself astray, but you can be brought together only by the Guide appointed for you. He will surely lead you to where God and His Son await your recognition. They are joined in giving you the gift of oneness, before which all separation vanishes. Unite with what you are.

Where God is, there are you. Such is the truth. Everything God created knows its Creator.

14.9. The Reflection of Holiness

You were created holy. Bringing illusion to truth, or the ego to God, is the Holy Spirit's only function.

Bringing the ego to God is but to bring error to truth, where it stands corrected because it is the opposite of what it meets. It is undone because the contradiction can no longer stand. How long can contradiction stand when its impossible nature is clearly revealed? What disappears in light is not attacked. It merely vanishes because it is not true.

You are not frail with God beside you. Yet without Him you are nothing. The Atonement offers you God. The gift that you refused is held by Him in you. The Holy Spirit holds it there for you. God has not left His altar, though His worshipers placed other gods upon it. The temple still is holy, for the Presence that dwells within it is Holiness.

In the temple, Holiness waits quietly for the return of them that love it. The Presence knows they will return to purity and to grace. The graciousness of God will take them gently in, and cover all their sense of pain and loss with the immortal assurance of their Father's Love. There, fear of death will be replaced with joy of life. For God is life, and they abide in life.

In this world you can become a spotless mirror, in which the Holiness of your Creator shines forth from you to all around you. You can reflect Heaven here. Yet no reflections of the images of other gods must dim the mirror that would hold God's reflection in it. Earth can reflect Heaven or hell; God or the ego. You need but leave the mirror clean and clear of all the images of hidden darkness you have drawn upon it. God will shine upon it of Himself. Only the clear reflection of Himself can be perceived upon it.

Reflections are seen in light. In darkness they are obscure, and their meaning seems to lie only in shifting interpretations, rather than in themselves. The reflection of God needs no interpretation. It is clear. Clean but the mirror, and the message that shines forth from what the mirror holds out for everyone to see, no one can fail to understand.

14.10. The Equality of Miracles

The reflections you accept into the mirror of your mind in time, but bring eternity nearer or farther. But eternity itself is beyond all time. Reach out of time and touch eternity, with the help of its reflection in you. And you will turn from time to holiness, as surely as the reflection of holiness calls everyone to lay all guilt aside. Reflect the peace of Heaven here, and bring this world to Heaven. For the reflection of truth draws everyone to truth, and as they enter into it they leave all reflections behind.

You classify some of your thoughts as more important, larger or better, wiser, or more productive and valuable than others. For some are reflections of Heaven, while others are motivated by the ego.

The result is a weaving, changing pattern that never rests and is never still. It shifts unceasingly across the mirror of your mind, and the reflections of Heaven last but a moment and grow dim, as darkness blots them out. Where there was light, darkness removes it in an instant, and alternating patterns of light and darkness sweep constantly across your mind. The little sanity that still remains is held together by a sense of order that you establish. Yet the very fact that you can do this, and bring any order into chaos shows you that you are not an ego, and that more than an ego must be in you. For the ego is chaos, and if it were all of you, no order at all would be possible. Yet though the order you impose upon your mind limits the ego, it also limits you. To order is to judge, and to arrange by judgment.

The only judgment involved is the Holy Spirit's one division into two categories; one of love, and the other the call for love. You cannot safely make this division, for you are much too confused either to recognize love, or to believe that everything else is nothing but a call for love. You are too bound to form, and not to content.

The ego is incapable of understanding *content*, and is totally unconcerned with it. To the ego, if the *form* is acceptable, the *content* must be. Otherwise it will attack the form. If you believe you understand something of the "dynamics" of the ego, let me assure you that you understand nothing of it. For of yourself you could not understand it. The study of the ego is not the study of the mind. In fact, the ego enjoys studying itself, and thoroughly approves the undertakings of students who would "analyze" it, thus approving its importance. Yet they but study form with meaningless content. For their teacher is senseless, though careful to conceal this fact behind impressive sounding words, but which lack any consistent sense when they are put together.

Separation therefore remains the ego's chosen condition.

As God communicates to the Holy Spirit in you, so does the Holy Spirit translate His communications through you, so you can understand them. God has no secret communications, for everything of Him is perfectly open and freely accessible to all, being for all. Nothing lives in secret, and what you would hide from the Holy Spirit is nothing. Every interpretation you would lay upon a brother is senseless. Let the Holy Spirit show him to you, and teach you both his love and his call for love. Neither his mind nor yours holds more than these two orders of thought.

The miracle is the recognition that this is true. Where there is love, your brother must give it to you because of what it is. But where there is a call for love, you must give it because of what you are. Earlier I said this course will teach you how to remember what you are, restoring to you your Identity. We have already learned that this Identity is shared. The miracle becomes the means of sharing It. By supplying your Identity wherever It is not recognized, you will recognize It. And God Himself, Who wills to be with His Son forever, will bless each recognition of His Son with all the Love He holds for him. Nor will the power of all His Love be absent from any miracle you offer to His Son.

14.11. The Test of Truth

Knowledge is power, and all power is of God. You who have tried to keep power for yourself have "lost" it. You still have the power, but you have interposed so much between it and your awareness of it that you cannot use it. Everything you have taught yourself has made your power more and more obscure to you. You know not what it is, nor where.

For you have taught yourself how to imprison the Son of God, a lesson so unthinkable that only the insane, in deepest sleep, could even dream of it.

Atonement teaches you how to escape forever from everything that you have taught yourself in the past, by showing you only what you are now. Nothing you have ever learned can help you understand the present, or teach you how to undo the past. Your past is what you have taught yourself. Let it all go. Do not attempt to understand any event or anything or anyone in its "light," for the darkness in which you try to see can only obscure. Put no confidence at all in darkness to illuminate your understanding, for if you do, you contradict the light, and thereby think you see the darkness. Yet darkness cannot be seen, for it is nothing more than a condition in which seeing becomes impossible.

Learn of God's happiness, which is yours. But to accomplish this, all your dark lessons must be brought willingly to truth, and joyously laid down by hands open to receive, not closed to take. Every dark lesson that you bring to Him Who teaches light, He will accept from you, because you do not want it. And He will gladly exchange each one for the bright lesson He has learned for you.

You have one test, as sure as God, by which to recognize if what you learned is true. If you are wholly free of fear of any kind, and if all those who meet or even think of you share in your perfect peace, then you can be sure that you have learned God's lesson, and not your own.

When your peace is threatened, or disturbed in any way, say to yourself:

I do not know what anything, including this, means.
And so I do not know how to respond to it.
And I will not use my own past learning as the light to guide me now.

You cannot be your guide to miracles, for it is you who made them necessary. The miracle acknowledges His changelessness by seeing His Son as He always was, and not as he would make himself. The miracle brings the effects that only guiltlessness can bring, and thus establishes the fact that guiltlessness must be.

Those who remember always that they know nothing, and who have become willing to learn everything, will learn it. But whenever they trust themselves, they will not learn. They have destroyed their motivation for learning by thinking they already know. Think not you understand anything until you pass the test of perfect peace, for peace and understanding go together and never can be found alone.

Call not upon the ego for anything; it is only this that you need do. The Holy Spirit will, of Himself, fill every mind that so makes room for Him.

Make way for peace, and it will come. For understanding is in you, and from it peace must come.

CHAPTER 15

THE HOLY INSTANT

15.1. The Two Uses of Time

Can you imagine what it means to have no cares, no worries, no anxieties, but merely to be perfectly calm and quiet all the time? Yet that is what time is for; to learn just that and nothing more. God's Teacher cannot be satisfied with His teaching until it constitutes all your learning. When this has happened, you will no longer need a teacher or time in which to learn.

The ego, like the Holy Spirit, uses "time" to convince you of the inevitability of the goal, the end of teaching. To the ego the goal is death, which is its end. But to the Holy Spirit the goal is life, which has no end.

The belief in hell is inescapable to those who identify with the ego. Their nightmares and their fears are all associated with it. The ego teaches that hell is in the future, for this is what all its teaching is directed to. Hell is its goal. The goal of death, which it craves for you, leaves it unsatisfied. No one who follows the ego's teaching is without the fear of death. Yet if death were thought merely as an end to pain, would it be feared? We have seen this strange paradox in the ego's thought system before, but never so clearly as here. For the ego must seem to keep fear from you to hold your allegiance. Yet it must engender fear in order to maintain itself. Again the ego tries, and all too frequently succeeds, in doing both, by using dissociation for holding its contradictory aims together so that they seem to be reconciled. The ego teaches thus: Death is the end as far as hope of Heaven goes. Yet because you and the ego cannot be separated, and because it cannot conceive of its own death, it will pursue you still, because guilt is eternal. Such is the ego's version of immortality. And it is this the ego's version of time supports.

How bleak and despairing is the ego's use of time! And how terrifying! For underneath its fanatical insistence that the past and future be the same is hidden a far more insidious threat to peace. The ego does not advertise its final threat, for it would have its worshipers still believe that it can offer them escape. But the belief in guilt must lead to the belief in hell, and always does.

The Holy Spirit teaches thus: There is no hell. Hell is only what the ego has made of the present. The belief in hell is what prevents you from understanding the present, because you are afraid of it. The Holy Spirit leads as steadily to Heaven as the ego drives to hell. For the Holy Spirit, Who knows only the present, uses it to undo the fear by which the ego would make the present useless. There is no escape from fear in the ego's use of time. For time, according to its teaching, is nothing but a teaching device for compounding guilt until it becomes all-encompassing, demanding vengeance forever.

The Holy Spirit would undo all of this now. Fear is not of the present, but only of the past and future, which do not exist. There is no fear in the present when each instant stands clear and separated from the past, without its shadow reaching out into the future. Each instant is a clean, untarnished birth, in which the Son of God emerges from the past into the present. And the present extends forever. It is so beautiful and so clean and free of guilt that nothing but happiness is there. No darkness is remembered, and immortality and joy are now.

This lesson takes no time. For what is time without a past and future? It has taken time to misguide you so completely, but it takes no time at all to be what you are. Begin to practice the Holy Spirit's use of time as a teaching aid to happiness and peace. Take this very instant, now, and think of it as all there is of time. Nothing can reach you here out of the past, and it is here that you are completely absolved, completely free and wholly without condemnation. From this holy instant wherein holiness was born again you will go forth in time without fear, and with no sense of change with time.

Time is inconceivable without change, yet holiness does not change. Learn from this instant more than merely that hell does not exist. In this redeeming instant lies Heaven. And Heaven will not change, for the birth into the holy present is salvation from change. Change is an illusion, taught by those who cannot see themselves as guiltless. There is no change in Heaven because there is no change in God. In the holy instant, in which you see yourself as bright with freedom, you will remember God. For remembering Him is to remember freedom.

How long is an instant? As long as it takes to re-establish perfect sanity, perfect peace and perfect love for everyone, for God and for yourself. As long as it takes to remember immortality, and your immortal creations who share it with you. As long as it takes to exchange hell for Heaven. Long enough to transcend all of the ego's making, and ascend unto your Father.

Time is your friend, if you leave it to the Holy Spirit to use. He needs but very little to restore God's whole power to you. He Who transcends time for you understands what time is for. Holiness lies not in time, but in eternity. There never was an instant in which God's Son could lose his purity. His changeless state is beyond time, for his purity remains forever beyond attack and without variability. Time stands still in his holiness, and changes not.

15.2. The End of Doubt

Do not be concerned with time, and fear not the instant of holiness that will remove all fear. For the instant of peace is eternal because it is without fear. It will come, being the lesson God gives you, through the Teacher He has appointed to translate time into eternity. Blessed is God's Teacher, Whose joy is to teach God's holy Son his holiness. His joy is not contained in time. His teaching is for you because His joy is yours. Through Him you stand before God's altar, where He gently translates hell into Heaven. For it is only in Heaven that God would have you be.

How long can it take to be where God would have you? The blessed instant reaches out to encompass time, as God extends Himself to encompass you.

The holy instant has not yet happened to you. Yet it will, and you will recognize it with perfect certainty. You can practice the mechanics of the holy instant, and will learn much from doing so.

Start now to practice your little part in separating out the holy instant. You will receive very specific instructions as you go along. To Learn to separate out this single second, and to experience it as timeless, is to begin to experience yourself as not separate. Fear not that you will not be given help in this. God's Teacher and His lesson will support your strength. It is only your weakness that will depart from you in this practice, for it is the practice of the power of God in you.

15.3. Littleness versus Magnitude

Be not content with littleness. But be sure you understand what littleness is, and why you could never be content with it. Littleness is the offering you give yourself. You offer this in place of magnitude, and you accept it. Everything in this world is little because it is a world made out of littleness, in the strange belief that littleness can content you. When you strive for anything in this world in the belief that it will bring you peace, you are belittling yourself and blinding yourself to glory. Littleness and glory are the choices open to your striving and your vigilance. You will always choose one at the expense of the other.

Yet what you do not realize, each time you choose, is that your choice is your evaluation of yourself. Choose littleness and you will not have peace, for you will have judged yourself unworthy of it. And whatever you offer as a substitute, is much too poor a gift to satisfy you. It is essential that you accept the fact there is no form of littleness that can ever content you. You are free to try as many as you wish, but all you will be doing is to delay your homecoming. For you will be content only in magnitude, which is your home.

Chapter 15

There is a deep responsibility you owe yourself, and one you must learn to remember all the time. The lesson may seem hard at first, but you will learn to love it when you realize that it is true and is but a tribute to your power. You who have sought and found littleness, remember this: Every decision you make stems from what you think you are, and represents the value that you put upon yourself. Believe the little can content you, and by limiting yourself you will not be satisfied. For your function is not little, and it is only by finding your function and fulfilling it that you can escape from littleness.

All striving must be directed against littleness, for it does require vigilance to protect your magnitude in this world. To hold your magnitude in perfect awareness in a world of littleness is a task the little cannot undertake. Yet it is asked of you, in tribute to your magnitude and not your littleness. Nor is it asked of you alone. The power of God will support every effort you make on behalf of His dear Son. Search for the little, and you deny yourself His power. God is not willing that His Son be content with less than everything. For He is not content without His Son, and His Son cannot be content with less than his Father has given him.

I asked you earlier, "Would you be hostage to the ego or host to God?" Let this question be asked you by the Holy Spirit every time you make a decision. For every decision you make does answer this, and invites sorrow or joy accordingly. Every decision you make is for Heaven or for hell, and brings you the awareness of what you decided for.

The Holy Spirit can hold your magnitude, clean of all littleness, clearly and in perfect safety in your mind, untouched by every little gift the world of littleness would offer you. But for this, you cannot side against Him in what He wills for you. Decide for God through Him. For littleness, and the belief that you can be content with littleness, are decisions you make about yourself. The power and the glory that lie in you from God are for all who, like you, perceive themselves as little, and believe that littleness can be blown up into a sense of magnitude that can content them. Neither give littleness, nor accept it. All honor is due the host of God. Your littleness deceives you, but your magnitude is of Him Who dwells in you, and in Whom you dwell.

When you have learned to accept what you are, you will make no more gifts to offer to yourself, for you will know you are complete, in need of nothing, and unable to accept anything for yourself. But you will gladly give, having received. The host of God needs not seek to find anything.

Call forth in everyone only the remembrance of God, and of the Heaven that is in him. For where you would have your brother be, there will you think you are. Hear not his appeal to hell and littleness, but only his call for Heaven and greatness. Forget not that his call is yours, and answer him with me. God's power is forever on the side of His host, for it protects only the peace in which He dwells. Lay not littleness before His holy altar, which rises above the stars and reaches even to Heaven, because of what is given it.

15.4. Practicing the Holy Instant

The holy instant is this instant and every instant. The one you want it to be *it* is. The one you would not have the holy instant be is lost to you. You must decide when *it* is. Delay *it* not. For beyond the past and future, where you will not find the holy instant, *it* stands in shimmering readiness for your acceptance. Yet, you cannot bring the holy instant into glad awareness while you do not want *it*, for *it* holds the whole release from littleness.

Your practice must therefore rest upon your willingness to let all littleness go. The instant in which magnitude dawns upon you, is but as far away as your desire for magnitude. As long as you do not desire magnitude and cherish littleness instead, by so much is the holy instant far from you. By so much as you want magnitude will you bring the holy instant nearer. Think not that you can find salvation in your own way and have it. Give over every plan you have made for your salvation in exchange for God's plan. His plan will content you, and nothing else can bring you peace. For peace is of God, and no one beside Him.

Be humble before Him, and yet great in Him. And value no plan of the ego before the plan of God. Every allegiance to a plan of salvation apart from Him diminishes the value of His Will for you in your own mind. And yet it is your mind that is the host to Him.

I stand within the holy instant, as clear as you would have me. I call to you to make the holy instant yours at once, for the release from littleness in the mind of the host of God depends on willingness, and not on time.

The reason this course is simple is that truth is simple. Complexity is of the ego, and is nothing more than the ego's attempt to obscure the obvious. You could live forever in the holy instant, beginning now and reaching to eternity, but for a very simple reason. Do not obscure the simplicity of this reason, for if you do, it will be only because you prefer not to recognize it and not to let it go. The simple reason, simply stated, is this: The holy instant is a time in which you receive and give perfect communication. This means, however, that it is a time in which your mind is open, both to receive and give. It is the recognition that all minds are in communication. It therefore seeks to change nothing, but merely to accept everything.

How can you do this when you would prefer to have private thoughts and keep them? The only way you could do that would be to deny the perfect communication that makes the holy instant what it is. You believe you can harbor thoughts you would not share, and that salvation lies in keeping thoughts to yourself alone. For in private thoughts, known only to yourself, you think you find a way to keep what you would have alone, and share what you would share. And then you wonder why it is that you are not in full communication with those around you, and with God Who surrounds all of you together.

Every thought you would keep hidden shuts communication off, because you would have it so. Ask yourself honestly, "Would I want to have perfect communication, and am I wholly willing to let everything that interferes with it go forever?"

For what you would hide is hidden from you. In your practice, then, try only to be vigilant against deception, and seek not to protect the thoughts you would keep to yourself. Let the Holy Spirit's purity shine them away, and bring all your awareness to the readiness for purity He offers you. Thus will He make you ready to acknowledge that you are host to God, and hostage to no one and to nothing.

15.5. The Holy Instant and Special Relationships

The holy instant is the Holy Spirit's most useful learning device for teaching you love's meaning. For its purpose is to suspend judgment entirely. Judgment always rests on the past, for past experience is the basis on which you judge. Judgment becomes impossible without the past, for without it you do not understand anything. You would make no attempt to judge, because it would be quite apparent to you that you do not understand what anything means. You are afraid of this because you believe that without the ego, all would be chaos. Yet I assure you that without the ego, all would be love.

The past is the ego's chief learning device, for it is in the past that you learned to define your own needs and acquired methods for meeting them on your own terms. If you seek to separate out certain aspects of the totality and look to them to meet your imagined needs, you are attempting to use separation to save you. How, then, could guilt not enter? For separation is the source of guilt, and to appeal to it for salvation is to believe you are alone. To be alone is to be guilty. For to experience yourself as alone is to deny the Oneness of the Father and His Son, and thus to attack reality.

All special relationships have elements of fear in them. This is why they shift and change so frequently. They are not based on changeless love alone. And love, where fear has entered, cannot be depended on because it is not perfect. In His function as Interpreter of what you made, the Holy Spirit uses special relationships, which you have chosen to support the ego, as learning experiences that point to truth. Under His teaching, every relationship becomes a lesson in love.

The Holy Spirit knows no one is special. Yet He also perceives that you have made special relationships, which He would purify and not let you destroy. However unholy the reason you made them may be, He can translate them into holiness by removing as much fear as you will let Him. You can place any relationship under His care and be sure that it will not result in pain, if you offer Him your willingness to have it serve no need but His. Do not, then, be afraid to let go your imagined needs, which would destroy the relationship. Your only need is His.

In the holy instant no one is special, for your personal needs intrude on no one to make your brothers seem different. Without the values from the past, you would see them all the same and like yourself. Nor would you see any separation between yourself and them. In the holy instant, you see in each relationship what it will be when you perceive only the present.

God knows you now. The holy instant reflects His knowing by bringing all perception out of the past, thus removing the frame of reference you have built by which to judge your brothers. Once this is gone, the Holy Spirit substitutes His frame of reference for it. His frame of reference is simply God. The Holy Spirit's timelessness lies only here. For in the holy instant, free of the past, you see that love is in you, and you have no need to look without and snatch love guiltily from where you thought it was.

God loves every brother as He loves you; neither less nor more. He needs them all equally, and so do you.

In the holy instant there is no conflict of needs, for there is only one. For the holy instant reaches to eternity, and to the Mind of God. And it is only there love has meaning, and only there can it be understood.

15.6. The Holy Instant and the Laws of God

It is impossible to use one relationship at the expense of another and not to suffer guilt. And it is equally impossible to condemn part of a relationship and find peace within it. Under the Holy Spirit's teaching all relationships are seen as total commitments, yet they do not conflict with one another in any way. Perfect faith in each one, for its ability to satisfy you completely, arises only from perfect faith in yourself. And this you cannot have while guilt remains. And there will be guilt as long as you accept the possibility, and cherish it, that you can make a brother into what he is not, because you would have him so.

You have so little faith in yourself because you are unwilling to accept the fact that perfect love is in you. And so you seek without for what you cannot find without. I offer you my perfect faith in you, in place of all your doubts. But forget not that my faith must be as perfect in all your brothers as it is in you, or it would be a limited gift to you. In the holy instant we share our faith in God's Son because we recognize, together, that he is wholly worthy of it, and in our appreciation of his worth we cannot doubt his holiness. And so we love him.

In the holy instant nothing happens that has not always been. Only the veil that has been drawn across reality is lifted. Nothing has changed. Yet the awareness of changelessness comes swiftly as the veil of time is pushed aside.

It is through us that peace will come.

There is no exclusion in the holy instant because the past is gone, and with it goes the whole basis for exclusion.

15.7. The Needless Sacrifice

The ego establishes relationships only to get something. And it would keep the giver bound to itself through guilt.

The sick attraction of guilt must be recognized for what it is. For having been made real to you, it is essential to look at it clearly, and by withdrawing your investment in it, to learn to let it go. No one would choose to let go what he believes has value. Yet the attraction of guilt has value to you only because you have not looked at what it is, and have judged it completely in the dark. As we bring it to light, your only question will be why it was you ever wanted it. You have nothing to lose by looking open-eyed, for ugliness such as this belongs not in your holy mind.

Anger takes many forms, but it cannot long deceive those who will learn that love brings no guilt at all, and what brings guilt cannot be love and must be anger. All anger is nothing more than an attempt to make someone feel guilty, and this attempt is the only basis the ego accepts for special relationships. Guilt is the only need the ego has, and as long as you identify with it, guilt will remain attractive to you. Yet remember this; to be with a body is not communication. And if you think it is, you will feel guilty about communication and will be afraid to hear the Holy Spirit, recognizing in His Voice your own need to communicate.

The illusion of the autonomy of the body, and its ability to overcome loneliness, is but the working of the ego's plan to establish its own autonomy. As long as you believe that to be with a body is companionship, you will be compelled to attempt to keep your brother in his body, held there by guilt. And you will see safety in guilt and danger in communication. For the ego will always teach that loneliness is solved by guilt, and that communication is the cause of loneliness. And despite the evident insanity of this lesson, many have learned it.

It is through the holy instant that what seems impossible is accomplished, making it evident that it is not impossible. In the holy instant guilt holds no attraction, since communication has been restored. And guilt, whose only purpose is to disrupt communication, has no function here. Here there is no concealment, and no private thoughts. The willingness to communicate attracts communication to it, and overcomes loneliness completely. There is complete forgiveness here, for there is no desire to exclude anyone from your completion, in sudden recognition of the value of his part in it. In the protection of your wholeness, all are invited and made welcome. And you understand that your completion is God's, Whose only need is to have you be complete. For your completion makes you His in your awareness. And here it is that you experience yourself as you were created, and as you are.

15.8. The Only Real Relationship

The holy instant does not replace the need for learning, for the Holy Spirit must not leave you as your Teacher until the holy instant has extended far beyond time. In the face of your fear of forgiveness, which He perceives as clearly as He knows forgiveness is release, He will teach you to remember that forgiveness is not loss, but your salvation. And that in complete forgiveness, in which you recognize that there is nothing to forgive, you are absolved completely.

Accept your sense of failure as nothing more than a mistake in who you are. For the holy host of God is beyond failure, and nothing that he wills can be denied.

Think but an instant on this: God gave the Sonship to you, to ensure your perfect creation. This was His gift, for as He withheld Himself not from you, He withheld not His creation. Nothing that ever was created but is yours. Your relationships are with the universe. And this universe, being of God, is far beyond the petty sum of all the separate bodies you perceive. For all its parts are joined in God through Christ, where they become like to their Father. Christ knows of no separation from His Father, Who is His one relationship, in which He gives as His Father gives to Him.

The Holy Spirit asks you to respond as God does, for He would teach you what you do not understand.

Leave, then, what seems to you to be impossible, because it is the will of God, and let Him Whose teaching is only of God teach you the only meaning of relationships. For God created the only relationship that has meaning, and that is His relationship with you.

15.9. The Holy Instant and the Attraction of God

As the ego would limit your perception of your brothers to the body, so would the Holy Spirit release your vision and let you see the Great Rays shining from them, so unlimited that they reach to God. It is this shift to vision that is accomplished in the holy instant. Yet it is needful for you to learn just what this shift entails, so you will become willing to make it permanent. Given this willingness it will not leave you, for it is permanent. Once you have accepted it as the only perception you want, it is translated into knowledge by the part that God Himself plays in the Atonement, for it is the only step in it He understands. Therefore, in this there will be no delay when you are ready for it. God is ready now, but you are not.

The body is the symbol of the ego, as the ego is the symbol of the separation. And both are nothing more than attempts to limit communication, and thereby to make it impossible.

In the holy instant, where the Great Rays replace the body in awareness, the recognition of relationships without limits is given you. But in order to see this, it is necessary to give up every use the ego has for the body, and to accept the fact that the ego has no purpose you would share with it. For the ego would limit everyone to a body for its own purposes, and while you think it has a purpose, you will choose to utilize the means by which it tries to turn its purpose into accomplishment.

If you would but let the Holy Spirit tell you of the Love of God for you, and the need your creations have to be with you forever, you would experience the attraction of the eternal. For it is your will to be in Heaven, where you are complete and quiet, in such sure and loving relationships that any limit is impossible. Would you not exchange your little relationships for this? For the body is little and limited, and only those whom you would see without the limits the ego would impose on them can offer you the gift of freedom.

Remember; the attraction of guilt opposes the attraction of God. His attraction for you remains unlimited, but because your power, being His, is as great as His, you can turn away from love. What you invest in guilt you withdraw from God. And your sight grows weak and dim and limited, for you have attempted to separate the Father from the Son, and limit their communication. Seek not Atonement in further separation. And limit not your vision of God's Son to what interferes with his release, and what the Holy Spirit must undo to set him free. For his belief in limits has imprisoned him.

When the body ceases to attract you, and when you place no value on it as a means of getting anything, then there will be no interference in communication and your thoughts will be as free as God's. As you let the Holy Spirit teach you how to use the body only for purposes of communication, and renounce its use for separation and attack which the ego sees in it, you will learn you have no need of a body at all. In the holy instant there are no bodies, and you experience only the attraction of God. Accepting it as undivided you join Him wholly, in an instant. The reality of this relationship becomes the only truth that you could ever want. All truth is here.

15.10 The Time of Rebirth

The holy instant is truly the time of Christ. For in this liberating instant no guilt is laid upon the Son of God, and his unlimited power is thus restored to him. Learn now that sacrifice of any kind is nothing but a limitation imposed on giving. And by this limitation you have limited acceptance of the gift I offer you.

The time of Christ is the time appointed for the gift of freedom, offered to everyone. And by your acceptance of it, you offer it to everyone.

It is in your power to make this season holy, for it is in your power to make the time of Christ be now. It is possible to do this all at once because there is but one shift in perception that is necessary, for you made but one mistake. It seems like many, but it is all the same. For though the ego takes many forms, it is always the same idea. What is not love is always fear, and nothing else.

It is not necessary to follow fear through all the circuitous routes by which it burrows underground and hides in darkness, to emerge in forms quite different from what it is. When you are willing to regard them, not as separate, but as different manifestations of the same idea, and one you do not want, they go together. The idea is simply this: You believe it is possible to be host to the ego or hostage to God. This is the choice you think you have, and the decision you believe that you must make. You see no other alternatives, for you cannot accept the fact that sacrifice gets nothing. Sacrifice is so essential to your thought system that salvation apart from sacrifice means nothing to you. Your confusion of sacrifice and love is so profound that you cannot conceive of love without sacrifice. And it is this that you must look upon; sacrifice is attack, not love. If you would accept but this one idea, your fear of love would vanish. Guilt cannot last when the idea of sacrifice has been removed. For if there is sacrifice, someone must pay and someone must get. And the only question that remains is how much is the price, and for getting what.

As host to the ego, you believe that you can give all your guilt away whenever you want, and thereby purchase peace. And the payment does not seem to be yours. While it is obvious that the ego does demand payment it never seems to be demanding it of you. You are unwilling to recognize that the ego, which you invited, is treacherous only to those who think they are its host. The ego will never let you perceive this, since this recognition would make it homeless. For when the recognition dawns clearly, you will not be deceived by any form the ego takes to protect itself from your sight. Each form will be recognized as but a cover for the one idea that hides behind them all; that love demands sacrifice, and is therefore inseparable from attack and fear. And that guilt is the price of love, which must be paid by fear.

How fearful, then, has God become to you, and how great a sacrifice do you believe His Love demands! For total love would demand total sacrifice. And so the ego seems to demand less of you than God, and of the two is judged as the lesser of two evils, one to be feared a little, perhaps, but the other to be destroyed. For you see love as destructive, and your only question is who is to be destroyed, you or another? You seek to answer this question in your special relationships, in which you seem to be both destroyer and destroyed in part, but able to be neither completely. And this you think saves you from God, Whose total Love would completely destroy you.

15.11. Christmas as the End of Sacrifice

The sign of Christmas is a star, a light in darkness. See the light not outside yourself, but shining in the Heaven within, and accept it as the sign the time of Christ has come. He comes demanding nothing. No sacrifice of any kind, of anyone, is asked by Him. In Christ's

Presence the whole idea of sacrifice loses all meaning. For Christ is Host to God. And you need but invite Christ in Who is there already, by recognizing that God's Host, Christ, is One, and no thought alien to God's Oneness can abide with Christ there.

This Christmas give the Holy Spirit everything that would hurt you. Let yourself be healed completely that you may join with Him in healing, and let us celebrate our release together by releasing everyone with us. Leave nothing behind, for release is total, and when you have accepted it with me you will give it with me. All pain and sacrifice and littleness will disappear in our relationship, which is as innocent as our relationship with our Father, and as powerful. Pain will be brought to us and disappear in our presence, and without pain there can be no sacrifice. And without sacrifice there love must be.

You who believe that sacrifice is love must learn that sacrifice is separation from love. For sacrifice brings guilt as surely as love brings peace. Guilt is the condition of sacrifice, as peace is the condition for the awareness of your relationship with God. Through guilt you exclude your Father and your brothers from yourself. Through peace you invite them back, realizing that they are where your invitation bids them be. What you exclude from yourself seems fearful, for you endow it with fear and try to cast it out, though it is part of you. Who can perceive part of himself as loathsome, and live within himself in peace? And who can try to resolve the "conflict" of Heaven and hell in him by casting Heaven out and giving it the attributes of hell, without experiencing himself as incomplete and lonely?

As long as you perceive the body as your reality, so long will you perceive yourself as lonely and deprived. And so long will you also perceive yourself as a victim of sacrifice, justified in sacrificing others.

In the holy instant the condition of love is met, for minds are joined without the body's interference, and where there is communication there is peace. The Prince of Peace was born to re-establish the condition of love by teaching that communication remains unbroken even if the body is destroyed, provided that you see not the body as the necessary means of communication. And if you understand this lesson, you will realize that to sacrifice the body is to sacrifice nothing, and communication, which must be of the mind, cannot be sacrificed. Where, then, is sacrifice? The lesson I was born to teach, and still would teach to all my brothers, is that sacrifice is nowhere and love is everywhere. For communication embraces everything, and in the peace it re-establishes, love comes of itself.

Let no despair darken the joy of Christmas, for the time of Christ is meaningless apart from joy. Let us join in celebrating peace by demanding no sacrifice of anyone, for so you offer me the love I offer you. What can be more joyous than to perceive we are deprived of nothing?

Chapter 16

The Forgiveness of Illusions

16.1. True Empathy

To empathize does not mean to join in suffering, for that is what you must refuse to understand. That is the ego's interpretation of empathy, and is always used to form a special relationship in which the suffering is shared. The capacity to empathize is very useful to the Holy Spirit, provided you let Him use it in His way. The Holy Spirit does not join in pain, understanding that healing pain is not accomplished by attempts to enter into it.

Yet of this you may be sure; if you will merely sit quietly by and let the Holy Spirit relate through you, you will empathize with strength, and will gain in strength and not in weakness.

All you have learned of empathy is from the past. And there is nothing from the past that you would share, for there is nothing from the past that you would keep. Do not use empathy to make the past real, and so perpetuate it. Step gently aside, and let healing be done for you. Keep but one thought in mind and do not lose sight of it, however tempted you may be to judge any situation, and to determine your response by judging it.

Focus your mind only on this:

> *I am not alone, and I would not intrude the past upon my Guest.*
> *I have invited Him, and He is here.*
> *I need do nothing except not to interfere.*

True empathy is of Him Who knows what it is. You will learn His interpretation of it if you let Him use your capacity for strength, and not for weakness. He will not desert you, but be sure that you desert not Him. Humility is strength in this sense only; that to recognize and accept the fact that you do not know is to recognize and accept the fact that He does know.

You are the learner; He the Teacher. Do not confuse your role with His, for this will never bring peace to anyone. Offer your empathy to Him for it is His perception and His strength that you would share. And let Him offer you His strength and His perception, to be shared through you.

16.2. The Power of Holiness

No evidence will convince you of the truth of what you do not want. Yet your relationship with Him is real. Regard this not with fear, but with rejoicing. The One you called upon is with you. Bid Him welcome, and honor the witnesses who bring you the glad tidings He has come. It is true, just as you fear, that to acknowledge Him is to deny all that you think you know. But what you think you know was never true. What gain is there to you in clinging to it, and denying the evidence for truth? For you have come too near to truth to renounce it now, and you will yield to its compelling attraction. You can delay this now, but only a little while. The Host of God has called to you, and you have heard. Never again will you be wholly willing not to listen.

This is a year of joy, in which your listening will increase and peace will grow with its increase. The power of holiness and the weakness of attack are both being brought into your awareness. And this has been accomplished in a mind firmly convinced that holiness is weakness and attack is power. But remember also that whenever you listened to His interpretation the results have brought you joy.

Do not interpret against God's Love, for you have many witnesses that speak of it so clearly that only the blind and deaf could fail to see and hear them. This year determine not to deny what has been given you by God, for that is the only reason He has called to you. His Voice has spoken clearly, and yet you have so little faith in what you heard, because you have preferred to place still greater faith in the disaster you have made. Today, let us resolve together to accept the joyful tidings that disaster is not real and that reality is not disaster. Reality is safe and sure, and wholly kind to everyone and everything. There is no greater love than to accept this and be glad. For love asks only that you be happy, and will give you everything that makes for happiness.

16.3. The Reward of Teaching

This is a course in how to know yourself. You have taught what you are, but have not let what you are, teach you. You have been very careful to avoid the obvious, and not to see the real "cause and effect" relationship that is perfectly apparent. What you accept into your mind does not really change it. Illusions are but beliefs in what is not there. And the seeming conflict between truth and illusion can only be resolved by separating yourself from the illusion and not from truth.

Though you seemed to suffer for it, the joy of teaching will yet be yours. For the joy of teaching is in the learner, who offers it to the teacher in gratitude, and shares it with him. As you learn, your gratitude to your Self, Who teaches you what He is, will grow and help you honor Him. And you will learn His power and strength and purity, and love Him as His Father does. His Kingdom has no limits and no end, and there is nothing in Him that is not perfect and eternal. All this is you, and nothing outside of this is you.

To your most holy Self all praise is due for what you are, and for what He is Who created you as you are. Sooner or later must everyone bridge the gap he imagines exists between his "selves". Each one builds this bridge, which carries him across the gap as soon as he is willing to expend some effort on behalf of bridging it.

Your bridge is built stronger than you think, and your foot is planted firmly on it. Have no fear that the attraction of those who stand on the other side and wait for you will not draw you safely across. For you will come where you would be, and where your Self awaits you.

16.4. The Illusion and the Reality of Love

Be not afraid to look upon the special hate relationship, for freedom lies in looking at it. Your salvation will rise clearly before your eyes as you look on this. You cannot limit hate. The special love relationship will not offset it, but will merely drive it underground and out of sight. It is essential to bring it into sight, and to make no attempt to hide it. For it is the attempt to balance hate with love that makes love meaningless to you. The extent of the split that lies in this you do not realize. And until you do, the split will remain unrecognized, and therefore unhealed.

You will go through this last undoing quite unharmed, and will at last emerge as yourself. This is the last step in the readiness for God. Be not unwilling now; you are too near, and you will cross the bridge in perfect safety, translated quietly from war to peace. For the illusion of love will never satisfy, but its reality, which awaits you on the other side, will give you everything.

The special love relationship is an attempt to limit the destructive effects of hate by finding a haven in the storm of guilt. It makes no attempt to rise above the storm, into the sunlight. On the contrary, it emphasizes the guilt outside the haven by attempting to build barricades against it, and keep within them.

Love is not an illusion. It is a fact. Where disillusionment is possible, there was not love but hate. For hate is an illusion.

Your task is not to seek for love, but merely to seek and find all of the barriers within yourself that you have built against it. It is not necessary to seek for what is true, but it is necessary to seek for what is false. Every illusion is one of fear, whatever form it takes. And the attempt to escape from one illusion into another must fail. If you seek love outside

Chapter 16

yourself you can be certain that you perceive hatred within, and are afraid of it. Yet peace will never come from the illusion of love, but only from its reality.

Heaven waits silently, and your creations are holding out their hands to help you cross and welcome them. For it is they you seek. You seek but for your own completion, and it is they who render you complete. The special love relationship is but a shabby substitute for what makes you whole in truth, not in illusion.

Across the bridge is your completion, for you will be wholly in God, willing for nothing special, but only to be wholly like to Him, completing Him by your completion. Fear not to cross to the abode of peace and perfect holiness. Only there is the completion of God and of His Son established forever.

The bridge that leads to union in yourself must lead to knowledge, for it was built with God beside you, and will lead you straight to Him where your completion rests, wholly compatible with His. Every illusion you accept into your mind by judging it to be attainable removes your own sense of completion, and thus denies the Wholeness of your Father. Every fantasy, be it of love or hate, deprives you of knowledge, for fantasies are the veil behind which truth is hidden. To lift the veil that seems so dark and heavy, it is only needful to value truth beyond all fantasy, and to be entirely unwilling to settle for illusion in place of truth.

Love calls, but hate would have you stay. Hear not the call of hate, and see the call of hate but the call for help, that rises from you to your Creator. He loves you, wholly without illusion, as you must love. For love is wholly without illusion, and therefore wholly without fear. Whom God remembers must be whole. And God has never forgotten what makes Him whole. In your completion lie the memory of His Wholeness and His gratitude to you for His completion. In His link with you lie both His inability to forget and your ability to remember. In Him are joined your willingness to love and all the Love of God, Who forgot you not.

The Holy Spirit is the Bridge to Him, made from your willingness to unite with Him and created by His joy in union with you. The journey that seemed endless is almost complete, for what is endless is very near. You have almost recognized the journey's end. Turn with me firmly away from all illusions now, and let nothing stand in the way of truth. We will take the last useless journey away from truth together, and then together we go straight to God, in joyous answer to His Call for His completion.

16.5. The Choice for Completion

In looking at the *special* relationship, it is necessary first to realize that it involves a great amount of pain. Anxiety, despair, guilt and attack all enter into it, broken into by periods, in which they seem to be gone. All these must be understood for what they are. Whatever form they take, they are always an attack on the self to make the other guilty. I have spoken of this before, but there are some aspects of what is really being attempted that have not been touched upon.

The special love relationship is the ego's chief weapon for keeping you from Heaven. It does not appear to be a weapon, but if you consider how you value it and why, you will realize what it must be.

The special love relationship is the ego's most boasted gift, and one which has the most appeal to those unwilling to relinquish guilt. The "dynamics" of the ego are clearest here, for counting on the attraction of special love's offering, the fantasies that center around it, are often quite overt. Here the fantasies are usually judged to be acceptable and even natural. No one considers it bizarre to love and hate together, and even those who believe that hate is sin merely feel guilty, but do not correct it.

This world is the opposite of Heaven, being made to be its opposite, and everything here takes a direction exactly opposite of what is true. In Heaven, where the meaning of love is known, love is the same as union. Here, in this world where the illusion of love is accepted in love's place, love is perceived as separation and exclusion.

It is in the special relationship, born of the hidden wish for special love from God, that the ego's hatred triumphs. For the special relationship is the renunciation of the Love of God, and the attempt to secure for the self the specialness that He denied. It is essential to the preservation of the ego that you believe this specialness is not hell, but Heaven. For the ego would never have you see that separation could only be loss. The state of separation is the one condition in which Heaven could not be.

To everyone, Heaven is completion. There can be no disagreement on this, because both the ego and the Holy Spirit accept that Heaven is completion. They are, however, in complete disagreement on what completion is, and how it is accomplished. The Holy Spirit knows that completion lies first in union, and then in the extension of union. To the ego completion lies in triumph, and in the extension of the "victory", even to the final triumph over God. In this it sees the ultimate freedom of the self, for nothing would remain to interfere with the ego. This is the ego's idea of Heaven.

The special relationship is a strange ego device for joining hell and Heaven, and making them indistinguishable. And the attempt to find the imagined "best" of both worlds has merely led to fantasies of both, and to the inability to perceive either hell or Heaven as it is. The special relationship is the triumph of this confusion. The special relationship is a kind of union from which union is excluded, and the basis for the attempt at union rests on exclusion. What better example could there be of the ego's maxim, "Seek but do not find"?

CHAPTER 16

Most curious of all is the concept of the self, which the ego fosters in the special relationship. This "self" seeks the relationship to make itself complete. Yet when this self finds the special relationship in which it thinks it can accomplish this, it gives itself away, and tries to "trade" itself for the self of another. This is not union, for there is no increase and no extension. Each partner tries to sacrifice the self he does not want for one he thinks he would prefer. And he feels guilty for the "sin" of taking, and of giving nothing of value in return. How much value can he place upon a self that he would give away to get a "better" one?

The "better" self the ego seeks is always one that is more special. And whoever seems to possess a special self is "loved" for what can be taken from him. Where both partners see this special self in each other, the ego sees "a union made in Heaven." For neither one will recognize that he has asked for hell, and so he will not interfere with the ego's illusion of Heaven.

The conviction of littleness lies in every special relationship, for only the deprived could value specialness. The demand for specialness, and the perception of the giving of specialness as an act of love, would make love hateful. The real purpose of the special relationship, in strict accordance with the ego's goals, is to destroy reality and substitute illusion. For the ego is itself an illusion, and only illusions can be the witnesses to its "reality."

If you perceived the special relationship as a triumph over God, would you want it? The central theme in separation's litany to sacrifice, is that God must die so you can live. And it is this theme that is acted out in the special relationship. Through the death of your little self, you think you can attack another self, and snatch the self from the other to replace the self that you despise. And you despise the little self because you do not think it offers the specialness that you demand. And hating it, you have made it little and unworthy, because you are afraid of it.

Whenever any form of special relationship tempts you to seek for love in the ritual of specialness, remember love is *content* and not *form* of any kind. The special relationship is a ritual of form, aimed at raising the form to take the place of God at the expense of content. There is no meaning in the form, and there will never be. The special relationship must be recognized for what it is; a senseless ritual.

See in the special relationship nothing more than a meaningless attempt to raise other gods before Him, and by worshiping them to obscure their tininess and His greatness. In the name of your completion you do not want this. For every idol that you raise to place before Him stands before you, in place of what you are.

Salvation lies in the simple fact that illusions are not fearful because they are not true. They but seem to be fearful to the extent to which you fail to recognize them for what they are; and you will fail to do this to the extent to which you want them to be true. And to the same extent you are denying truth, and so are failing to make the simple choice between truth and illusion; God and fantasy. Remember this, and you will have no difficulty in perceiving the decision as just what it is, and nothing more.

The core of the separation illusion lies simply in the fantasy of the destruction of love's meaning. And unless love's meaning is restored to you, you cannot know yourself who share its meaning. Separation is only the decision not to know yourself. This whole thought system is a carefully contrived learning experience, designed to lead away from truth and into fantasy. Yet for every learning that would hurt you, God offers you correction and complete escape from all its consequences.

The decision whether or not to listen to this course and follow it is but the choice between truth and illusion. For here is truth, separated from illusion and not confused with it at all. How simple does this choice between truth and illusion become when it is perceived as only what it is. For only fantasies make confusion in choosing possible, and they are totally unreal.

This year is thus the time to make the easiest decision that ever confronted you, and also the only one. You will cross the bridge into reality simply because you will recognize that God is on the other side, and nothing at all is here.

16.6. The Bridge to the Real World

The search for the special relationship is the sign that you equate yourself with the ego and not with God. For the special relationship has value only to the ego. To the ego, unless a relationship has special value it has no meaning, for it perceives all love as special.

The special relationship is totally meaningless without a body. If you value it, you must also value the body. And what you value you will keep. The special relationship is a device for limiting your self to a body, and for limiting your perception of others to theirs.

You see the world you value. On this side of the bridge you see the world of separate bodies, seeking to join each other in separate unions and to become one by losing. When two individuals seek to become one, they are trying to decrease their magnitude. Each would deny his power, for the separate union excludes the universe.

Across the bridge, in Heaven, it is so different! For a time the body is still seen, but not exclusively, as it is seen here in this world. Once you have crossed the bridge, the value of the body is so diminished in your sight that you will see no need at all to magnify it. For you will realize that the only value the body has is to enable you to bring your brothers to the bridge with you, and to be released together there.

The bridge itself is nothing more than a transition in the perspective of reality. On this world's side, everything you see is grossly distorted and completely out of perspective.

What is little and insignificant is magnified, and what is strong and powerful cut down to littleness. In the transition there is a period of confusion, in which a sense of actual disorientation may occur. But fear it not, for it means only that you have been willing to let go your hold on the distorted frame of reference that seemed to hold your world together. This frame of reference is built around the special relationship. Without this illusion there could be no meaning you would still seek here.

The new perspective you will gain from crossing over will be the understanding of where Heaven is. From this world's side, Heaven seems to be outside and across the bridge. Yet as you cross to join Heaven, it will join with you and become one with you. And you will think, in glad astonishment, that for all this you gave up nothing! The joy of Heaven, which has no limit, is increased with each light that returns to take its rightful place within Heaven. Wait no longer, for the Love of God and you. And may the *holy instant* speed you on the way, as it will surely do if you but let it come to you.

The Holy Spirit asks only this little help of you: Whenever your thoughts wander to a special relationship which still attracts you, enter with Him into a holy instant, and there let Him release you. The Holy Spirit needs only your willingness to share His perspective to give it to you completely. And your willingness need not be complete because His is perfect. It is the Holy Spirit's task to atone for your unwillingness by His perfect faith, and it is His faith you share with Him there. Out of your recognition of your unwillingness for your release, His perfect willingness is given you. Call upon Him, for Heaven is at His Call. And let Him call on Heaven for you.

16.7. The End of Illusions

It is impossible to let the past go without relinquishing the special relationship. For the special relationship is an attempt to re-enact the past and change it. Imagined slights, remembered pain, past disappointments, perceived injustices and deprivations all enter into the special relationship, which becomes a way in which you seek to restore your wounded self-esteem. What basis would you have for choosing a special partner without the past? Every such choice is made because of something "evil" in the past to which you cling, and for which must someone else atone.

Do not underestimate the intensity of the ego's drive for vengeance on the past. It is completely savage and completely insane. For the ego remembers everything you have done that has offended it, and seeks retribution of you. The fantasies the ego brings to its chosen relationships in which to act out its hate are fantasies of your destruction. For the ego holds the past against you, and in your escape from the past it sees itself deprived of the vengeance it believes you so justly merit. Yet without your alliance in your own destruction, the ego could not hold you to the past. In the special relationship you are allowing your destruction to be.

The past is gone; seek not to preserve it in the special relationship that binds you to it, and would teach you that salvation is in the past, and so you must return to the past to find salvation.

The one thing the ego *never* allows to reach awareness is that the special relationship is the acting out of vengeance on yourself. In seeking the special relationship, you look *not* for glory in yourself. You have denied that glory is there within you, and the substitute becomes your substitute for it. And vengeance becomes your substitute for Atonement.

Against the ego's insane notion of salvation, the Holy Spirit gently lays the *holy instant*. We said before that the Holy Spirit must teach through comparisons, and uses opposites to point to truth. The holy instant is the opposite of the ego's fixed belief in salvation through vengeance for the past. In the holy instant it is understood that the past is gone, and with its passing the drive for vengeance has been uprooted and has disappeared. The stillness and the peace of *now* enfold you in perfect gentleness. Everything is gone except the truth.

Remember that you always choose between truth and illusion; between the real Atonement that would heal, and the ego's "atonement" that would destroy. The power of God and all His Love, without limit, will support you as you seek only your place in the plan of Atonement arising from His Love. Be an ally of God and not the ego in seeking how Atonement can come to you. His help suffices, for His Messenger understands how to restore the Kingdom to you, and to place all your investment in salvation in your relationship with Him.

Seek and find His message in the holy instant, where all illusions are forgiven. From there the miracle extends to bless everyone and to resolve all problems, be they perceived as great or small, possible or impossible. To join in close relationship with Him is to accept relationships as real, and through their reality to give over all illusions for the reality of your relationship with God. Praise be to your relationship with Him and to no other.

> *Forgive us our illusions, Father, and help us to accept our true relationship with You, in which there are no illusions, and where none can ever enter. Our holiness is Yours. What can there be in us that needs forgiveness when Yours is perfect? The sleep of forgetfulness is only the unwillingness to remember Your forgiveness and Your Love. Let us not wander into temptation, for the temptation of the Son of God is not Your Will. And let us receive only what You have given, and accept but this into the minds which You created and which You love. Amen.*

Chapter 17

Forgiveness and the Holy Relationship

17.1. Bringing Fantasy to Truth

The betrayal of the Son of God lies only in illusions, and all his "sins" are but his own imagining. His reality is forever sinless. He need not be forgiven but awakened. In his dreams he has betrayed himself, his brothers and his God. Yet what is done in dreams has not been really done. It is impossible to convince the dreamer that this is so, for dreams are what they are because of their illusion of reality. Only in waking is the full release from them, for only then does it become perfectly apparent that they had no effect upon reality at all, and did not change it. Fantasies change reality. That is their purpose. They cannot do so in reality, but they can do so in the mind that would have reality be different.

Think you that you can bring truth to fantasy, and learn what truth means from the perspective of illusions? Truth has no meaning in illusion. The frame of reference for its meaning must be itself. When you try to bring truth to illusions, you are trying to make illusions real, and keep them by justifying your belief in them.

Be willing, then, to give all you have held outside the truth to Him Who knows the truth, and in Whom all is brought to truth. Be not concerned with anything except your willingness to have this be accomplished; He will accomplish it; not you. But forget not this: When you become disturbed and lose your peace of mind because another is attempting to solve his problems through fantasy, you are refusing to forgive yourself for just this same attempt. And you are holding both of you and your brother away from truth and from salvation. As you forgive him, you restore to truth what was denied by both of you. And you will see forgiveness where you have given it.

17.2. The Forgiven World

Can you imagine how beautiful those you forgive will look to you? In no fantasy have you ever seen anything so lovely. Nothing you see here, sleeping or waking, comes near to such loveliness. Nothing that you remember that made your heart sing with joy has ever brought you even a little part of the happiness this sight will bring you. For you will see the Son of God. You will behold the beauty the Holy Spirit loves to look upon, and which He thanks the Father for. He was created to see this for you, until you learned to see the loveliness for yourself. And all His teaching leads to seeing it and giving thanks with Him.

This loveliness is not a fantasy. It is the real world, bright and clean and new, with everything sparkling under the open sun. Nothing is hidden here, for everything has been forgiven and there are no fantasies to hide the truth. The bridge between that world and this is so little and so easy to cross, that you could not believe it is the meeting place of worlds so different. Yet this little bridge is the strongest thing that touches on this world at all. This little step, so small it has escaped your notice, is a stride through time into eternity, beyond all ugliness into beauty that will enchant you, and will never cease to cause you wonderment at its perfection.

The stars will disappear in light, and the sun that opened up the world to beauty will vanish. Perception will be meaningless when it has been perfected, for everything that has been used for learning will have no function. The perception of the real world will be so short that you will barely have time to thank God for it. For God will take the last step swiftly, when you have reached the real world and have been made ready for Him.

The real world is attained simply by the complete forgiveness of the old; the world you see without forgiveness. The great Transformer of perception will undertake with you the careful searching of the mind that made this world, and uncover to you the seeming reasons for your making it. In the light of the real reason that He brings, as you follow Him, He will show you that there is no reason here at all. Each spot His reason touches grows alive with beauty, and what seemed ugly in the darkness of your lack of reason is suddenly released to loveliness. Not even what the Son of God made in insanity could be without a hidden spark of beauty that gentleness could release.

All this beauty will rise to bless your sight as you look upon the world with forgiving eyes. For forgiveness literally transforms vision, and lets you see the real world reaching quietly and gently across chaos, removing all illusions that had twisted your perception and fixed it on the past. The smallest leaf becomes a thing of wonder, and a blade of grass a sign of God's perfection.

From the forgiven world the Son of God is lifted easily into his home. And there he knows that he has always rested there in peace. Even salvation will become a dream, and vanish from his mind. For salvation is the end of dreams, and with the closing of the dream will have no meaning.

17.3. Shadows of the Past

To forgive is merely to remember only the loving thoughts you gave in the past, and those that were given you. All the rest must be forgotten. Forgiveness is a selective remembering, based not on your selection. For the shadow figures you would make immortal are "enemies" of reality. The shadow figures are the witnesses you bring with you to demonstrate he did what he did not. Because you bring them, you will hear them. And you who keep them by your own selection do not understand how they came into your mind, and what their purpose is. They represent the evil that you think was done to you. You bring them with you only that you may return evil for evil, hoping that their witness will enable you to think guiltily of another and not harm yourself. They speak so clearly for the separation that no one not obsessed with keeping separation could hear them. They offer you the "reasons" why you should enter into unholy alliances to support the ego's goals, and make your relationships the witness to its power.

The shadow figures always speak for vengeance, and all relationships into which they enter are totally insane. Without exception, these relationships have as their purpose the exclusion of the truth about the other, and of yourself. This is why you see in both what is not there, and make of both the slaves of vengeance. And why whatever reminds you of your past grievances attracts you, and seems to go by the name of love, no matter how distorted the associations by which you arrive at the connection may be. And finally, why all such relationships become attempts at union through the body, for only bodies can be seen as means for vengeance. That bodies are central to all unholy relationships is evident. Your own experience has taught you this. But what you may not realize are all the reasons that go to make the relationship unholy.

The Holy Spirit wants only to make His resolutions complete and perfect, and so He seeks and finds the source of problems where the problem is, and there undoes the problem. And with each step in His undoing is the separation more and more undone, and union brought closer. The Holy Spirit is not at all confused by any "reasons" for separation. All He perceives in separation, is that the separation must be undone. Let the Holy Spirit uncover the hidden spark of beauty in your relationships, and show it to you. The spark's loveliness will so attract you that you will be unwilling ever to lose the sight of it again. And you will let this spark transform the relationship so you can see it more and more. For you will want it more and more, and become increasingly unwilling to let it be hidden from you. And you will learn to seek for and establish the conditions in which this beauty can be seen.

All this you will do gladly, if you but let Him hold the spark before you, to light your way and make it clear to you. God's Son is One. Whom God has joined as one, the ego cannot put asunder.

It is still up to you to choose to join with truth or with illusion. The spark of beauty or the veil of ugliness, the real world or the world of guilt and fear, truth or illusion, freedom or slavery. For you can never choose except between God and the ego. Thought systems are but true or false, and all their attributes come simply from what they are.

My holy brother, I would enter into all your relationships, and step between you and your fantasies. Let my relationship to you be real to you, and let me bring reality to your perception of your brothers.

17.4. The Two Pictures

The holy instant is a miniature of Heaven, sent you from Heaven. It is a picture set in a frame. If you accept this gift you will not see the frame at all, because the gift can only be accepted through your willingness to focus all your attention on the picture. The holy instant is a miniature of eternity. It is a picture of timelessness, set in a frame of time.

Two gifts are offered you, illusion or truth. Each is a picture seen very differently. You cannot compare their value by comparing a picture to a frame. It must be the pictures only that you compare, or the comparison is wholly without meaning. Remember that it is the picture that is the gift. Look at the pictures. Both of them. One is a tiny picture, hard to see at all beneath the heavy shadows of its enormous and disproportionate enclosure. The other is lightly framed and hung in light, lovely to look upon for what it is.

You who have tried so hard, and are still trying, to fit the better picture into the wrong frame and so combine what cannot be combined, accept this and be glad: These pictures are each framed perfectly for what they represent. One is framed to be out of focus and not seen. The other is framed for perfect clarity.

The *picture of illusion*, darkness and of death grows less convincing as you search it out amid its wrappings. As each senseless stone that seems to shine from the frame in darkness is exposed to light, it becomes dull and lifeless, and ceases to distract you from the picture. And finally, you look upon the picture itself, seeing at last, that unprotected by the frame the picture has no meaning.

The p*icture of truth* is lightly framed, for time cannot contain eternity. There is no distraction here. The picture of Heaven and eternity grows more convincing as you look at it. And now, by real comparison, a transformation of both pictures can at last occur. And each is given its rightful place when both are seen in relation to each other. The dark picture, brought to light, is not perceived as fearful, but the fact that it is just a picture. And what you see there you will recognize as what it is; a picture of what you thought was real, and nothing more. For beyond this picture of darkness, you will see nothing.

The picture of light, in clear-cut and unmistakable contrast, is transformed into what lies beyond the picture. As you look on this, you realize that it is not a picture, but a reality. This is no figured representation of a thought system, but the Thought itself. What it represents is there. The frame fades gently and God rises to your remembrance, offering you the whole of creation in exchange for your little picture.

As God ascends into His rightful place and you to yours, you will experience again the *meaning* of relationship and know it to be true. Let us ascend in peace together to the Father, by giving Him ascendance in our minds. We will gain everything by giving Him the power and the glory, and keeping no illusions of where they are. They are in us, through His ascendance. What He has given is His. It shines in every part of Him, as in the whole. The whole reality of your relationship with Him lies in our relationship to one another. The holy instant shines alike on all relationships, for in it they are one. For here is only healing, already complete and perfect.

17.5. The Healed Relationship

The holy relationship is the expression of the holy instant in living in this world. Like everything about salvation, the holy instant is a practical device, witnessed to by its results. The holy relationship is a constant reminder of the experience in which the relationship became what it is. And as the unholy relationship is a continuing hymn of hate in praise of its maker, so is the holy relationship a happy song of praise to the Redeemer of relationships.

The holy relationship, a major step toward the perception of the real world, is learned. It is the old, unholy relationship, transformed and seen anew. The holy relationship is a phenomenal teaching accomplishment. For here, the goal of the relationship is abruptly shifted to the exact opposite of what it was. This is the first result of offering the relationship to the Holy Spirit, to use for His purposes.

At once His goal replaces yours. This is accomplished very rapidly, but it makes the relationship seem disturbed, disjunctive and even quite distressing. The reason is quite clear. For the relationship as it is, is out of line with its own goal, and clearly unsuited to the purpose that has been accepted for it. In its unholy condition, your goal was all that seemed to give it meaning. Now it seems to make no sense. Many relationships have been broken off at this point, and the pursuit of the old goal re-established in another relationship. For once the unholy relationship has accepted the goal of holiness, it can never again be what it was.

The temptation of the ego becomes extremely intense with this shift in goals. Yet now the goal will not be changed. Set firmly in the unholy relationship, there is no course except to

Chapter 17

change the relationship to fit the goal. Until this happy solution is seen and accepted as the only way out of the conflict, the relationship may seem to be severely strained.

This is the time for faith. You let this goal be set for you. That was an act of faith. Do not abandon faith, now that the rewards of faith are being introduced.

You undertook, together, to invite the Holy Spirit into your relationship. He could not have entered otherwise. Although you may have made many mistakes since then, you have also made enormous efforts to help Him do His work. And He has not been lacking in appreciation for all you have done for Him. Nor does He see the mistakes at all. Have you consistently appreciated the good efforts, and overlooked mistakes? Or has your appreciation flickered and grown dim in what seemed to be the light of the mistakes? Perhaps you are now entering upon a campaign to blame your brother for the discomfort of the situation in which you find yourself. And by this lack of thanks and gratitude you make yourself unable to express the holy instant, and thus lose sight of it.

To give thanks to one another is to appreciate the holy instant, and thus enable its results to be accepted and shared. To attack your brother is not to lose the instant, but to make it powerless in its effects.

You have received the holy instant, but you may have established a condition in which you cannot use it. As a result, you do not realize that it is with you still. And by cutting yourself off from its expression, you have denied yourself its benefit. You reinforce this every time you attack your brother, for the attack must blind you to yourself.

You and your brother stand together in the holy presence of truth itself. Here is the goal, together with you. And you will share the gladness of the Sonship that it is so.

As you begin to recognize and accept the gifts you have so freely given to your brother, you will also accept the effects of the holy instant and use them to correct all your mistakes and free you from their results. And learning this, you will have also learned how to release all the Sonship, and offer it in gladness and thanksgiving to Him Who gave you your release, and Who would extend it through you.

17.6. Setting the Goal

In any situation in which you are uncertain, the first thing to consider, very simply, is "What do I want to come of this? What is it for?" The clarification of the goal belongs at the beginning, for it is this which will determine the outcome. In the ego's procedure this is reversed. The situation becomes the determiner of the outcome, which can be anything. The reason for this disorganized approach is evident. The ego does not know what it wants to come of the situation. It is aware of what it does not want, but only that. It has no positive goal at all.

Without a clear-cut positive goal set at the outset, the situation just seems to happen, and makes no sense until it has already happened. The absence of a criterion for outcome (set in advance) makes understanding doubtful and evaluation impossible.

The value of deciding in advance what you want to happen is simply that you will perceive the situation as a means to make it happen. You will therefore make every effort to overlook what interferes with the accomplishment of your objective, and concentrate on everything that helps you meet it.

The goal of truth has further practical advantages. If the situation is used for truth and sanity, its outcome must be peace. And this is quite apart from what the outcome is. If peace is the condition of truth and sanity, and cannot be without them, where peace is they must be. Truth comes of itself. If you experience peace, it is because the truth has come to you and you will see the outcome truly, for deception cannot prevail against you.

The goal of truth requires faith. Faith is implicit in the acceptance of the Holy Spirit's purpose, and this faith is all-inclusive. Where the goal of truth is set, there faith must be. The Holy Spirit sees the situation as a whole. The goal establishes the fact that everyone involved in it will play his part in its accomplishment. This is inevitable. No one will fail in anything. This seems to ask for faith beyond you, and beyond what you can give. Yet this is so only from the viewpoint of the ego, for the ego believes in "solving" conflict through fragmentation, and does not perceive the situation as a whole. Therefore, it seeks to split off segments of the situation and deal with them separately, for it has faith in separation and not in wholeness.

17.7. The Call for Faith

There is no problem in any situation that faith will not solve. Is it not possible that all your problems have been solved, but you have removed yourself from the solution?

A situation is a relationship, being the joining of thoughts. If problems are perceived, it is because the thoughts are judged to be in conflict. Faithlessness brought to faith will never interfere with truth. But faithlessness used against truth will always destroy faith. If you lack faith, ask that it be restored where it was lost.

Every situation in which you find yourself is but a means to meet the purpose set for your relationship. See the situation as something else and you are faithless. Use not your faithlessness. If you let it enter, look upon it calmly, but do not use it. Faithlessness is the servant of illusion, and wholly faithful to its master. Use faithlessness, and it will carry you straight to illusions. Be tempted not by what it offers you.

The power set in you in whom the Holy Spirit's goal has been established is so far beyond your little conception of the infinite that you have no idea how great the strength that goes with you. And you can use this in perfect safety. Yet for all its might, so great it reaches past the stars and to the universe that lies beyond them, your little faithlessness can make it useless.

Yet think on this, and learn the cause of faithlessness: You think you hold against your brother what he has done to you. But what you really blame him for is what you did to him. It is not his past but yours you hold against him. And you lack faith in him because of what you were. Yet you are as innocent of what you were as he is.

You call for faith because of Him Who walks with you in every situation. You are no longer wholly insane, nor no longer alone. For loneliness in God must be a dream. You whose relationship shares the Holy Spirit's goal are set apart from loneliness because the truth has come. Truth's call for faith is strong. Use not your faithlessness against truth, for it calls you to salvation and to peace.

17.8. The Conditions of Peace

The holy instant is nothing more than a special case, or an extreme example, of what every situation is meant to be. The meaning that the Holy Spirit's purpose has given the holy instant is also given to every situation. It calls forth just the same suspension of faithlessness, withheld and left unused, that faith might answer to the call of truth. The holy instant is the shining example, the clear and unequivocal demonstration of the meaning of every relationship and every situation, seen as a whole. Faith has accepted every aspect of the situation, and faithlessness has not forced any exclusion on it. The holy instant is a situation of perfect peace, simply because you have let it be what it is.

Let truth encompass every situation and bring you peace.

Let truth enter, and truth will call forth and secure for you the faith you need for peace.

Chapter 18

The Passing of the Dream

18.1. The Substitute Reality

To substitute is to accept in place of.

The Holy Spirit never uses substitutes. Where the ego perceives one person as a replacement for another, the Holy Spirit sees them joined and indivisible. He does not judge between them, knowing they are one. Being united, they are one because they are the same. Substitution is clearly a process in which they are perceived as different. One would unite; the other separate. Nothing can come between what God has joined and what the Holy Spirit sees as one. But everything seems to come between the fragmented relationships the ego sponsors to destroy.

The one emotion in which substitution is impossible is love. Fear involves substitution by definition, for it is love's replacement. Fear is both a fragmented and fragmenting emotion. No one is seen complete.

You who believe that God is fear, made but one substitution. This one substitution has taken many forms, because it was "the substitution of illusion for truth"; of fragmentation for wholeness. That one error, which brought truth to illusion, infinity to time, and life to death, was all you ever made. Your whole world rests upon it. Everything you see reflects it, and every special relationship that you have ever made is part of it.

You do not realize the magnitude of that one error. It was so vast and so completely incredible, that from it, a world of total unreality had to emerge. Nothing you have seen begins to show you the enormity of the original error, which seemed to cast you out of Heaven, to shatter knowledge into meaningless bits of disunited perceptions, and to force you to make further substitutions.

That was the first projection of error outward. The world arose to hide it, and became the screen on which it was projected and drawn between you and the truth. Call this error not sin but madness, for such it was and so it still remains. Invest it not with guilt, for guilt implies it was accomplished in reality. And above all, be not afraid of it.

When you seem to see some twisted form of the original error rising to frighten you, say only, "God is not fear, but Love," and it will disappear. The truth will save you. It has not left you, to go out into the mad world and so depart from you. Inward is sanity; insanity is outside you. You but believe it is the other way; that truth is outside, and error and guilt within. Your little, senseless substitutions, touched with insanity and swirling lightly off on a mad course like feathers dancing insanely in the wind, have no substance.

Let them all go, dancing in the wind, dipping and turning till they disappear from sight, far, far outside of you. And turn you to the stately calm within, where in holy stillness dwells the living God you never left, and Who never left you. The Holy Spirit takes you gently by the hand, and retraces with you your mad journey outside yourself, leading you gently back to the truth and safety within. He brings all your insane projections and the wild substitutions that you have placed outside you to the truth. Thus he reverses the course of insanity and restores you to reason.

In you there is no separation, and no substitute can keep you from your brother. Your reality was God's creation, and has no substitute. You are so firmly joined in truth that only God is there. And he would never accept something else instead of you. He loves you both, equally and as one. And as he loves you, so you are.

The universe within you stands with you, together. And Heaven looks with love on what is joined in it, along with its Creator.

The peace of God is given you with the glowing purpose in which you join. The holy light that brought you together must extend, as you accepted it.

18.2. The Basis of the Dream

Dreams are chaotic because they are governed by your conflicting wishes, and therefore they have no concern with what is true. They are the best example you could have of how perception can be utilized to substitute illusions in the place of truth. They are a way of looking at the world, and changing it to suit the ego better.

You do not find the differences between what you see in sleep and on awaking disturbing. In dreams you arrange everything. People become what you would have them be. For a time it seems as if the world were given you, to make it what you wish. You do not realize you are attacking it, trying to triumph over it and make it serve you.

Dreams are perceptual temper tantrums, in which you literally scream, "I want it thus!" And thus it seems to be. And yet the dream cannot escape its origin. Anger and fear pervade it, and in an instant the illusions of satisfaction is invaded by the illusion of terror. For the dream of your ability to control reality by substituting a world that you prefer is terrifying.

And while you see it, you do not doubt that it is real. Yet here is a world, clearly within your mind, that seems to be outside.

The Holy Spirit, ever practical in His wisdom, accepts your dreams and uses them as means for waking. You would have used them to remain asleep. I said before that the first change, before dreams disappear, is that your dreams of fear are changed to happy dreams.

It will be a happy dream, and one which you will share with all who come within your sight. Through it, the blessing the Holy Spirit has laid upon it will be extended. Think not that He has forgotten anyone in the purpose He has given you. And think not that He has forgotten you to whom He gave the gift. He uses everyone who calls on Him as means for the salvation of everyone. And He will waken everyone through you who offered your relationship to Him.

You are so used to choosing among dreams you do not see that you have made, at last, the choice between the truth and all illusions.

Heaven is sure. This is no dream. Its coming means that you have chosen truth.

18.3. Light in the Dream

The light is in you. Darkness can cover it, but cannot put it out.

The goal you accepted is the goal of knowledge, for which you signified your willingness. Fear seems to live in darkness, and when you are afraid you have stepped back. Let us then join quickly in an instant of light, and it will be enough to remind you that your goal is light.

Truth has rushed to meet you since you called upon it. If you knew Who walks beside you on the way that you have chosen, fear would be impossible. You are advancing to love's meaning, and away from all illusions in which you have surrounded love. When you retreat to the illusion your fear increases, for in illusion is little doubt that what you think love means is fearful.

18.4. The Little Willingness

The holy instant is the result of your determination to be holy. The desire and the willingness to let it come precede its coming. You prepare your mind for it only to the extent of recognizing that you want it above all else. It is not necessary that you do more; indeed, it is necessary that you realize that you cannot do more. Do not attempt to give the Holy Spirit what He does not ask, or you will add the ego to Him and confuse the two. He asks but little. It is He who adds the greatness and the might. He joins with you to make the holy instant far greater than you can understand. It is your realization that you need do so little that enables Him to give so much.

Trust not your good intentions. They are not enough. Come to the holy instance not in arrogance, assuming that you must achieve the state its coming brings with it. The miracle of the holy instant lies in your willingness to let it be what it is. And in your willingness for this lies also your acceptance of yourself as you were meant to be.

Humility will never ask that you remain content with littleness. Your difficulty with the holy instant arises from your fixed conviction that you are not worthy of it. And what is this but the determination to be as you would make yourself? God did not create His dwelling place unworthy of Him.

The holy instant does not come from your little willingness alone. It is always the result of your small willingness combined with the unlimited power of God's Will. You have been wrong in thinking that it is needful to prepare yourself for Him. It is impossible to make arrogant preparations for holiness, and not believe that it is up to you to establish the conditions for peace.

You merely ask the question. The answer is given. Seek not to answer, but merely to receive the answer as it is given. In preparing for the holy instant, do not attempt to make yourself holy to be ready to receive it. That is but to confuse your role with God's. Atonement cannot come to those who think that they must first atone, but only to those who offer it nothing more than simple willingness to make way for it. Purification is of God alone, and therefore for you. Rather than seek to prepare yourself for Him, try to think thus:

> I who am host to God am worthy of Him.
> He Who established His dwelling place in me created it as He would have it be.
> It is not needful that I make it ready for Him,
> but only that I do not interfere with His plan to restore to me my own awareness of my readiness, which is eternal.
> I need add nothing to His plan.
> But to receive it, I must be willing not to substitute my own in place of it.

And that is all. Add more, and you will merely take away the little that is asked. The preparation for the holy instant belongs to Him Who gives it. Release yourself to Him Whose function is release. Do not assume His function for Him. Give Him but what He asks, that you may learn how little is your part, and how great is His.

Salvation is easy just because it asks nothing you cannot give right now.

18.5. The Happy Dream

Happy dreams come true, not because they are dreams, but only because they are happy. And so they must be loving. Their message is, "Thy Will be done," and not, "I want it otherwise."

It is no dream to love your brother as yourself. Nor is your holy relationship a dream.

When you feel the holiness of your relationship is threatened by anything, stop instantly and offer the Holy Spirit your willingness, in spite of fear, to let Him exchange this instant for the holy instant that you would rather have. Forget not that your relationship is one, and so it must be that whatever threatens the peace of one is an equal threat to the other.

Whoever is saner at the time the threat is perceived should remember how deep is his indebtedness to the other and how much gratitude is due him, and be glad that he can pay his debt by bringing happiness to both. Let him remember this, and say:

> I desire this holy instant for myself, that I may share it with my brother, whom I love.
> It is not possible that I can have it without him, or he without me.
> Yet it is wholly possible for us to share it now.
> And so I choose this instant as the one to offer to the Holy Spirit, that His blessing may descend on us, and keep us both in peace.

18.6. Beyond the Body

There is nothing outside you. That is what you must ultimately learn, for it is that realization the Kingdom of Heaven is restored to you. For God created only this, and He did not depart from it nor leave it separate from Himself. The Kingdom of Heaven is the dwelling place of the Son of God, who left not his Father and dwells not apart from Him. Heaven is not a place nor a condition. It is merely an awareness of perfect Oneness, and the knowledge that there is nothing else; nothing outside this Oneness, and nothing else within.

What could God give but knowledge of Himself? What else is there to give? The belief that you could give and get something else, something outside yourself, has cost you the awareness of Heaven and of your Identity. And you have done a stranger thing than you yet realize. You have displaced your guilt to your body from your mind. Yet a body cannot be guilty, for it can do nothing of itself. You who think you hate your body deceive yourself. You hate your mind, for guilt has entered into it.

Guilt is projected to the body, which suffers and dies because it is attacked to hold the separation in the mind, and let it not know its Identity. Mind cannot attack, but it can make fantasies and direct the body to act them out. Yet it is never what the body does that seems to satisfy. Unless the mind believes the body is actually acting out its fantasies, it will attack the body by increasing the projection of its guilt upon it.

Chapter 18

It is insane to use the body as the scapegoat for guilt.

This thing, you call the body, you made to serve your guilt stands between you and other minds. You see yourself locked in a separate prison, removed and unreachable, incapable of reaching out as being reached. You hate this prison you have made.

The place you set aside to house your hate is not a prison, but an illusion of yourself. Mind reaches to itself. Within itself it has no limits, and there is nothing outside it. It encompasses you entirely; you within it and it within you. There is nothing else, anywhere or ever.

The body is outside you, and but seems to surround you, shutting you off from others and keeping you apart from them. It is not there. There is no barrier between God and His Son. You cannot put a barrier around yourself, because God placed none between Himself and you.

You are surrounded only by Him. What limits can there be on you whom He encompasses?

Everyone has experienced what he would call a sense of being transported beyond himself. This feeling of liberation far exceeds the dream of freedom sometimes hoped for in special relationships. It is a sense of actual escape from limitations. If you will consider what this "transportation" really entails, you will realize that it is a sudden unawareness of the body, and a joining of yourself and something else in which your mind enlarges to encompass it. This joining becomes part of you, as you unite with it. And both become whole, as neither is perceived as separate. What really happens is that you have given up the illusion of a limited awareness, and lost your fear of union. The love that instantly replaces the illusion extends to what has freed you, and that love unites with that joining. And while this lasts you are not uncertain of your Identity, and would not limit It. You have escaped from fear to peace, asking no questions of reality, but merely accepting it. You have accepted this instead of the body, and have let yourself be one with something beyond the body, simply by not letting your mind be limited by it.

In these instants of release from physical restrictions, you experience much of what happens in the holy instant; the lifting of the barriers of time and space, the sudden experience of peace and joy, and, above all, the lack of awareness of the body, and of the questioning whether or not all this is possible.

It is possible because you want it. The sudden expansion of awareness that takes place with your desire for this joining is the irresistible appeal the holy instant holds. The awareness calls to you to be yourself, within its safe embrace. There are the laws of limit lifted for you, to welcome you to openness of mind and freedom. Come to this place of refuge, where you can be yourself in peace.

18.7. I Need Do Nothing

You still have too much faith in the body as a source of strength. What plans do you make that do not involve its comfort or protection or enjoyment in some way? This makes the body an end and not a means in your interpretation, and this always means you still find sin attractive. No one accepts Atonement for himself who still accepts sin as his goal. You have thus not met your one responsibility. Atonement is not welcomed by those who prefer pain and destruction.

It is extremely difficult to reach Atonement by fighting against sin. Nor is a lifetime of contemplation and long periods of meditation aimed at detachment from the body necessary. All such attempts will ultimately succeed because of their purpose. Yet the means are tedious and very time consuming, for all of them look to the future for release from a state of present unworthiness and inadequacy.

When peace comes at last to those who wrestle with temptation and fight against the giving in to sin; when the light comes at last into the mind given to contemplation; or when the goal is finally achieved by anyone, it always comes with just one happy realization; "I need do nothing."

Save time for me by only this one preparation, and practice doing nothing else. "I need do nothing" is a statement of allegiance, a truly undivided loyalty. Believe it for just one instant, and you will accomplish more than is given to a century of contemplation, or of struggle against temptation.

To do anything involves the body. And if you recognize you need do nothing, you have withdrawn the body's value from your mind. Here is the quick and open door through which you slip past centuries of effort, and escape from time. This is the way in which sin loses all attraction right now. For here is time denied, and past and future gone. Who needs do nothing has no need for time. To do nothing is to rest, and make a place within you where the activity of the body ceases to demand attention. Into this place the Holy Spirit comes, and there abides. He will remain when you forget, and the body's activities return to occupy your conscious mind.

Yet there will always be this place of rest to which you can return. And you will be more aware of this quiet center of the storm than all its raging activity. This quiet center, in which you do nothing, will remain with you, giving you rest in the midst of every busy doing on which you are sent. For from this center will you be directed how to use the body sinlessly. It is this center, from which the body is absent, that will keep it so in your awareness of it.

18.8. The Little Garden

It is only the awareness of the body that makes love seem limited. For the body is a limit on love. Everything you recognize you identify with externals, something outside itself. You cannot even think of God without a body, or in some form you think you recognize.

While you limit your awareness to its tiny senses, you will not see the grandeur that surrounds you. God cannot come into a body, nor can you join Him there. Limits on love will always seem to shut Him out, and keep you apart from Him. The body is a tiny fence around a little part of a glorious and complete idea. It draws a circle, infinitely small, around a very little segment of Heaven, splintered from the whole, proclaiming that within it is your kingdom, where God can enter not.

Within this splintered kingdom, the ego rules, and cruelly. And to defend this little speck of dust it bids you fight against the universe. This fragment of your mind is such a tiny part of it that, could you but appreciate the whole, you would see instantly that this small kingdom is like the smallest sunbeam to the sun, or like the faintest ripple on the surface of the ocean. In its amazing arrogance, this tiny sunbeam has decided it is the sun; this almost imperceptible ripple hails itself as the ocean. Think how alone and frightened is this little thought, this infinitesimal illusion, holding itself apart against the universe. The sun becomes the sunbeam's "enemy" that would devour it, and the ocean terrifies the little ripple and wants to swallow it.

Yet neither sun nor ocean is even aware of all this strange and meaningless activity. They merely continue, unaware that they are feared and hated by a tiny segment of themselves. Even that segment is not lost to them, for it could not survive apart from them. And what it thinks it is in no way changes its total dependence on them for its being. Its whole existence still remains in them. Without the sun the sunbeam would be gone; the ripple without the ocean is inconceivable.

Such is the strange position in which those in a world inhabited by bodies seem to be. Each body seems to house a separate mind, a disconnected thought, living alone and in no way joined to the Thought by which it was created. Each tiny fragment seems to be self-contained, needing another for some things, but by no means totally dependent on its one Creator for everything; needing the whole to give it any meaning, for by itself it does mean nothing. Nor has each tiny fragment any life apart and by itself.

Like to the sun and ocean your Self continues, unmindful that this tiny part regards itself as you. It is not missing; it could not exist if it were separate, nor would the Whole be whole without it. It is not a separate kingdom, ruled by an idea of separation from the rest. Nor does a fence surround it, preventing it from joining with the rest, and keeping it apart from its Creator. This little aspect is no different from the whole, being continuous with the whole, and at one with it. This tiny part leads no separate life, because its life is the oneness in which its being was created.

Do not accept this little, fenced-off aspect as yourself. The sun and ocean are as nothing beside what you are. The sunbeam sparkles only in the sunlight, and the ripple dances as it rests upon the ocean. Yet in neither sun nor ocean is the power that rests in you. Would you remain within your tiny kingdom, a sorry king, a bitter ruler of all that he surveys, who looks on nothing yet who would still die to defend it? This little self is not your kingdom. Arched high above it and surrounding it with love is the glorious whole, which offers all its happiness and deep content to every part.

The Thought of God surrounds your little kingdom, waiting at the barrier you built to come inside and shine upon the barren ground. See how life springs up everywhere! The desert becomes a garden, green and deep and quiet, offering rest to those who lost their way and wander in the dust. Give them a place of refuge, prepared by love for them where once a desert was. And everyone you welcome will bring love with him from Heaven for you. They enter one by one into this holy place, but they will not depart as they had come, alone. The love they brought with them will stay with them, as it will stay with you. And under its beneficence your little garden will expand, and reach out to everyone who thirsts for living water, but has grown too weary to go on alone.

Go out and find them, for they bring your Self with them. And lead them gently to your quiet garden, and receive their blessing there. So will it grow and stretch across the desert, leaving no lonely little kingdoms locked away from love, and leaving you inside. And you will recognize yourself, and see your little garden gently transformed into the Kingdom of Heaven, with all the Love of its Creator shining upon it.

The holy instant is your invitation to love, to enter into your bleak and joyless kingdom, and to transform it into a garden of peace and welcome. Love's answer is inevitable. It will come because you came without the body, and interposed no barriers to interfere with its glad coming. In the holy instant, you ask of love only what it offers everyone, neither less nor more. Asking for everything, you will receive it. And your shining Self will lift the tiny aspect that you tried to hide from Heaven straight to Heaven. No part of love calls on the whole in vain. No Son of God remains outside his Fatherhood.

You have reached the end of an ancient journey, not realizing yet that it is over. You are still worn and tired, and the desert's dust still seems to cloud your eyes and keep you sightless. Yet He Whom you welcomed has come to you, and would welcome you. He has waited long to give you this. Receive it now of Him, for He would have you know Him. Only a little wall of dust still stands between you. Blow on it lightly and with happy laughter, and it will fall away. And walk into the garden love has prepared for both of you.

Chapter 18

18.9. The Two Worlds

You have been told to bring the darkness to the light, and guilt to holiness. And you have also been told that error must be corrected at its source. Therefore, it is the tiny part of yourself, the little thought that seems split off and separate, the Holy Spirit needs. The rest is fully in God's keeping, and needs no guide. Yet this wild and delusional thought needs help because, in its delusions, it thinks it is the Son of God, whole and omnipotent, sole ruler of the kingdom it set apart to tyrannize by madness into obedience and slavery. This is the little part you think you stole from Heaven. Give it back to Heaven. Heaven has not lost it, but you have lost sight of Heaven. Let the Holy Spirit remove it from the withered kingdom in which you set it off, surrounded by darkness, guarded by attack and reinforced by hate. Within its barricades is still a tiny segment of the Son of God, complete and holy, serene and unaware of what you think surrounds it.

From the **world of bodies**, the circle of fear lies just below the level the body sees, and seems to be the whole foundation on which the world is based. Here are all the illusions, all the twisted thoughts, all the insane attacks, the fury, the vengeance and betrayal that were made to keep the guilt in place, so that the world of illusions could rise and keep the real world of Heaven hidden. Yet truth's intensity is veiled by guilt's heavy coverings, and kept apart from what was made to keep the truth hidden. The body cannot see this, for the body arose from guilt for the ego's protection, which depends on keeping the real world not seen. The body's eyes will never look on truth. Yet they will see what the ego dictates.

From the **world of light**, this circle of brightness is the real world, where guilt meets with forgiveness. Here the world outside is seen anew, without the shadow of guilt upon it. Here is the new perception, where everything is bright and shining with innocence, washed in the waters of forgiveness, and cleansed of every evil thought you laid upon the outside world. Here, in the real world, there is no attack upon the Son of God, and you are welcome. Here is your innocence, waiting to clothe you and protect you, and make you ready for the final step in the journey inward. Here are the dark and heavy garments of guilt laid by, and gently replaced by purity and love.

Love is not learned. Its meaning lies within itself. And learning ends when you have recognized all that love is not.

Forgiveness removes only the untrue, lifting the shadows from the world and carrying it, safe and sure within forgiveness's gentleness, to the bright world of new and clean perception. There is your purpose now. And it is there in the new perception that peace awaits you.

Chapter 19

The Attainment of Peace

19.1. Healing and Faith

Every situation, properly perceived, becomes an opportunity to heal the Son of God.

Faithlessness is the perception of a brother as a body. If, then, you see your brother as a body, you have established a condition in which uniting with him becomes impossible. Your faithlessness to him has separated you from him, and kept you both apart from being healed. Your faithlessness has thus opposed the Holy Spirit's purpose, and brought illusions, centered on the body, to stand between you.

The inevitable compromise is the belief that the body must be healed, and not the mind.

To have faith is to heal. By faith, you offer the gift of freedom from the past, which you received. You do not use anything your brother has done before to condemn him now. You freely choose to overlook his errors, looking past all barriers between yourself and him, and seeing them as one.

Faith is the opposite of fear. Faith is the gracious acknowledgment of everyone as a Son of your most loving Father, loved by him like you, and therefore loved by you as yourself.

Faith is the gift of God, through the Holy Spirit Whom God has given you. Faithlessness looks upon the Son of God, and judges him unworthy of forgiveness. But through the eyes of faith, the Son of God is seen already forgiven, free of all the guilt he laid upon himself. Faith sees him only *now* because it looks not to the past to judge him, but would see in him only what it would see in you.-

Grace is not given to a body, but to a mind. And the mind that receives grace looks instantly beyond the body, and sees the holy place where the mind was healed. And there it is that you will realize that there is nothing faith cannot forgive.

Chapter 19

For faith brings peace. For faith is still a learning goal, no longer needed when the lesson of faith has been learned.

19.2. Sin versus Error

It is essential that error be not confused with sin, and it is this distinction that makes salvation possible. For error, can be corrected, and the wrong made right. But sin, were it possible, would be irreversible. Sin calls for punishment, as error for correction, and the belief that punishment is correction, is clearly insane.

Sin is the proclamation that attack is real and guilt is justified. It assumes the Son of God is guilty, and has thus succeeded in losing his innocence and making himself what God created not. Thus, is creation seen as not eternal, and the Will of God open to opposition and defeat. Sin is the grand illusion underlying all the ego's grandiosity. For by it God himself is changed, and rendered incomplete.

The Son of God can be mistaken; he can deceive himself; he can even turn the power of his mind against himself. But he cannot sin. There is nothing he can do that would really change his reality in any way, nor make him really guilty. That is what sin would do, for such is its purpose. For the wages of sin is death, and how can the immortal die?

It can indeed be said the ego made its world on sin. This is the strange illusion that makes the clouds of guilt seem heavy and impenetrable. For sin, has changed creation from an idea of God to an ideal the ego wants; a world it rules, made up of bodies, mindless and capable of complete corruption and decay.

There is no stone in all the ego's embattled citadel that is more heavily defended than the idea that sin is real. To the ego, this is no mistake. For this is its reality; this is the "truth" from which escape will always be impossible.

19.3. The Unreality of Sin

When you are tempted to believe that sin is real, remember this: If sin is real, God must be at war with Himself. He must be split, and torn between good and evil; partly sane and partially insane. For He must have created what wills to destroy Him, and has the power to do so. Is it not easier to believe that you have been mistaken than to believe in this?

While you believe that your reality or your brother's is bounded by a body, you will believe in sin. For sin would prove what God created holy, could not prevail against it. Sin is perceived as mightier than God, before which God Himself must bow, and offer His creation to its conqueror, which is sin.

If sin is real, it must forever be beyond the hope of healing. For there would be a power beyond God's, capable of making another will that could attack his will and overcome it; and give His Son a will apart from His, and stronger.

You will not see sin long. For in the *new* perception the mind corrects sin. And you will help each other overcome mistakes by joyously releasing each other from the belief in sin.

In the holy instant, you will see the smile of Heaven shining on both of you. And you will shine upon each other, in glad acknowledgment of the grace that has been given you. For sin, will not prevail against a union Heaven has smiled upon. The barriers to Heaven will disappear before your holy sight, for you who were sightless have been given vision, and you can see. Look not for what has been removed, but for the glory that has been restored for you to see.

Look upon your Redeemer, and behold what he would show you in your brother, and let not sin arise again to blind your eyes. For sin would keep you separate, but your Redeemer would have you look upon your brother as yourself. Your relationship is now a temple of healing; a place where all the weary ones can come and rest. Here is the rest that waits for all, after the journey. And it is brought nearer to all by your relationship.

19.4. The Obstacles to Peace

As peace extends from deep inside yourself to embrace all the Sonship and give it rest, it will encounter many obstacles. Some of them you will try to impose. Others will seem to arise from elsewhere; from your brothers, and from various aspects of the world outside. Yet peace will gently cover them, extending past completely unencumbered. The extension of the Holy Spirit's purpose from your relationship to others, to bring them gently in, will quietly extend to every aspect of your lives, surrounding each of you with glowing happiness and the calm awareness of complete protection. And you will carry its message of love and safety and freedom to everyone who draws nigh unto your temple, where healing waits for him.

All this will you do. Yet the peace that already lies deeply within must first expand, and flow across the obstacles you placed before it.

When the peace in you has been extended to encompass everyone, the Holy Spirit's function here will be accomplished.

19.4.a. The First Obstacle: The Desire to Get Rid of It

The first obstacle that peace must flow across is your desire to get rid of peace. If you would make peace homeless, how can it abide within the Son of God?

Why would you want peace homeless? What seems to be the cost you are so unwilling to pay? The little barrier of sand still stands between you and your brother. Would you

CHAPTER 19

reinforce it now? Would you let a little bank of sand, a wall of dust, a tiny seeming barrier, stand between your brothers and salvation? And yet, this little remnant of attack still against each other is the first obstacle the peace in you encounters in its going forth. This little wall of hatred would still oppose the Will of God, and keep it limited.

Fear not this little obstacle. It cannot contain the Will of God. Peace will flow across it, and join you without hindrance. The little wall will fall away so quietly beneath the wings of peace. For peace, will send its messengers from you to all the world.

For in the miracle of your holy relationship, without this barrier, is every miracle contained. Guilt can raise no real barriers against it. And all that seems to stand between you and your brother must fall away because of the appeal you answered. His home is in your holy relationship. Do not attempt to stand between him and his holy purpose, for it is yours. But let him quietly extend the miracle of your relationship to everyone contained in it.

There is a hush in Heaven, a happy expectancy, a little pause of gladness in acknowledgment of the journey's end. For Heaven knows you well, as you know Heaven. No illusions stand between you now. Look not upon the little wall of shadows. The sun has risen over it. How can a shadow keep you from the sun? No more can you be kept by shadows from the light in which illusions end. Every miracle is but the end of an illusion. Such was the journey; such its ending. And in the goal of truth which you accepted, must all illusions end.

The Attraction of Guilt

The attraction of guilt produces fear of love, for love would never look on guilt at all. It is the nature of love to look upon only the truth, for there it sees itself, with which it would unite in holy union and completion. As love must look past fear, so must fear see love not. For love contains the end of guilt, as surely as fear depends on it. Overlooking guilt completely, it sees no fear. Being wholly without attack, it could not be afraid. Fear is attracted to what love sees not, and each believes that what the other looks upon does not exist. Fear looks on guilt with just the same devotion that love looks on itself. And each has messengers which they send forth, and which return to them with messages written in the language in which their going forth was asked.

Love's messengers are gently sent, and return with messages of love and gentleness. The messengers of fear are harshly ordered to seek out guilt, and cherish every scrap of evil and of sin that they can find. Perception cannot obey two masters, each asking for messages of different things in different languages. What fear would feed upon, love overlooks. What fear demands, love cannot even see. The fierce attraction that guilt holds for fear is wholly absent from love's gentle perception. What love would look upon is meaningless to fear, and quite invisible.

Relationships in this world are the result of how the world is seen. And this depends on which emotion was called on to send its messengers to look upon the world, and return with word of what either love or fear saw. The Holy Spirit has given you love's messengers to send, instead of those you trained through fear.

If you send forth only the messengers the Holy Spirit gives you, wanting no messages but theirs, you will see fear no more. The world will be transformed before your sight, cleansed of all guilt and softly brushed with beauty. The Holy Spirit has given you his messengers to send to your brother and return to you with what love sees. And they go forth to signify the end of fear.

Love, too, would set a feast before you, on a table covered with a spotless cloth, set in a quiet garden where no sound but singing and a softly joyous whispering is ever heard. This is a feast that honors your holy relationship, and at which everyone is welcomed as an honored guest. And in a holy instant, grace is said by everyone together, as they join in gentleness before the table of communion. And I will join you there, as long ago I promised and promise still. For in your new relationship am I made welcome. And where I am made welcome, there I am.

19.4.b. The Second Obstacle: The Belief the Body is Valuable for What It Offers

We said that peace must first surmount the obstacle of your desire to get rid of it. Where the attraction of guilt holds sway, peace is not wanted. The second obstacle that peace must flow across, and closely related to the first, is the belief that the body is valuable for what it offers. For here is the attraction of guilt made manifest in the body, and seen in it.

What has the body really given you that justifies your strange belief that in it lies salvation? Do you not see that this is the belief in death?

You want communion, not the feast of fear. You want salvation, not the pain of guilt. And you want your Father, not a little mound of clay, to be your home.

You have paid very dearly for your illusions, and nothing you have paid for brought you peace. There is no obstacle that you can place before our union, for in your holy relationship I am there already. We will surmount all obstacles together, for we stand within the gates and not outside. How easily the gates are opened from within, to let peace through to bless the tired world! Can it be difficult for us to walk past barriers together, when you have joined the limitless? The end of guilt is in your hands to give.

Let me be to you the symbol of the end of guilt, and look upon your brother as you would look upon me. Forgive me all the sins you think the Son of God committed. And in the light of your forgiveness he will remember who he is, and forget what never was. I ask for your forgiveness, for if you are guilty, so must I be. But if I surmounted guilt and overcame the

CHAPTER 19

world, you were with me. Would you see in me the symbol of guilt or the end of guilt, remembering that what I signify to you, you see within yourself?

The Attraction of Pain

The body can bring you neither peace nor turmoil; neither joy nor pain. It is a means, and not an end. It has no purpose of itself, but only what is given to it. The body will seem to be whatever is the means for reaching the goal that you assign to it. Peace and guilt are both conditions of the mind, to be attained. And these conditions are the home of the emotion that calls them forth, and therefore is compatible with them.

Under fear's orders the body will pursue guilt, serving its master whose attraction to guilt maintains the whole illusion of its existence. This, then, is the attraction of pain. Ruled by this perception the body becomes the servant of pain, seeking it dutifully and obeying the idea that pain is pleasure. It is this idea that underlies all of the ego's heavy investment in the body. And it is this insane relationship that the ego keeps hidden, and yet feeds upon. To you the ego teaches that the body's pleasure is happiness. Yet to itself it whispers, "It is death."

Why should the body be anything to you? Certainly, what it is made of, is not precious. And just as certainly it has no feeling. It transmits to you the feelings that you want. Like any communication medium the body receives and sends the messages that it is given. It has no feeling for them. All of the feeling with which they are invested is given by the sender and the receiver. The ego and the Holy Spirit both recognize this, and both also recognize that here the sender and receiver are the same. The Holy Spirit tells you this with joy. The ego hides it, for it would keep you unaware of it. Who would send messages of hatred and attack if he but understood he sends them to himself? Who would accuse, make guilty and condemn himself?

Like the ego, the Holy Spirit is both the sender and the receiver. For what is sent through Him returns to Him, seeking itself along the way, and finding what it seeks. So does the ego find the death it seeks, returning it to you.

19.4.c. The Third Obstacle: The Attraction of Death

No one can die unless he chooses death. What seems to be the fear of death is really its attraction. Guilt, too, is feared and fearful. Yet it could have no hold at all except on those who are attracted to it and seek it out. And so it is with death. Made by the ego, its dark shadow falls across all living things, because the ego is the "enemy" of life.

And yet a shadow cannot kill. What is a shadow to the living? They but walk past and it is gone. Your dedication is not to death, nor to its master. When you accepted the Holy Spirit's purpose in place of the ego's you renounced death, exchanging it for life. We know that an idea leaves not its source. And death is the result of the thought we call the ego, as surely as life is the result of the Thought of God.

The Incorruptible Body

From the ego came sin and guilt and death, in opposition to life and innocence, and to the Will of God Himself.

The arrogance of sin, the pride of guilt, the sepulcher of separation, all are part of your unrecognized dedication to death.

The body can but serve your purpose. As you look on it, so will it seem to be.

Those who fear death see not how often and how loudly they call to it, and bid it come to save them from communication. For death is seen as safety, the great dark savior from the light of truth, the answer to the Answer, the silencer of the Voice that speaks for God. Yet the retreat to death is not the end of conflict. Only God's Answer is its end. The obstacle of your seeming love for death that peace must flow across seems to be very great. For in it lie hidden all the ego's secrets, all its strange devices for deception, all its sick ideas and weird imaginings.

When anything seems to you to be a source of fear, when any situation strikes you with terror and makes your body tremble and the cold sweat of fear comes over it, remember it is always for one reason; the ego has perceived your body as a symbol of fear, a sign of sin and death. Remember, then, that neither sign nor symbol should be confused with *source*, for both sign and symbol stand for something other than themselves. Their meaning cannot lie in them, but must be sought in what they represent. And they may thus mean everything or nothing, according to the truth or falsity of the idea which they reflect. Confronted with such seeming uncertainty of meaning, judge not the sign or symbol. Remember the holy Presence of the One given to you to be the Source of judgment. Give it to Him to judge for you, and say:

> *Take this from me and look upon it, judging it for me.*
> *Let me not see it as a sign of sin and death, nor use it for destruction.*
> *Teach me how not to make of it an obstacle to peace,*
> *but let You use it for me, to facilitate its coming.*

19.4.d. The Fourth Obstacle: The Fear of God

The fourth obstacle to be surmounted hangs like a heavy veil before the face of Christ.

This is the darkest veil, upheld by the belief in death and protected by its attraction. The dedication to death and to its sovereignty is but the solemn vow, the promise made in secret to the ego never to lift this veil, not to approach it, nor even to suspect that it

Chapter 19

is there. This is the secret bargain made with the ego to keep what lies beyond the veil forever blotted out and unremembered.

See how the belief in death would seem to "save" you. For if this were gone, what could you fear but life? It is the attraction of death that makes life seem to be ugly, cruel and tyrannical.

Every obstacle that peace must flow across is surmounted in just the same way; the fear that raised it yields to the love beyond. The exaltation of the body is given up in favor of the spirit, which you love as you could never love the body. And the appeal of death is lost forever as love's attraction stirs and calls to you. From beyond each of the obstacles to love, Love Itself has called. And each has been surmounted by the power of the attraction of what lies beyond. Your wanting fear seemed to be holding them in place. Yet when you heard the Voice of Love beyond them, you answered and they disappeared.

All that will occur is you will leave the world forever. This is the re-establishment of your will. Look upon it, open-eyed, and you will nevermore believe that you are at the mercy of things beyond you, forces you cannot control, and thoughts that come to you against your will. It is your will to look on this. No mad desire, no trivial impulse to forget again, no stab of fear nor the cold sweat of seeming death can stand against your will. For what attracts you from beyond the veil is also deep within you, unseparated from it and completely one.

The Lifting of the Veil

You are afraid of God because you fear your brother.

Behold your friend, the Christ who stands beside you. How holy and beautiful he is!

Think who your brother is, before you would condemn him. And offer thanks to God that he is holy, and has been given the gift of holiness for you. Join him in gladness, and remove all trace of guilt from his disturbed and tortured mind. Help your brother to lift the heavy burden of sin you laid upon him and he accepted as his own, and toss it lightly and with happy laughter away from him. Press it not like thorns against his brow, nor nail him to it, unredeemed and hopeless.

Free your brother here, as I freed you. Offer your brother freedom and complete release from sin, here in the garden of seeming agony and death.

Together we will disappear into the Presence beyond the veil, not to be lost but found; not to be seen but known. And knowing, nothing in the plan God has established for salvation will be left undone. This is the journey's purpose, without which is the journey meaningless. Here is the peace of God, given to you eternally by him. Here is the rest and quiet that you seek, the reason for the journey from its beginning. Heaven is the gift you owe your brother, the debt of gratitude you offer to the Son of God in thanks for what he is, and what his Father created him to be.

The crucified give pain because they are in pain. But the redeemed give joy because they have been healed of pain. Everyone gives as he receives, but he must choose what it will be that he receives. And he will recognize his choice by what he gives, and what is given him.

You came this far because the journey was your choice. And no one undertakes to do what he believes is meaningless. What you had faith in still is faithful, and watches over you in faith so gentle yet so strong that it would lift you far beyond the veil, and place the Son of God safely within the sure protection of his Father. Here is the only purpose that gives this world, and the long journey through this world, whatever meaning lies in them. It is given you to see this purpose in your holy Friend, and recognize it as your own.

Chapter 20

The Vision of Holiness

20.1. Holy Week

This is Palm Sunday, the celebration of victory and the acceptance of the truth. Let us not spend this holy week brooding on the crucifixion of God's Son, but happily in the celebration of his release. For Easter is the sign of peace, not pain. A slain Christ has no meaning. But a risen Christ becomes the symbol of the Son of God's forgiveness on himself; the sign he looks upon himself as healed and whole.

This week we celebrate life, not death. And we honor the perfect purity of the Son of God, and not his sins. Offer your brother the gift of lilies, not the crown of thorns; the gift of love and not the "gift" of fear. You stand beside your brother, thorns in one hand and lilies in the other, uncertain which to give. Join now with me and throw away the thorns, offering the lilies to replace them. This Easter I would have the gift of your forgiveness offered by you to me, and returned by me to you. We cannot be united in crucifixion and in death. Nor can the resurrection be complete till your forgiveness rests on Christ, along with mine.

The time of Easter is a time of joy, and not of mourning. Look on your risen Friend, and celebrate his holiness along with me. For Easter is the time of your salvation, along with mine.

20.2. The Gift of Lilies

Look upon all the trinkets made to hang upon the body, or to cover it or for its use. See all the useless things made for its eyes to see. Think on the many offerings made for its pleasure, and remember, all these were made to make seem lovely what you hate.

Gifts are not made through bodies, if they be truly given and received. For bodies can neither offer nor accept; hold out nor take. Only the mind can value, and only the mind decides on what it would receive and give. And every gift it offers depends on what it wants. Each gift is an evaluation of the receiver and the giver.

You have the vision now to look past all illusions. It has been given you to see no thorns, no strangers and no obstacles to peace. The fear of God is nothing to you now. Who is afraid to look upon illusions, knowing his savior stands beside him? With him, your vision has become the greatest power for the undoing of illusion that God Himself could give. For what God gave the Holy Spirit, you have received. The Son of God looks unto you for his release. For you have asked for and been given the strength to look upon this final obstacle, and see no thorns nor nails to crucify the Son of God, and crown him king of death.

Your chosen home is on the other side, beyond the veil. In you the knowledge lies, ready to be unveiled and freed from all the terror that kept it hidden. There is no fear in love. The song of Easter is the glad refrain the Son of God was never crucified. Let us lift up our eyes together, not in fear but faith. And there will be no fear in us, for in our vision will be no illusions; only a pathway to the open door of Heaven, the home we share in quietness and where we live in gentleness and peace, as one together.

We go beyond the veil of fear, lighting each other's way. The holiness that leads us is within us, as is our home. So will we find what we were meant to find by Him Who leads us.

This is the way to Heaven and to the peace of Easter, in which we join in glad awareness that the Son of God is risen from the past, and has awakened to the present. Your gift has saved your brother from the thorns and nails, and his strong arm is free to guide you safely through them and beyond. Walk with your brother now rejoicing, for the savior from illusions has come to greet you, and lead you home with him.

20.3. Sin as an Adjustment

An adjustment is a change; a shift in perception, or a belief that what was *so* before and has been made different.

The ego's fixed belief that all relationships depend upon adjustments, to make of them what it would have them be. Direct relationships, in which there are no interferences, are always seen as dangerous. The ego is the self-appointed mediator of all relationships, making whatever adjustments it deems necessary and interposing them between those who would meet, to keep them separate and prevent their union. It is this studied interference that makes it difficult for you to recognize your holy relationship for what it is.

A simple question yet remains, and needs an answer. Do you like what you have made? --a world of murder and attack, through which you thread your timid way through constant dangers, alone and frightened, hoping at most that death will wait a little longer before it overtakes you and you disappear. You made this up. It is a picture of what you think you are; of how you see yourself. A murderer is frightened, and those who kill, fear death. All these are but the fearful thoughts of those who would adjust themselves to a world made fearful by their adjustments. And they look out in sorrow from what is sad within, and see the sadness there.

Have you not wondered what the world is really like; how it would look through happy eyes? The world you see is but a judgment on yourself. It is not there at all. Yet judgment lays a sentence on it, justifies it and makes it real. Such is the world you see; a judgment on yourself, and made by you. This sickly picture of yourself is carefully preserved by the ego, whose image it is and which it loves, and placed outside you in the world. And to this world must you adjust as long as you believe this picture is outside, and has you at its mercy. This world is merciless, and were it outside you, you should indeed be fearful. Yet it was you who made it merciless, and now if mercilessness seems to look back at you, it can be corrected.

Prisoners bound with heavy chains for years, starved and emaciated, weak and exhausted, and with eyes so long cast down in darkness they remember not the light, do not leap up in joy the instant they are made free. It takes a while for them to understand what freedom is. You groped but feebly in the dust and found your brother's hand, uncertain whether to let it go or to take hold on life so long forgotten. Strengthen your hold and raise your eyes unto your strong companion, in whom the meaning of your freedom lies. Your brother seemed to be crucified beside you. And yet his holiness remained untouched and perfect, and with him beside you, you shall this day enter with him to Paradise, and know the peace of God.

Such is my will for you, and for each of you for one another and for himself. Here there is only holiness and joining without limit. For what is Heaven but union, direct and perfect, and without the veil of fear upon it? Here are we one, looking with perfect gentleness upon each other and on ourselves. Here all thoughts of any separation between us become impossible. You who were prisoners in separation are now made free in Paradise. And here would I unite with you, my friends, my brothers and my Self.

Your gift unto your brother has given me the certainty our union will be soon. Share, then, this faith with me, and know that it is justified. There is no fear in perfect love because it knows no sin, and it must look on others as on itself. Looking with charity within, what can it fear without? The innocent see safety, and the pure in heart see God within His Son, and look unto the Son to lead them to the Father. And where else would they go but where they will to be? Each of you now will lead the other to the Father as surely as God created His Son holy, and kept him so. In your brother is the light of God's eternal promise of your immortality. See him as sinless, and there can be no fear in you.

20.4. Entering the Ark

The ark of peace is entered two by two, yet the beginning of another world goes with them. Each holy relationship must enter here, to learn its special function in the Holy Spirit's plan, now that it shares His purpose. And as this purpose is fulfilled, a new world rises in which sin can enter not, and where the Son of God can enter without fear and where he rests a while, to forget imprisonment and to remember freedom. How can he enter, to rest and to remember, without you? Except you be there, he is not complete. And it is his completion that he remembers there.

This is the purpose given you. Think not that your forgiveness of your brother serves but you two alone. For the whole new world rests in the hands of every two who enter here to rest. And as they rest, the face of Christ shines on them and they remember the laws of God, forgetting all the rest and yearning only to have His laws perfectly fulfilled in them and all their brothers.

20.5. Heralds of Eternity

In this world, God's Son comes closest to himself in a *holy* relationship. There he begins to find the certainty his Father has in him. And there he finds his function of restoring his Father's laws to what was held outside them, and finding what was lost. Only in time can anything be lost, and never lost forever. So do the parts of God's Son gradually join in time, and with each joining is the end of time brought nearer. Each miracle of joining is a mighty herald of eternity.

Each herald of eternity sings of the end of sin and fear. Each speaks in time of what is far beyond it. Two voices raised together call to the hearts of everyone, to let them beat as one. And in that single heartbeat is the unity of love proclaimed and given welcome. Peace to your holy relationship, which has the power to hold the unity of the Son of God together. You give to one another for everyone, and in your gift is everyone made glad.

Be comforted, and feel the Holy Spirit watching over you in love and perfect confidence in what He sees. He knows the Son of God, and shares his Father's certainty the universe rests in his gentle hands in safety and in peace.

20.6. The Temple of the Holy Spirit

The Holy Spirit's temple is not a body, but a relationship. The body is an isolated speck of darkness; a hidden secret room, a tiny spot of senseless mystery, a meaningless enclosure carefully protected, yet hiding nothing. Here the *unholy* relationship escapes reality, and seeks for crumbs to keep itself alive.

You cannot make the body the Holy Spirit's temple, and it will never be the seat of love. It is the home of the idolater, and of love's condemnation. For here is love made fearful and hope abandoned.

The body is the ego's idol; the belief in sin made flesh and then projected outward. This produces what seems to be a wall of flesh around the mind, keeping it prisoner in a tiny spot of space and time, beholden unto death, and given but an instant in which to sigh and grieve and die in honor of its master. And this unholy instant seems to be life; an instant of despair, a tiny island of dry sand, bereft of water and set uncertainly upon oblivion. Here does the Son of God stop briefly by, to offer his devotion to death's idols and then pass on. And here he is more dead than living. Yet it is also here he makes his choice again between idolatry and love. Here it is given him to choose to spend this instant paying tribute to the body, or let himself be given freedom from it. Here he can accept the holy instant, offered him to replace the unholy one he chose before. And here can he learn relationships are his salvation, and not his doom.

The holy instant is of greater value now to you than its unholy seeming counterpart, and you have learned you really want but one. This is no time for sadness. Perhaps you fear your brother a little yet; perhaps a shadow of the fear of God remains with you. Yet what is that to those who have been given one true relationship beyond the body?

20.7. The Consistency of Means and End

It is impossible to see your brother as sinless if you look upon him as a body.

Who sees a brother's body has laid a judgment on him, and sees him not. He does not really see him as sinful; he does not see him at all. In the darkness of sin he is invisible. He can but be imagined in the darkness, and it is here that the illusions you hold about him are not held up to his reality. Here are illusions and reality kept separated. Here are illusions never brought to truth, and always hidden from it. And here, in darkness, is your brother's reality imagined as a body, in unholy relationships with other bodies, serving the cause of sin an instant before he dies.

Your question should not be, "How can I see my brother without the body?" Ask only, "Do I really wish to see him sinless?" And as you ask, forget not that his sinlessness is your escape from fear. Salvation is the Holy Spirit's goal. The means is vision. For what the seeing look upon is sinless. No one who loves can judge, and what he sees is free of condemnation. And what he sees he did not make, for it was given him to see, as was the vision that made his seeing possible.

20.8. The Vision of Sinlessness

Your brother's sinlessness is given you in shining light, to look on with the Holy Spirit's vision and to rejoice in along with Him. For peace will come to all who ask for it with real desire and sincerity of purpose, shared with the Holy Spirit and at one with Him on what salvation is. Be willing, then, to see your brother sinless, that Christ may rise before your vision and give you joy. And place no value on your brother's body, which holds him to illusions of what he is. It is his desire to see his sinlessness, as it is yours. And bless the Son of God in your relationship, nor see in him what you have made of him.

Chapter 20

The body is the sign of weakness, vulnerability and loss of power. Look through the body's eyes, and everything will stand condemned before you. All that could save you, you will never see.

Judgment is but a toy, a whim, the senseless means to play the idle game of death in your imagination. But true vision sets all things right, bringing them gently within the kindly sway of Heaven's laws. What if you recognized this world is but an hallucination?

Hallucinations disappear when they are recognized for what they are. This is the healing and the remedy. Believe them not and they are gone. And all you need to do is recognize that you did this. Once you accept this simple fact and take unto yourself the power you gave them, you are released from them. One thing is sure; hallucinations serve a purpose, and when that purpose is no longer held they disappear. Therefore, the question never is whether you want them, but always, do you want the purpose that they serve? This world seems to hold out many purposes, each different and with different values. Yet they are all the same.

Only two purposes are possible. And one is sin, the other holiness. Nothing is in between, and which you choose determines what you see. For what you see is merely how you elect to meet your goal. Hallucinations serve to meet the goal of madness. They are the means by which the outside world, projected from within, adjusts to sin and seems to witness to its reality. It still is true that nothing is without. Yet upon nothing are all projections made. For it is the projection that gives the "nothing" all the meaning that it holds.

When you have looked on what seemed terrifying, and seen it change to sights of loveliness and peace; when you have looked on scenes of violence and death, and watched them change to quiet views of gardens under open skies, with clear, life-giving water running happily beside them in dancing brooks that never waste away; who need persuade you to accept the gift of vision? And after vision, who is there who could refuse what must come after? Think but an instant just on this; you can behold the holiness God gave His Son. And never need you think that there is something else for you to see.

Chapter 21

Reason and Perception

Introduction

Projection makes perception. The world you see is what you gave it, nothing more than that. It is the witness to your state of mind, the outside picture of an inward condition. As a man thinketh, so does he perceive. Therefore, seek not to change the world, but choose to change your mind about the world. Perception is a result and not a cause.

Damnation is your judgment on yourself, and this you will project upon the world. See it as damned, and all you see is what you did to hurt the Son of God. If you behold disaster and catastrophe, you tried to crucify him. If you see holiness and hope, you joined the Will of God to set him free. There is no choice that lies between these two decisions. And you will see the witness to the choice you made, and learn from this to recognize which one you chose.

21.1. The Forgotten Song

There is no need to learn through pain. And gentle lessons are acquired joyously, and are remembered gladly. What gives you happiness, you want to learn and not forget.

The blind become accustomed to their world by their adjustments to it. They think they know their way about in it. They learned it, not through joyous lessons, but through the stern necessity of limits they believed they could not overcome. And still believing this, they hold those lessons dear, and cling to them because they cannot see. They do not understand the lessons keep them blind. This they do not believe. And so they keep the world they learned to "see" in their imagination, believing that their choice is that or nothing. They hate the world they learned through pain. And everything they think is in it serves to remind them that they are incomplete and bitterly deprived.

CHAPTER 21

Thus they define their life and where they live, adjusting to it as they think they must, afraid to lose the little that they have. And so it is with all who see the body as all they have and all their brothers have. They try to reach each other, and they fail, and fail again. And they adjust to loneliness, believing that to keep the body is to save the little that they have. Listen, and try to think if you remember what we will speak of now.

Listen: perhaps you catch a hint of an ancient state not quite forgotten; dim, perhaps, and yet not altogether unfamiliar, like a song whose name is long forgotten, and the circumstances in which you heard completely unremembered. Not the whole song has stayed with you, but just a little wisp of melody, attached not to a person or a place or anything particular. But you remember, from just this little part, how lovely was the song, how wonderful the setting where you heard it, and how you loved those who were there and listened with you.

The notes are nothing. Yet you have kept them with you, not for themselves, but as a soft reminder of what would make you weep if you remembered how dear the song was to you. You could remember, yet you are afraid, believing you would lose the world you learned since then. And yet you know that nothing in the world you learned is half so dear as this. Listen, and see if you remember an ancient song you knew so long ago and held more dear than any melody you taught yourself to cherish since.

Beyond the body, beyond the sun and stars, past everything you see and yet somehow familiar, is an arc of golden light that stretches as you look into a great and shining circle. And all the circle fills with light before your eyes. The edges of the circle disappear, and what is in it is no longer contained at all. The light expands and covers everything, extending to infinity forever shining and with no break or limit anywhere. Within it everything is joined in perfect continuity. Nor is it possible to imagine that anything could be outside, for there is nowhere that this light is not.

21.2. The Responsibility for Sight

I am responsible for what I see.
I choose the feelings I experience, and I decide upon the goal I would achieve.
And everything that seems to happen to me I ask for, and receive as I have asked.

Deceive yourself no longer that you are helpless in the face of what is done to you. Acknowledge but that you have been mistaken, and all effects of your mistakes will disappear.

It is impossible the Son of God be merely driven by events outside of him. It is impossible that happenings that come to him were not his choice. His power of decision is the determiner of every situation in which he seems to find himself by chance or accident. No accident nor chance is possible within the universe as God created it, outside of which is nothing. Suffer, and you decided sin was your goal. Be happy, and you gave the power of decision to Him Who must decide for God for you. This is the little gift you offer to the Holy Spirit, and even this He gives to you to give yourself. For by this gift is given you the power to release your savior, that he may give salvation unto you.

You must perceive that what is strong enough to make a world can let it go, and can accept correction if it is willing to see that it was wrong.

All that the ego is, is an idea that it is possible that things should happen to the Son of God without his will; and thus without the Will of his Creator, Whose Will cannot be separate from his own. This is the Son of God's replacement for his will, a mad revolt against what must forever be. This is the statement that he has the power to make God powerless and so to take it for himself, and leave himself without what God has willed for him. This is the mad idea you have enshrined upon your altars, and which you worship. And everything that threatens this seems to attack your faith, for here is it invested. Think not that you are faithless, for your belief and trust in this is strong indeed.

The Holy Spirit can give you faith in holiness and vision to see it easily enough. But you have not left open and unoccupied the altar where the gifts belong. Where they should be, you have set up your idols to something else. This other "will," which seems to tell you what must happen, you give reality. And what would show you otherwise must therefore seem unreal. All that is asked of you is to make room for truth. You are not asked to make or do what lies beyond your understanding. All you are asked to do is let it in; only to stop your interference with what will happen of itself; simply to recognize again the presence of what you thought you gave away.

It is as needful that you recognize you made the world you see, as that you recognize that you did not create yourself. They are the same mistake. Nothing created not by your Creator has any influence over you. And if you think what you have made can tell you what you see and feel, and place your faith in its ability to do so, you are denying your Creator and believing that you made yourself. For if you think the world you made has power to make you what it wills, you are confusing Son and Father; effect and Source.

Yet the truth in you and your bother were created by a loving Father, Who created you together and as one. See what "proves" otherwise, and you deny your whole reality. But grant that everything that seems to stand between you, keeping you from each other and separate from your Father, you made in secret, and the instant of release has come to you. All separation's effects are gone, because its source has been uncovered. It is its seeming independence of its egoic source that keeps you prisoner. This is the same mistake as thinking you are independent of the Source by which you were created, and have never left.

21.3. Faith, Belief and Vision

No one allows a purpose to be replaced while he desires it, for nothing is so cherished and protected as is a goal the mind accepts. This it will follow, grimly or happily, but always with faith and with the persistence that faith inevitably brings.

Faith can keep the Son of God in chains as long as he believes he is in chains. And when he is released from them it will be simply because he no longer believes in them, withdrawing faith that they can hold him, and placing it in his freedom instead. It is impossible to place equal faith in opposite directions. What faith you give to sin you take away from holiness. And what you offer holiness has been removed from sin.

Faith and belief and vision are the means by which the goal of holiness is reached. Through them the Holy Spirit leads you to the real world, and away from all illusions where your faith was laid. This is His direction; the only one He ever sees. And when you wander, He reminds you there is but one. His faith and His belief and vision are all for you. And when you have accepted them completely instead of yours, you will have need of them no longer. For faith and vision and belief are meaningful only before the state of certainty is reached. In Heaven they are unknown. Yet Heaven is reached through them.

It is impossible that the Son of God lacks faith, but he can choose where he would have it be. Faithlessness is not a lack of faith, but faith in nothing. Faith given to illusions does not lack power, for by it does the Son of God believe that he is powerless. Thus is he faithless to himself, but strong in faith in his illusions about himself. For faith, perception and belief you made, as means for losing certainty and finding sin. This mad direction was your choice, and by your faith in what you chose, you made what you desired.

The Holy Spirit sees perception as a means to teach you that the vision of a holy relationship is all you want to see. Then will you give your faith to holiness, desiring and believing in it because of your desire.

Faith and belief become attached to vision, as all the means that once served sin are redirected now toward holiness. For what you think is sin is limitation, and whom you try to limit to the body you hate because you fear. In your refusal to forgive your brother, you would condemn him to the body because the means for sin are dear to you. And so the body has your faith and your belief. But holiness would set your brother free, removing hatred by removing fear, not as a symptom, but at its source.

Those who would free their brothers from the body can have no fear. They have renounced the means for sin by choosing to let all limitations be removed. As they desire to look upon their brothers in holiness, the power of belief and faith goes far beyond the body, supporting vision, not obstructing it. But first they chose to recognize how much their faith had limited their understanding of the world, desiring to place its power elsewhere should another point of view be given them. The miracles that follow this decision are also born of faith. For all who choose to look away from sin are given vision, and are led to holiness.

Those who believe in sin must think the Holy Spirit asks for sacrifice, for this is how they think their purpose is accomplished. Brother, the Holy Spirit knows that sacrifice brings nothing. He makes no bargains. And if you seek to limit Him, you will hate Him because you are afraid. The gift that He has given you is more than anything that stands this side of Heaven.

Your faith in sacrifice has given it great power in your sight; except you do not realize you cannot see because of it. The intention of sacrifice is in the mind, which tries to use the body to carry out the means for sin, in which the mind believes. Thus, is the joining of mind and body an inescapable belief of those who value sin. And so is sacrifice invariably a means for limitation, and thus for hate.

The body was made to be a sacrifice to sin, and in the darkness so it still is seen. Yet in the light of vision it is looked upon quite differently. You can have faith in the body to serve the Holy Spirit's goal, and give it power to serve as means to help the blind to see. But in their seeing the blind must look past the body, as do you. The faith and the belief you gave the body belongs beyond. You gave perception and belief and faith from mind to body. Let them now be given back to what produced them, and can use them still to save itself from what it made.

21.4. The Fear to Look Within

The Holy Spirit will never teach you that you are sinful. Errors He will correct, but this makes no one fearful. You are indeed afraid to look within and see the sin you think is there. This you would not be fearful to admit. The ego has no fear to let you feel ashamed. It doubts not your belief and faith in sin. Your faith that sin is there but witnesses to your desire that it be there to see. This merely seems to be the source of fear.

Loudly the ego tells you not to look inward, for if you do your eyes will light on sin, and God will strike you blind. This you believe, and so you do not look. Yet this is not the ego's hidden fear, nor yours who serve it. Loudly indeed the ego claims it is; too loudly and too often. For underneath this constant shout and frantic proclamation, the ego is not certain it is so. Beneath your fear to look within because of sin is yet another fear, and one which makes the ego tremble.

What if you looked within and saw no sin? This "fearful" question is one the ego never asks.

The Holy Spirit's purpose was accepted by the part of your mind the ego knows not of. No more did you. And yet this part, with which you now identify, is not afraid to look upon itself. It knows no sin. How, otherwise, could it have been willing to see the Holy Spirit's purpose as its own?

And now the ego is afraid. Yet what it hears in terror, the other part hears as the sweetest music; the song the other part longed to hear since first the ego came into your mind. The song of freedom, which sings the praises of another world, brings to it hope of peace. For the other part remembers Heaven, and now it sees that Heaven has come to earth at last, from which the ego's rule has kept it out so long. Heaven has come because it found a home in your relationship on earth. And earth can hold no longer what has been given Heaven as its own.

21.5. The Function of Reason

Perception selects, and makes the world you see. It literally picks it out as the mind directs. The still, small Voice for God is not drowned out by all the ego's raucous screams and senseless ravings to those who want to hear It. Perception is a choice and not a fact. But on this choice depends far more than you may realize as yet. For on the voice you choose to hear, and on the sights you choose to see, depends entirely your whole belief in what you are. Perception is a witness but to what you believe, and never to reality. Yet perception can show you the conditions in which awareness of reality is possible, or those where it could never be.

Reality needs no cooperation from you to be itself. But your awareness of it needs your help, because it is your choice. Listen to what the ego says, and see what it directs you see, and it is sure that you will see yourself as tiny, vulnerable and afraid. You will experience depression, a sense of worthlessness, and feelings of impermanence and unreality. You will believe that you are helpless prey to forces far beyond your own control, and far more powerful than you. And you will think the world you made directs your destiny.

You do not realize the whole extent to which the idea of separation has interfered with reason.

God's plan is simple; never circular and never self-defeating. He has no thoughts except the Self-extending, and in this your will must be included. Thus, there must be a part of you that knows His Will and shares it. It is not meaningful to ask if what must be is so. But it is meaningful to ask why you are unaware of what is so, for this must have an answer if the plan of God for your salvation is complete.

Reason is a means that serves the Holy Spirit's purpose in its own right. It is not reinterpreted and redirected from the goal of sin, as are the others. For reason is beyond the ego's range of means.

Faith and perception and belief can be misplaced, and serve the great deceiver's needs as well as truth. But reason has no place at all in madness, nor can it be adjusted to fit its end. Faith and belief are strong in madness, guiding perception toward what the mind has valued. But reason enters not at all in this. For the perception would fall away at once, if reason were applied. There is no reason in insanity, for it depends entirely on reason's absence. The ego never uses it, because it does not realize that it exists. The partially insane have access to it, and only they have need of it. Knowledge does not depend on it, and madness keeps it out.

The part of mind where reason lies was dedicated, by your will in union with your Father's, to the undoing of insanity. Here was the Holy Spirit's purpose accepted and accomplished, both at once. Reason is alien to insanity, and those who use it have gained a means which cannot be applied to sin. Knowledge is far beyond attainment of any kind. But reason can serve to open doors you closed against it.

You have come very close to this. Faith and belief have shifted, and you have asked the question the ego will never ask. Faith and belief, upheld by reason, cannot fail to lead to changed perception. And in this change, is room made way for vision. Vision extends beyond itself, as does the purpose that it serves, and all the means for its accomplishment.

21.6 Reason versus Madness

Reason cannot see sin but can see errors, and leads to their correction. Reason does not value errors, but does value their correction. Reason will also tell you that when you think you sin, you call for help. Yet if you will not accept the help you call for, you will not believe that this help is yours to give. And so you will not give it, thus maintaining the belief that you have sinned. For uncorrected error of any kind deceives you about the power that is in you to make correction. If the power within can correct, and you allow it not to do so, you deny the power within to yourself and to your brother. And if he shares this same belief you both will think that you are damned. This you could spare him and yourself. For reason would not make way for correction in you alone.

Correction cannot be accepted or refused by you without your brother. Sin would maintain it can. Yet reason tells you that you cannot see your brother or yourself as sinful and still perceive the other innocent. Who looks upon himself as guilty and sees a sinless world? And who can see a sinful world and look upon himself apart from it? Sin would maintain you must be separate.

The home of madness cannot be the home of reason. Yet it is easy to leave the home of madness if you see reason. You do not leave insanity by going somewhere else. You leave it simply by accepting reason where madness was. Madness and reason see the same things, but it is certain that they look upon them differently.

Madness is an attack on reason that drives it out of mind, and takes its place. Reason does not attack, but takes the place of madness quietly, replacing madness if it be the choice of the insane to listen to it. But the insane know not their will, for they believe they see the body, and let their madness tell them it is real. Reason would be incapable of this. And if you would defend the body against your reason, you will not understand the body or yourself.

Reason, like love, would reassure you, and seeks not to frighten you. The power to heal the Son of God is given you because your brother must be one with you. Reason is given you to understand that this is so. For reason leads steadily away from madness toward the goal of truth. That you and your brother are joined is your salvation; the gift of Heaven, not the gift of fear.

Reason assures you Heaven is what you want, and all you want. Listen to Him Who speaks with reason, and brings your reason into line with His. Be willing to let reason be the means by which He would direct you how to leave insanity behind. Hide not behind insanity in order to escape from reason. What madness would conceal, the Holy Spirit still holds out for everyone to look upon with gladness.

You are your brother's savior. He is yours.

21.7. The Last Unanswered Question

Do you not see that all your misery comes from the strange belief that you are powerless? Being helpless is the cost of sin. Helplessness is sin's condition; the one requirement that it demands to be believed. Only the helpless could believe in it.

Hate must have a target. There can be no faith in sin without an enemy. Who that believes in sin would dare believe he has no enemy? Could he admit that no one made him powerless? Reason would surely bid him seek no longer what is not there to find. Yet first he must be willing to perceive a world where it is not. It is not necessary that he understand how he can see it. Nor should he try. For if he focuses on what he cannot understand, he will but emphasize his helplessness, and let sin tell him that his enemy must be himself. But let him only ask himself these questions, which he must decide, to have it done for him:

> *Do I desire a world I rule instead of one that rules me?*
> *Do I desire a world where I am powerful instead of helpless?*
> *Do I desire a world in which I have no enemies and cannot sin?*
> *And do I want to see what I denied because it is the truth?*

You may already have answered the first three questions, but not yet the last. For this one still seems fearful, and unlike the others. Yet reason would assure you they are all the same. This final question, still seems to hold a threat the rest have lost for you. And this imagined difference attests to your belief that truth may be the enemy you yet may find. Here, then, would seem to be the last remaining hope of finding sin, and not accepting power.

Forget not that the choice of sin or truth, helplessness or power, is the choice of whether to attack or heal. For healing comes of power, and attack of helplessness. Whom you attack you cannot want to heal. And whom you would have healed must be the one you chose to be protected from attack. And what is this decision but the choice whether to see him through the body's eyes, or let him be revealed to you through vision? How this decision leads to its effects is not your problem. But what you want to see must be your choice. This is a course in cause and not effect.

Consider carefully your answer to the last question you have left unanswered still. And let your reason tell you that it must be answered, and is answered in the other three. And then it will be clear to you that, as you look on the effects of sin in any form, all you need do is simply ask yourself:

Is this what I would see? Do I want this?

This is your one decision; this the condition for what occurs. It is irrelevant to how it happens, but not to why. You have control of this. And if you choose to see a world without an enemy, in which you are not helpless, the means to see it will be given you.

Why is the final question so important? Reason will tell you why. It is the same as are the other three, except in time. The others are decisions that can be made, and then unmade and made again. But truth is constant, and implies a state where vacillations are impossible. You can desire a world you rule that rules you not, and change your mind. You can desire to exchange your helplessness for power, and lose this same desire as a little glint of sin attracts you. And you can want to see a sinless world, and let an "enemy" tempt you to use the body's eyes and change what you desire.

In *content* all the questions are the same. For each one asks if you are willing to exchange the world of sin for what the Holy Spirit sees, since it is this the world of sin denies. And therefore those who look on sin are seeing the denial of the real world. Yet the last question adds the wish for constancy in your desire to see the real world, so the desire becomes the only one you have. By answering the final question "yes," you add sincerity to the decisions you have already made to all the rest. For only then have you renounced the option to change your mind again.

Elusive happiness, or happiness in changing *form* that shifts with time and place, is an illusion that has no meaning. Happiness must be constant, because it is attained by giving up the wish for the inconstant. Joy cannot be perceived except through constant vision. And constant vision can be given only those who wish for constancy. The power of the Son of God's desire remains the proof that he is wrong who sees himself as helpless.

21.8. The Inner Shift

The constancy of joy is a condition quite alien to your understanding. Yet if you could even imagine what it must be, you would desire it although you understand it not. The constancy of happiness has no exceptions; no change of any kind. It is unshakable as is the Love of God for His creation. Sure in its vision as its Creator is in what He knows, happiness looks on everything and sees everything is the same. It sees not the ephemeral, for it desires everything be like itself, and sees it so.

You who complete God's Will and are His happiness, whose will is powerful as His, a power that is not lost in your illusions, think carefully why you have not yet decided how you would answer the final question. Your answer to the others has made it possible to help you be already partly sane. And yet it is the final one that really asks if you are willing to be wholly sane.

Chapter 22

Salvation and the Holy Relationship

Introduction

Who has need for sin? Only the lonely and alone, who see their brothers different from themselves. For an unholy relationship is based on differences, where each one thinks the other has what he has not. They come together, each to complete himself and rob the other. They stay until they think that there is nothing left to steal, and then move on. And so they wander through a world of strangers, unlike themselves, living with their bodies perhaps under a common roof that shelters neither; in the same room and yet a world apart.

A *holy* relationship starts from a different premise. Each one has looked within and seen no lack. Accepting his completion, he would extend it by joining with another, whole as himself. He sees no difference between these selves, for differences are only of the body. Therefore, he looks on nothing he would take. Think what a holy relationship can teach! Here is belief in differences undone. Here is the faith in differences shifted to sameness.

22.1. The Message of the Holy Relationship

Christ comes to what is like Himself; the same, not different. For He is always drawn unto Himself. And what draws you together draws Him to you. Here are His sweetness and His gentle innocence protected from attack. And here can He return in confidence, for faith in one another is always faith in Him. You are indeed correct in looking on each other as His chosen home. And who is drawn to Christ is drawn to God as surely as Both are drawn to every holy relationship, the home prepared for them as earth is turned to Heaven.

22.2. Your Brother's Sinlessness

The opposite of illusions is not disillusionment but truth. Only to the ego, to which truth is meaningless, do they appear to be the only alternatives, and different from each other. In truth illusions and disillusionments are the same. Both bring the same amount of misery, though each one seems to be the way to lose the misery the other brings. Every illusion carries pain and suffering in the dark folds of the heavy garments in which it hides its nothingness. Yet by these dark and heavy garments are those who seek illusions covered, and hidden from the joy of truth.

Truth is the opposite of illusions because it offers joy. What else but joy could be the opposite of misery? To leave one kind of misery and seek another is hardly an escape. To change illusions is to make no change. The search for joy in misery is senseless, for how could joy be found in misery? All that is possible in the dark world of misery is to select some aspects out of it, see the aspects as different, and define the difference as joy. Yet to perceive a difference where none exists will surely fail to make a difference.

Illusions carry only guilt and suffering, sickness and death, to their believers. The *form* in which they are accepted is irrelevant. No form of misery in reason's eyes can be confused with joy. Joy is eternal. Reason will tell you that the only way to escape from misery is to recognize it and go the other way.

The ego will assure you now that it is impossible for you to see no guilt in anyone. This is a crucial period in this course, for here the separation of you and the ego must be made complete. Now must you choose between yourself and an illusion of yourself. Not both, but one. There is no point in trying to avoid this one decision. It must be made. Faith and belief can fall to either side, but reason tells you misery lies only on one side and joy upon the other.

Forsake not now your brother. For you who are the same will not decide alone nor differently. Either you give each other life or death; either you are each other's savior or his judge, offering him sanctuary or condemnation.

Let us look closer at the whole illusion that what you made has power to enslave its maker. Nothing you made has any power over you unless you still would be apart from your Creator, and with a will opposed to His. For only if you would believe His Son could be His enemy does it seem possible that what you made is yours. You would condemn His joy to misery, and make Him different. And all the misery you made has been your own. Are you not glad to learn it is not true? Is it not welcome news to hear not one of the illusions that you made replaced the truth?

Beyond the body that you interposed between you and your brother is your holy relationship, beloved of God Himself. Every illusion brought to its forgiveness is gently overlooked and disappears. For at its center, Christ has been reborn, to light His home with vision that overlooks the world. Would you not have this holy home be yours as well? No misery is here, but only joy.

All you need do to dwell in quiet here with Christ is share His vision. Quickly and gladly is His vision given anyone who is but willing to see his brother sinless. Look on your holy brother, sinless as yourself, and let him lead you there.

22.3. Reason and the Forms of Error

The introduction of reason into the ego's thought system is the beginning of its undoing, for reason and the ego are contradictory.

The ego's whole continuance depends on its belief you cannot learn this course. Share this belief, and reason will be unable to see your errors and make way for their correction. For reason sees through errors, telling you what you thought was real is not. Reason can see the difference between sin and mistakes, because it wants correction. Therefore, it tells you what you thought was uncorrectable can be corrected, and thus it must have been an error. The ego's opposition to correction leads to its fixed belief in sin and disregard of errors. It looks on nothing that can be corrected. Thus does the ego damn, and reason save.

Reason is not salvation in itself, but it makes way for peace and brings you to a state of mind in which salvation can be given to you. "Sin" is a block, set like a heavy gate, locked and without a key, across the road to peace. No one who looks on it without the help of reason would try to pass it. The body's eyes behold it as solid granite, so thick it would be madness to attempt to pass it. Yet reason sees through sin easily, because it is an error. The form it takes cannot conceal its emptiness from reason's eyes.

Everything the body's eyes can see is a mistake, an error in perception, a distorted fragment of the whole without the meaning that the whole would give. And yet mistakes, regardless of their form, can be corrected. Sin is but error in a special form that the ego venerates. It would preserve all errors and make them sins. For here is the ego's own stability, its heavy anchor in the shifting world it made; the rock on which its church is built, and where its worshipers are bound to bodies, believing the body's freedom is their own.

The body's eyes see only form. They cannot see beyond what they were made to see. And they were made to look on error and not see past it. Theirs is indeed a strange perception, for they can see only illusions, unable to look beyond the granite block of sin, and stopping at the outside form of nothing. To this distorted form of vision, the wall that stands between you and the truth, is wholly true. Yet how can sight that stops at nothingness, as if it were a solid wall, see truly? It is held back by *form*, having been made to guarantee that nothing else but form will be perceived.

These eyes, made not to see, will never see. See how the body's eyes rest on externals and cannot go beyond. Watch how they stop at nothingness, unable to go beyond the form to meaning. Nothing so blinding, as perception of form. For sight of form means understanding has been obscured.

Reason will tell you that if form is not reality it must be an illusion, and is not there to see. And if you see it you must be mistaken, for you are seeing what can not be real as if it were. What cannot see beyond what is not there must be distorted perception, and must perceive illusions as the truth. Could these eyes, then, recognize the truth?

Let your awareness of your brother not be blocked by your perception of his sins and of his body. What is there in him that you would attack except what you associate with his body, which you believe can sin? Beyond his errors is his holiness and your salvation. You gave him not his holiness, but tried to see your sins in him to save yourself. And yet, his holiness is your forgiveness. Can you be saved by making sinful the one whose holiness is your salvation?

A holy relationship, however newly born, must value holiness above all else. Unholy values will produce confusion. Reason sees a holy relationship as what it is; a common state of mind, where both give errors gladly to correction, that both may happily be healed as one.

22.4. The Branching of the Road

When you come to the place where the branch in the road is quite apparent, you cannot go ahead. You must go either one way or the other. For now if you go straight ahead, the way you went before you reached the branch, you will go nowhere. The whole purpose of coming this far was to decide which branch you will take now. The way you came no longer matters. It can no longer serve. No one who reaches this far can make the wrong decision, although he can delay. And there is no part of the journey that seems more hopeless and futile than standing where the road branches, and not deciding on which way to go.

It is but the first few steps along the right way that seem hard, although you still may think you can go back and make the other choice.

And so you and your brother stand here, in this holy place, before the veil of sin that hangs between you and the face of Christ. The Love of Christ will light your faces, and shine from them into a darkened world that needs the light.

Think of the loveliness that you will see, who walk with Him! And think how beautiful will each of you look to the other! How happy you will be to be together, after such a long and lonely journey where you walked alone. The gates of Heaven, open now for you, and now you will open to the sorrowful. And none who looks upon the Christ in you but will rejoice. How beautiful the sight you saw beyond the veil, which you will bring to light the tired eyes of those as weary now as once you were. How thankful will they be to see you come among them, offering Christ's forgiveness to dispel their faith in sin.

Those who would let illusions be lifted from their minds are this world's saviors, walking the world with their Redeemer, and carrying His message of hope and freedom and release from suffering to everyone who needs a miracle to save him.

How easy is it to offer this miracle to everyone! For by receiving it, he learned it was not given him alone. Such is the function of a holy relationship; to receive together and give as you received. Standing before the veil, it still seems difficult. But hold out your joined hands and touch this heavy-seeming block, and you will learn how easily your fingers slip through its nothingness. It is no solid wall. And only an illusion stands between you and the holy self you share.

22.5. Weakness and Defensiveness

How does one overcome illusions? Surely not by force or anger, nor by opposing them in any way. Merely by letting reason tell you that they contradict reality. Everything that needs defense you do not want, for anything that needs defense will weaken you.

God rests with you in quiet, undefended and wholly undefending, for in this quiet state alone is strength and power. Here can no weakness enter, for here is no attack and therefore no illusions. Love rests in certainty. Only uncertainty can be defensive. And all uncertainty is doubt about yourself.

How weak is fear; how little and how meaningless. How insignificant before the quiet strength of those whom love has joined! This is your "enemy,"--a frightened mouse that would attack the universe. How likely is it that it will succeed? Can it be difficult to disregard its feeble squeaks that tell of its omnipotence, and would drown out the hymn of praise to its Creator that every heart throughout the universe forever sings as one? Which is the stronger? Is it this tiny mouse or everything that God created? You are not joined together by this mouse, but by the Will of God. And can a mouse betray whom God has joined?

If you but recognized how little stands between you and your awareness of your union! Be not deceived by the illusions it presents of size and thickness, weight, solidity and firmness of foundation. Yes, to the body's eyes it looks like an enormous solid body, immovable as is a mountain. Yet within you is a Force that no illusions can resist. This body only seems to be immovable; this Force is irresistible in truth. What, then, must happen when they come together?

Forget not, when you feel the need arise to be defensive about anything, you have identified yourself with an illusion. And therefore, feel that you are weak because you are alone. This is the cost of all illusions.

22.6. The Light of the Holy Relationship

Do you want freedom of the body or of the mind? For both you cannot have. Which do you value? Which is your goal? For one you see as means; the other, end. And one must serve the other and lead to its predominance, increasing its importance by diminishing its own. Means serve the end, and as the end is reached the value of the means decreases, eclipsed entirely when they are recognized as functionless. No one but yearns for freedom and tries to find it. Yet he will seek for it where he believes it is and can be found. He will believe it possible of mind or body, and he will make the other serve his choice as means to find it.

Where freedom of the body has been chosen, the mind is used as means whose value lies in its ability to contrive ways to achieve the "body's freedom". Yet freedom of the body has no meaning, and so the mind is dedicated to serve illusions. This is a situation so contradictory and so impossible that anyone who chooses this has no idea of what is valuable. Yet even in this confusion, so profound it cannot be described, the Holy Spirit waits in gentle patience, as certain of the outcome as He is sure of His Creator's Love. He knows this mad decision was made by one as dear to His Creator as love is to itself.

This holy relationship, lovely in its innocence, mighty in strength, and blazing with a light far brighter than the sun that lights the sky you see, is chosen of your Father as a means for His Own plan.

Child of peace, the light has come to you. The light you bring you do not recognize, and yet you will remember. Who can deny himself the vision that he brings to others? And who would fail to recognize a gift he let be laid in Heaven through himself? The gentle service that you give the Holy Spirit is service to yourself. You who are now His means must love all that He Loves. And what you bring is your remembrance of everything that is eternal. No trace of anything in time can long remain in minds that serve the timeless. And no illusion can disturb the peace of a relationship that has become the means of peace.

When you have looked upon your brother with complete forgiveness, from which no error is excluded and nothing kept hidden, what mistake can there be anywhere you cannot overlook? What form of suffering could block your sight, preventing you from seeing past it? And what illusion could be there you will not recognize as a mistake; a shadow through which you walk completely undismayed? God would let nothing interfere with those whose wills are His, and serve it willingly.

You will see your value through your brother's eyes, and each one is released as he beholds his brother as savior in place of the attacker who he thought was there. Through this releasing is the world released. This is your part in bringing peace. For you have asked what is your function here, and have been answered that your function is to forgive. Seek not to change it, nor to substitute another goal. Accept this function to forgive and serve it willingly, for what the Holy Spirit does with gifts you give each other, to whom He offers them, and where and when, is up to Him. He will bestow these gifts where they are received and welcomed. He will use every one of these gifts of forgiveness for peace. Nor will one little smile or willingness to overlook the tiniest mistake be lost to anyone.

What can it be but universal blessing to look on what your Father loves with charity? Extension of forgiveness is the Holy Spirit's function. Leave this to Him. Let your concern be only that you give to Him that which can be extended. Save no dark secrets that He cannot use, but offer Him the tiny gifts He can extend forever. He will take each gift of forgiveness and make of it a potent force for peace. He will withhold no blessing from it, nor limit it in any way. He will join to each gift all the power that God has given Him, to make each little gift of love a source of healing for everyone. Each little gift you offer to your brother lights up the world. Be not concerned with darkness; look away from it and toward each other. And let the darkness be dispelled by Him Who knows the light, and lays it gently in each quiet smile of faith and confidence, with which you bless each other.

The light that joins you shines throughout the universe, and because it joins you, so it makes you one with your Creator.

Chapter 23

The War Against Yourself

Introduction

No one is strong who has an enemy, and no one can attack unless he thinks he has. Belief in enemies is therefore the belief in weakness, and what is weak is not the Will of God.

How strange indeed becomes this war against yourself!

Walk you in glory, with your head held high, and fear no evil. The innocent are safe because they share their innocence. Nothing they see is harmful, for their awareness of the truth releases everything from the illusion of harmfulness. And what seemed harmful now stands shining in their innocence, released from sin and fear and happily returned to love. They share the strength of love because they looked on innocence. And every error disappeared because they saw it not.

Let not the little interferers pull you to littleness. There can be no attraction of guilt in innocence. Think what a happy world you walk, with truth beside you! Do not give up this world of freedom for a little sigh of seeming sin, nor for a tiny stirring of guilt's attraction. Would you, for all these meaningless distractions, lay Heaven aside? Your destiny and purpose are far beyond them, in the clean place where littleness does not exist.

Let us not let littleness lead God's Son into temptation. The Son of God's glory is beyond it, measureless and timeless as eternity. Do not let time intrude upon your sight of God's Son. Leave him not frightened and alone in his temptation, but help him rise above it and perceive the light of which he is a part. Your innocence will light the way to his, and so is yours protected and kept in your awareness. For who can know his glory, and perceive the little and the weak about him? Who can walk trembling in a fearful world, and realize that Heaven's glory shines on him?

Chapter 23

Nothing around you is but part of you. Look on it lovingly, and see the light of Heaven in it. So will you come to understand all that is given you. In kind forgiveness will the world sparkle and shine, and everything you once thought sinful now will be reinterpreted as part of Heaven. How beautiful it is to walk, clean and redeemed and happy, through a world in bitter need of the redemption that your innocence bestows upon it! What can you value more than this? For here is your salvation and your freedom.

23.1. The Irreconcilable Beliefs

The memory of God comes to the quiet mind. It cannot come where there is conflict, for a mind at war against itself remembers not eternal gentleness. The means of war are not the means of peace, and what the warlike would remember is not love. War is impossible unless belief in victory is cherished. Conflict within you must imply that you believe the ego has the power to be victorious. Why else would you identify with it? Surely you realize the ego is at war with God.

Do you not realize a war against yourself would be a war on God? Is victory conceivable? And if it were, is this a victory that you would want? The death of God, if it were possible, would be your death. Is this a victory? The ego always marches to defeat, because it thinks that triumph over you is possible. And God thinks otherwise. This is no war; only the mad belief the Will of God can be attacked and overthrown. You may identify with this belief, but never will it be more than madness. And fear will reign in madness, and will seem to have replaced love there. This is the conflict's purpose. And to those who think that it is possible, the means seem real.

Be certain that it is impossible God and the ego, or your Self and the ego, will ever meet. You seem to meet, and make your strange alliances on grounds that have no meaning. For your beliefs converge upon the body, the ego's chosen home, which you believe is yours. You meet at a mistake; an error in your self-appraisal. The ego joins with an illusion of yourself you share with it. And yet illusions cannot join. The ego joins with nothing, being nothing. The victory it seeks is meaningless as is itself.

Brother, the war against yourself is almost over. The journey's end is at the place of peace. Would you not now accept the peace offered you here? This "enemy" you fought as an intruder on your peace is here transformed, before your sight, into the giver of your peace. Your "enemy" was God Himself, to Whom all conflict, triumph and attack of any kind are all unknown. He loves you perfectly, completely and eternally.

The war against yourself was undertaken to teach the Son of God that he is not himself, and not his Father's Son. For this, the memory of his Father must have been forgotten. It is forgotten in the body's life, and if you think you are a body, you will believe you have forgotten it. Yet truth can never be forgotten by itself, and you have not forgotten what you are.

What you remember is a part of you. For you must be as God created you. Truth does not fight against illusions, nor do illusions fight against the truth. Illusions battle only with themselves. Being fragmented, they fragment. You will remember what you know when you have learned you cannot be in conflict. One illusion about yourself can battle with another, yet the war of two illusions is a state where nothing happens. There is no victor and there is no victory. And truth stands radiant, apart from conflict, untouched and quiet in the peace of God.

Conflict must be between two forces. It cannot exist between one power and nothingness. There is nothing you could attack that is not part of you. And by attacking it you make two illusions of yourself, in conflict with each other. And this occurs whenever you look on anything that God created with anything but love. Conflict is fearful, for it is the birth of fear. Yet what is born of nothing cannot win reality through battle. Why would you fill your world with conflicts with yourself? Let all this madness be undone for you, and turn in peace to the remembrance of God, still shining in your quiet mind.

See how the conflict of illusions disappears when it is brought to truth! Thus, conflict is the choice between illusions, one to be crowned as real, the other vanquished and despised.

You who are beloved of Him are no illusion, being as true and holy as Himself. The stillness of your certainty of Him and of yourself is home to Both of You, Who dwell as One and not apart. Open the door of His most holy home, and let forgiveness sweep away all trace of the belief in sin that keeps God homeless. You are not a stranger in the house of God. Illusions have no place where love abides, protecting you from everything that is not true. You dwell in peace as limitless as its Creator, and everything is given those who would remember Him.

The meeting of illusions leads to war. Peace, looking on itself, extends itself. War is the condition in which fear is born, and grows and seeks to dominate. Peace is the state where love abides, and seeks to share itself. Conflict and peace are opposites. Where one abides the other cannot be; where either goes the other disappears. So is the memory of God obscured in minds that have become illusions' battleground. Yet far beyond this senseless war it shines, ready to be remembered when you side with peace.

23.2. The Laws of Chaos

The "laws" of chaos can be brought to light. They *appear* to be an *obstacle* to reason and to truth. Let us, then, look upon them calmly, that we may look beyond them, understanding what they are, not what they would maintain. It is essential it be understood what they are for, because it is their purpose to attack the truth. They govern nothing, and need not be broken; merely looked upon and gone beyond.

CHAPTER 23

The *first* chaotic law is that - the truth is different for everyone.

The *second* law of chaos is that - each one must sin, and therefore deserves attack and death.

The *third* preposterous belief - to make chaos eternal.

The *fourth* law of chaos is the belief - you have what you have taken.

And here a *final* principle of chaos - it holds there is a substitute for love.

These are the laws you made for your "salvation". They hold in place the substitute for Heaven.

No one wants madness, nor does anyone cling to his madness if he sees that this is what it is. What protects madness is the belief that it is true. It is the function of insanity to take the place of truth. It must be seen as truth to be believed.

Chaos is lawlessness. To be believed, its seeming laws must be perceived as real, their goal of madness must be seen as sanity.

Can an attack in any form be love? What form of condemnation is a blessing? Be not deceived when madness takes a form you think is lovely. What is intent on your destruction is not your friend.

There is no life outside of Heaven. Where God created life, there life must be. In any state apart from Heaven life is illusion. Outside of Heaven, only the conflict of illusion stands; senseless, impossible and beyond all reason, and yet perceived as an eternal barrier to Heaven. Illusions are but forms. Their content is never true.

And lack of faith in love, in any form, attests to chaos as reality.

Brother, take not one step in the descent to hell. For having taken one, you will not recognize the rest for what they are. And they will follow. Attack in any form has placed your foot upon the twisted stairway that leads from Heaven. Yet any instant it is possible to have all this undone. How can you know whether you chose the stairs to Heaven or the way to hell? Quite easily. How do you feel? Is peace in your awareness? Are you certain which way you go? If not, you walk alone. Ask, then, your Friend to join with you, and give you certainty of where you go.

23.3. Salvation without Compromise

Salvation is no compromise of any kind. To compromise is to accept but part of what you want; to take a little and give up the rest. Salvation gives up nothing. It is complete for everyone.

23.4. Above the Battleground

Do not remain in conflict, for there is no war without attack. The fear of God is fear of life, and not of death. Yet He remains the only place of safety. In Him is no attack, and no illusion in any form stalks Heaven. You are not asked to fight against your wish to murder. But you are asked to realize the form it takes conceals the same intent, which is the attack upon the truth. And it is this you fear, and not the form. What is not love is murder. What is not loving must be an attack. Every illusion is an assault on truth.

Each form of murder and attack that still attracts you and that you do not recognize for what it is, limits the healing and the miracles you have the power to extend to all. He understands how your relationship is raised above the battleground, in it no more. The overlooking of the battleground is now your purpose.

Be lifted up, and from a higher place look down upon it. From there will your perspective be quite different. Here in the midst of it, it does seem real. Here you have chosen to be part of it. Here murder is your choice. Yet from above, the choice is miracles instead of murder. And the perspective coming from this choice shows you the battle is not real, and easily escaped. Bodies may battle, but the clash of *forms* is meaningless. And it is over when you realize it never was begun. How can a battle be perceived as nothingness when you engage in it? How can the truth of miracles be recognized if murder is your choice?

When the temptation to attack rises to make your mind darkened and murderous, remember you can see the battle from above. Even in forms you do not recognize, the signs you know. There is a stab of pain, a twinge of guilt, and above all, a loss of peace. This you know well. When they occur leave not your place on high, but quickly choose a miracle instead of murder. And God Himself and all the lights of Heaven will gently lean to you, and hold you up. For you have chosen to remain where He would have you, and no illusion can attack the peace of God together with His Son.

Think what is given those who share their Father's purpose, and who know that it is theirs. They want for nothing. Sorrow of any kind is inconceivable. Only the light they love is in awareness, and only love shines upon them forever. It is their past, their present and their future; always the same, eternally complete and wholly shared. They know it is impossible

Chapter 23

their happiness could ever suffer change of any kind. Perhaps you think the battleground can offer something you can win. Can it be anything that offers you a perfect calmness, and a sense of love so deep and quiet that no touch of doubt can ever mar your certainty?

Those with the strength of God in their awareness could never think of battle. What could they gain but loss of their perfection? For everything fought for on the battleground is of the body; something it seems to offer or to own. No one who knows that he has everything could seek for limitation, nor could he value the body's offerings. The senselessness of conquest is quite apparent from the quiet sphere above the battleground. Who with the Love of God upholding him could find the choice of miracles or murder hard to make?

Chapter 24

The Goal of Specialness

Introduction

Forget not that the motivation for this course is the attainment and the keeping of the state of peace. Given this state the mind is quiet, and the condition in which God is remembered is attained. Peace will be yours because it is His Will. Can you believe a shadow can hold back the Will that holds the universe secure? And what illusion that idly seems to drift between Them has the power to defeat what is Their Will?

To learn this course requires willingness to question every value that you hold. Not one can be kept hidden and obscure, it will jeopardize your learning. No belief is neutral. Every one has the power to dictate each decision you make. For a decision is a conclusion based on everything that you believe. It is the outcome of belief. There is no substitute for peace.

24.1. Specialness as a Substitute for Love

What God created cannot be attacked, for there is nothing in the universe unlike itself. But what is different calls for judgment, and this must come from someone "better," someone incapable of being like what he, the judge, condemns. The judge, "above" what he judges, is "sinless" by comparison with it. And thus, does specialness become a means and end at once. For specialness not only sets apart, but serves as grounds from which attack on those who seem "beneath" the special one is "natural" and "just." Those who judge, the special ones, feel weak and frail because of differences, for what would make them special is their enemy.

Specialness is the great dictator of the wrong decisions. For what your brother must become to keep your specialness is an illusion. He who is "worse" than you must be attacked, so that your specialness can live on his defeat. For specialness is triumph, and its victory is his defeat and shame.

Would it be possible for you to hate your brother if you were like him? Could you attack him if you realized you journey with him, to a goal that is the same? Would you not help him reach the same goal in every way you could, if his attainment of it were perceived as yours? You are his enemy in specialness; his friend in a shared purpose. Specialness can never share, for specialness depends on goals that you alone can reach. And he must never reach them, or your goal is jeopardized. Can love have meaning where the goal is triumph over your brother?

Your brother is your friend because his Father created him like you. There is no difference. Could you attack your brother if you chose to see no specialness of any kind between you and him? Look fairly at whatever makes you give your brother only partial welcome, or would let you think that you are better off apart.

The fear of God and of your brother comes from each unrecognized belief in specialness. For you demand your brother bow to it against his will. Every twinge of malice, or stab of hate or wish to separate arises here. For here the purpose that you and your brother share becomes obscured from both of you. You would oppose this course because it teaches you, you and your brother are alike.

He is your friend because you are the same.

24.2. The Treachery of Specialness

Comparison must be an ego device, for love makes none. Specialness always makes comparisons. It is established by a lack seen in another, and maintained by searching for, and keeping clear in sight, all lacks it can perceive. Lack in another does it seek, and this it looks upon. And always whom it thus diminishes would be your savior, had you not chosen to make of your brother a tiny measure of your specialness instead. Against the littleness you see in him, you stand as tall and stately, clean and honest, pure and unsullied, by comparison with what you see. Nor do you understand it is yourself that you diminish thus.

Pursuit of specialness is always at the cost of peace. You have a function in salvation. Its pursuit will bring you joy. But the pursuit of specialness must bring you pain. Here is a goal that would defeat salvation, and thus run counter to the Will of God.

You are not special. If you think you are, and would defend your specialness against the truth of what you really are, how can you know the truth? What answer that the Holy Spirit gives can reach you, when it is your specialness to which you listen, and which asks and answers? Its tiny answer, soundless in the melody that pours from God to you, eternally in loving praise of what you are, is all you listen to. And that vast song of honor and of love for what you are seems silent and unheard before its "mightiness." You strain your ears to hear its soundless voice, and yet the Call of God Himself is soundless to you.

You can defend your specialness, but never will you hear the Voice for God beside it. They speak a different language and they fall on different ears. The special messages the special hear, convince them they are different and apart; each in his special sins and "safe" from love, which does not see his specialness at all. Christ's vision is their "enemy," for it sees not what they would look upon, and it would show them that the specialness they think they see is an illusion.

What would they see instead? The shining radiance of the Son of God, so like his Father that the memory of Him springs instantly to mind. And with this memory, the Son remembers his own creations, as like to him as he is to his Father. And all the world he made, and all his specialness, and all the sins he held in its defense against himself, will vanish as his mind accepts the truth about himself, as it returns to take their place.

Think of the loveliness that you will see within yourself, when you have looked on your brother as on a friend. Here is your savior from your specialness. Specialness is the seal of treachery upon the gift of love.

The hope of specialness makes it seem possible God made the body as the prison house that keeps His Son from Him. For it demands a special place God cannot enter, and a hiding place where none is welcome but your tiny self. Nothing is sacred here but unto you, and you alone, apart and separate from all your brothers; safe from all intrusions of sanity upon illusions; safe from God and safe in conflict everlasting. Here are the gates of hell you closed upon yourself, to rule in madness and in loneliness, your special kingdom apart from God, away from truth and from salvation.

The death of specialness is not your death, but your awaking into life eternal. You but emerge from an illusion of what you are to the acceptance of yourself as God created you.

24.3. The Forgiveness of Specialness

Forgiveness is the end of specialness.

Specialness is not the truth in you. It can be thrown off balance by anything. What rests on nothing never can be stable. However large and overblown it seems to be, it still must rock and turn and whirl about with every breeze. Without foundation nothing is secure. Would God have left His Son in such a state, where safety has no meaning? No, His Son is safe, resting on Him.

Here, in the illusions of your specialness, is the hell you chose to be your home. He chose not this for you. Ask not He enter this hell. The way is barred to love and to salvation. Yet if you would release your brother from the depths of hell, you will rest forever in the arms of peace, in perfect safety, and without the heat and malice of one thought of specialness to mar your rest.

The "special" ones are all asleep, surrounded by a world of loveliness they do not see. Freedom and peace and joy stand there, beside the bier on which they sleep, and call them to come forth and waken from their dream of death. Yet they hear nothing. They are lost in dreams of specialness. Open your eyes a little; see the savior God gave to you that you might look on your brother, and give him back his birthright. It is also yours.

24.4. Specialness versus Sinlessness

Specialness is a lack of trust in anyone except yourself. Faith is invested in yourself alone. Everything else becomes your enemy; feared and attacked, deadly and dangerous, hated and worthy only of destruction. Whatever gentleness it offers is but deception, but its hate is real. In danger of destruction it must kill, and you are drawn to it to kill it first. And such is guilt's attraction. Here is death enthroned as savior; crucifixion is now redemption, and salvation can only mean destruction of the world, except yourself.

What could the purpose of the body be but specialness? And it is this that makes it frail and helpless in its own defense. It was conceived to make you frail and helpless. The goal of separation is its curse. Yet bodies have no goal. Purpose is of the mind. And minds can change as they desire. What minds are, and all their attributes, they cannot change. But what minds hold as purpose can be changed, and body *states* must shift accordingly. Of itself the body can do nothing. See it as means to hurt, and it is hurt. See it as means to heal, and it is healed.

For miracles are merely change of purpose, from hurt to healing. This shift in purpose does "endanger" specialness, but only in the sense that all illusions are "threatened" by the truth. What you have given specialness has left you bankrupt and your treasure house barren and empty, with an open door inviting everything that would disturb your peace to enter and destroy.

Do not defend this senseless dream, in which God is bereft of what He loves, and you remain beyond salvation. Only this is certain in this shifting world that has no meaning in reality: When peace is not with you entirely, and when you suffer pain of any kind, you have beheld some sin within your brother, and have rejoiced at what you thought was there. Your specialness seemed safe because of it. And thus you saved what you appointed to be your savior, and crucified the one whom God has given you instead. So are you bound with him, for you are one. And so is specialness his "enemy," and yours as well.

24.5. The Christ in You

The Christ in you is very still. He looks on what He loves, and knows it as Himself. And thus does He rejoice at what He sees, because He knows that it is one with Him and with His Father.

The Goal of Specialness

Where could your peace arise, but from forgiveness? The Christ in you looks only on the truth, and sees no condemnation that could need forgiveness. He is at peace because He sees no sin. Identify with Him, and what has He that you have not? He is your eyes, your ears, your hands, your feet. How gentle are the sights He sees, the sounds He hears. How beautiful His hand that holds His brother's, and how lovingly He walks beside him, showing him what can be seen and heard, and where he will see nothing and there is no sound to hear.

Rejoice you have no eyes with which to see; no ears to listen, and no hands to hold nor feet to guide. Be glad that only Christ can lend you His, while you have need of them. They are illusions, too, as much as yours. And yet because they serve a different purpose, the strength their purpose holds is given them. And what they see and hear and hold and lead is given light, that you may lead as you were led.

The Christ in you is very still. He knows where you are going, and He leads you there in gentleness and blessing all the way. His Love for God replaces all the fear you thought you saw within yourself. His Holiness shows you Himself in your brother whose hand you hold, and whom you lead to Him. And what you see is like yourself. For what but Christ is there to see and hear and love and follow home? He looked upon you first, but recognized that you were not complete. And so He sought for your completion in each living thing that He beholds and loves. And seeks it still, that each might offer you the Love of God.

Yet is He quiet, for He knows that love is in you now, and safely held in you by that same hand that holds your brother's in your own. Christ's hand holds all His brothers in Himself. He gives them vision for their sightless eyes, and sings to them of Heaven, that their ears may hear no more the sound of battle and of death. He reaches through them, holding out His hand, that everyone may bless all living things, and see their holiness. And He rejoices that these sights are yours, to look upon with Him and share His joy. His perfect lack of specialness He offers you, that you may save all living things from death, receiving from each one the gift of life that your forgiveness offers to your Self. The sight of Christ is all there is to see. The song of Christ is all there is to hear. The hand of Christ is all there is to hold. There is no journey but to walk with Him.

You who would be content with specialness, and seek salvation in a war with love, consider this: God, the holy Lord of Heaven, has Himself come down to you, to offer you your own completion. What is Gods, is yours, because in your completion is His Own.

There must be doubt before there can be conflict. And every doubt must be about yourself. Christ has no doubt, and from His certainty His quiet comes. He will exchange His certainty for all your doubts, if you agree that He is One with you, and that this Oneness is endless, timeless, and within your grasp because your hands are His. He is within you, yet He walks beside you and before, leading the way that He must go to find Himself complete. His quietness becomes your certainty. And where is doubt when certainty has come?

24.6. Salvation from Fear

Before your brother's holiness the world is still, and peace descends on it in gentleness and blessing so complete that not one trace of conflict still remains to haunt you in the darkness of the night. He is your savior from the dreams of fear. He is the healing of your sense of sacrifice and fear that what you have will scatter with the wind and turn to dust. In him is your assurance God is here, and with you now. For He could never leave His Own creation. And the sign that this is so lies in your brother, offered you that all your doubts about yourself may disappear before his holiness. See in him God's creation. For in him his Father waits for your acknowledgment that He created you as part of Him.

Without you there would be a lack in God, a Heaven incomplete, a Son without a Father. There could be no universe and no reality. For what God wills is whole, and part of Him because His Will is One. Nothing alive that is not part of Him, and nothing is but is alive in Him. Your brother's holiness shows you that God is One with him and you; that what he has is yours because you are not separate from him nor from his Father.

Nothing is lost to you in all the universe. Nothing that God created has He failed to lay before you lovingly, as yours forever. And no Thought within His Mind is absent from your own. It is His Will you share His Love for you, and look upon yourself as lovingly as He conceived of you before the world began, and as He knows you still. God changes not His Mind about His Son with passing circumstance which has no meaning in eternity where He abides, and you with Him. Your brother is as He created him. And it is this that saves you from a world that He created not.

Forget not that the healing of God's Son is all the world is for. That is the only purpose the Holy Spirit sees in it, and thus the only one it has. Let not your eyes be blinded by the veil of specialness that hides the face of Christ from your brother, and you as well.

Think, then, how great the Love of God for you must be, that He has given you a part of Him to save from pain and give you happiness. And never doubt but that your specialness will disappear before the Will of God, Who loves each part of Him with equal love and care. The Christ in you can see your brother truly.

Specialness is the function that you gave yourself. It stands for you alone, as self-created, self-maintained, in need of nothing, and unjoined with anything beyond the body. In its eyes you are a separate universe, with all the power to hold itself complete within itself, with every entry shut against intrusion, and every window barred against the light. Always attacked and always furious, with anger always fully justified, you have pursued this goal with vigilance you never thought to yield, and effort that you never thought to cease. And all this grim determination was for this; you wanted specialness to be the truth.

Now you are merely asked that you pursue another goal with far less vigilance; with little effort and with little time, and with the power of God maintaining it, and promising success. Yet of the two, it is this one you find more difficult. The "sacrifice" of self you understand, nor do you deem this cost too heavy. But a tiny willingness, a nod to God, a greeting to the Christ in you, you find a burden wearisome and tedious, too heavy to be borne. Yet to the dedication to the truth as God established it no sacrifice is asked, no strain called forth, and all the power of Heaven and the might of truth itself is given to provide the means, and guarantee the goal's accomplishment.

24.7. The Meeting Place

How bitterly does everyone tied to this world defend the specialness he wants to be the truth! His wish is law to him, and he obeys. Nothing his specialness demands does he withhold. Nothing it needs does he deny to what he loves. And while it calls to him he hears no other Voice.

How can you know your worth, while specialness claims you instead? How can you fail to know it in his holiness? Seek not to make your specialness the truth, for if it were you would be lost indeed. Be thankful, rather, it is given you to see his holiness because it is the truth. And what is true in him must be as true in you.

The Father keeps what He created safe. You cannot touch it with the false ideas you made, because it was created not by you. Let not your foolish fancies frighten you.

The test of everything on earth is simply this; "What is it for?" The answer makes it what it is for you. It has no meaning of itself, yet you can give reality to it, according to the purpose that you serve. Here you are but means, along with it. God is a Means as well as End. In Heaven, means and end are one, and one with Him. This is the state of true creation, found not within time, but in eternity.

This course makes no attempt to teach what cannot easily be learned. Its scope does not exceed your own, except to say that what is yours will come to you when you are ready. Here are the means and the purpose separate because they were so made and so perceived. Perception does not seem to be a means. And it is this that makes it hard to grasp the whole extent to which it must depend on what you see it for. Perception seems to teach you what you see. Yet it but witnesses to what you taught. It is the outward picture of a wish; an image that you wanted to be true.

Look at yourself, and you will see a body. Look at this body in a different light and it looks different. And without a light it seems that it is gone. Yet you are reassured that it is there because you still can feel it with your hands and hear it move. Here is an image that you

Chapter 24

want to be yourself. It is the means to make your wish come true. It gives the eyes with which you look on it, the hands that feel it, and the ears with which you listen to the sounds it makes. It proves its own reality to you.

Thus is the body made a theory of yourself, with no provisions made for evidence beyond itself, and no escape within its sight. Its course is sure, when seen through its own eyes. It grows and withers, flourishes and dies. And you cannot conceive of you apart from it. You brand it sinful and you hate its acts, judging it evil.

The Son of God retains his Father's Will. The "son of man" perceives an alien will and wishes it were so. And thus, does his perception serve his wish by giving this alien will the appearances of truth. Yet perception can serve another goal. It is not bound to specialness, but by your choice. And it is given you to make a different choice, and use perception for a different purpose. And what you see will serve that purpose well, and prove its own reality to you.

Chapter 25

The Justice of God

Introduction

The Christ in you inhabits not a body. Yet He is in you. And thus it must be that you are not within a body. What is within you cannot be outside. And it is certain that you cannot be apart from what is at the very center of your life. What gives you life cannot be housed in death. No more can you. Christ is within a frame of Holiness whose only purpose is that He may be made manifest to those who know Him not, that He may call to them to come to Him and see Him where they thought their bodies were. Then will their bodies melt away, that they may frame His Holiness in them.

No one who carries Christ in him can fail to recognize the Christ everywhere. Except in bodies. And as long as he believes he is in a body, where he thinks he is, Christ cannot be. And so, he carries Christ unknowingly, and does not make Him manifest. And thus he does not recognize Christ where He is.

The body needs no healing. But the mind that thinks it is a body is sick indeed! And it is here in the mind that Christ sets forth the remedy. His purpose folds the body in His light, and fills it with the Holiness that shines from Him. And nothing that the body says or does but makes Him manifest. To those who know Him not His light carries Him in gentleness and love, to heal their minds. Such is the mission that your brother has for you. And such it must be that your mission is for your brother.

25.1. The Link to Truth

It cannot be that it is hard to do the task that Christ appointed you to do, since it is He Who does it. And in the doing of it will you learn the body merely seems to be the means to do it. For the Mind is His. And so it must be yours. His Holiness directs the body through the mind at one with Him.

CHAPTER 25

Perception tells you, you are manifest in what you see. Behold the body, and you will believe that you are there. And every body that you look upon reminds you of yourself; your sinfulness, your evil, and above all, your death. And would you not despise the one who tells you that you are a sinful body, and seek your brother's death instead? The message and the messenger are one. And you must see your brother as yourself. Set in your brother's holiness, the Christ in him proclaims Himself as you.

Perception is a choice of what you want yourself to be; the world you want to live in, and the state in which you think your mind will be content and satisfied. It chooses where you think your safety lies, at your decision. It reveals yourself to you as you would have you be. And always is it faithful to your purpose, from which it never separates, nor gives the slightest witness unto anything the purpose in your mind upholdeth not. Perception is a part of what it is your purpose to behold, for means and end are never separate.

You are the means for God; not separate, nor with a life apart from His. His life is manifest in you who are His Son. The veil is lifted through its gentleness, and nothing hides the face of Christ from its beholders. You and your brother stand before Him now, to let Him draw aside the veil that seems to keep you separate and apart.

Since you believe that you are separate, Heaven presents itself to you as separate, too. Christ and His Father never have been separate, and Christ abides within your understanding, in the part of you that shares His Father's Will. The Holy Spirit *links* the other part (the tiny, mad desire to be separate, different and special) to the Christ, to make the oneness clear to what is really one. In this world this is not understood, but can be taught.

The Holy Spirit serves Christ's purpose in your mind, so that the aim of specialness can be corrected where the error lies. Because His purpose still is one with Both the Father and the Son, He knows the Will of God and what you really will. But this is understood by mind perceived as one, aware that it is one, and so experienced. It is the Holy Spirit's function to teach you how this oneness is experienced, what you must do that it can be experienced, and where you should go to do it.

It is apparent that a mind so split could never be the Teacher of a Oneness which unites all things within Itself. And so What is within this mind, and does unite all things together, must be its Teacher. Yet must It use the language that this mind can understand, in the condition in which it thinks it is. And It must use all learning to transfer illusions to the truth, taking all false ideas of what you are, and leading you beyond them to the truth that is beyond them.

> *What is the same can not be different,*
> *and what is one can not have separate parts.*

25.2 The Savior from the Dark

Is it not evident that what the body's eyes perceive fills you with fear? Perhaps you think you find a hope of satisfaction there. Perhaps you fancy to attain some peace and satisfaction in the world as you perceive it. Yet it must be evident the outcome does not change. Despite your hopes and fancies, always does despair result. And there is no exception, nor will there ever be. The only value that the past can hold is that you learn it gave you no rewards which you would want to keep. For only thus will you be willing to relinquish it, and have it gone forever.

Is it not strange that you should cherish still some hope of satisfaction from the world you see?

Is it not also true that you have found some hope apart from this; some glimmering, yet dimly seen, that hopefulness is warranted on grounds that are not in this world? And yet your hope that they may still be here prevents you still from giving up the hopeless and unrewarding task you set yourself. Can it make sense to hold the fixed belief that there is reason to uphold pursuit of what has always failed, on grounds that it will suddenly succeed and bring what it has never brought before?

A frame is but a means to hold the picture up, so that it can be seen. A frame that hides the picture has no purpose. It cannot be a frame if it is what you see. Without the picture is the frame without its meaning. Its purpose is to set the picture off, and not itself.

Who hangs an empty frame upon a wall and stands before it, deep in reverence, as if a masterpiece were there to see? Yet if you see your brother as a body, it is but this you do. The masterpiece that God has set within this frame is all there is to see. The body holds it for a while, without obscuring it in any way. Yet what God has created needs no frame, for what He has created He supports and frames within Himself. His masterpiece He offers you to see. And would you rather see the frame instead of this? And see the picture not at all?

The Holy Spirit is the frame God set around the part of Him that you would see as separate. Yet its frame is joined to its Creator, One with Him and with His masterpiece. This is its purpose, and you do not make the frame into the picture when you choose to see it in its place. The frame that God has given it but serves His purpose, not yours apart from His. It is your separate purpose that obscures the picture, and cherishes the frame instead of it. Yet God has set His masterpiece within a frame that will endure forever, when yours has crumbled into dust. But think you not the picture is destroyed in any way. What God creates is safe from all corruption, unchanged and perfect in eternity.

Accept God's frame instead of yours. Its holiness lights up the sinlessness the frame of darkness hides, and casts a veil of light across the picture's face which but reflects the light that shines from it to its Creator. Think not this face was ever darkened because you saw it in a frame of death. God kept it safe that you might look on it, and see the holiness that He has given it.

You and your brother are the same as God Himself is One, and not divided in His Will. And you must have one purpose, since He gave the same to both of you. See not in your brother the sinfulness he sees, but give your brother honor that you may esteem yourself and him. To you and your brother is given the power of salvation, that escape from darkness into light be yours to share; that you may see as one what never has been separate, nor apart from all God's Love as given equally.

25.3. Perception and Choice

To the extent to which you value guilt, to that extent will you perceive a world in which attack is justified. To the extent to which you recognize that guilt is meaningless, to that extent you will perceive attack cannot be justified. This is in accord with perception's fundamental law: You see what you believe is there, and you believe it is there because you want it there. Perception has no other law than this. The rest but stems from this, to hold it up and offer it support. This is perception's form, adapted to this world, of God's more basic law; that love creates itself, and nothing but itself.

Perception rests on choosing.

The Maker of the world of gentleness has perfect power to offset the world of violence and hate that seems to stand between you and His gentleness.

The Son of God could never sin, but he can wish for what would hurt him. And he has the power to think he can be hurt. What could this be except a mis-perception of himself? Is this a sin or a mistake, forgivable or not? Does he need help or condemnation? Is it your purpose that he be saved or damned? Forgetting not that what he is to you will make this choice your future? For you make it now, the instant when all time becomes a means to reach a goal. Make, then, your choice. But recognize that in this choice the purpose of the world you see is chosen, and will be justified.

25.4. The Light You Bring

Minds that are joined and recognize they are, can feel no guilt. For they cannot attack, and they rejoice that this is so, seeing their safety in this happy fact. Their joy is in the innocence they see. And thus they seek for it, because it is their purpose to behold it and rejoice. Everyone seeks for what will bring him joy as he defines it.

Perception's basic law could thus be said, "You will rejoice at what you see because you see it to rejoice." And while you think that suffering and sin will bring you joy, so long will they be there for you to see. Nothing is harmful or beneficent apart from what you wish. It is your wish that makes it what it is in its effects on you. Because you chose it as a means to gain these same effects, believing them to be the bringers of rejoicing and of joy.

Would you not do this for the Love of God? And for yourself? For think what it would do for you. Your "evil" thoughts that haunt you now will seem increasingly remote and far away from you. And they go farther and farther off, because the sun in you has risen that they may be pushed away before the light. They linger for a while, a little while, in twisted forms too far away for recognition, and are gone forever. And in the sunlight you will stand in quiet, in innocence and wholly unafraid. And from you will the rest you found extend, so that your peace can never fall away and leave you homeless. Those who offer peace to everyone have found a home in Heaven the world cannot destroy. For it is large enough to hold the world within its peace.

In you is all of Heaven. Every leaf that falls is given life in you. Each bird that ever sang will sing again in you. And every flower that ever bloomed has saved its perfume and its loveliness for you. What aim can supersede the Will of God and of His Son, that Heaven be restored to him for whom it was created as his only home? How better could your own mistakes be brought to truth than by your willingness to bring the light of Heaven with you, as you walk beyond the world of darkness into light?

25.5. The State of Sinlessness

The state of sinlessness is merely this: The whole desire to attack is gone, and so there is no reason to perceive the Son of God as other than he is. The need for guilt is gone because it has no purpose, and is meaningless without the goal of sin. Attack and sin are bound as one illusion, each the cause and aim and justifier of the other. Each is meaningless alone, but seems to draw a meaning from the other. Attack and sin each depends upon the other for whatever sense it seems to have. And no one could believe in one unless the other were the truth, for each attests the other must be true.

It is no sacrifice that your brother be saved, for by his freedom will you gain your own. To let his function be fulfilled is but the means to let yours be. And so you walk toward Heaven or toward hell, but not alone. How beautiful his sinlessness will be when you perceive it! And how great will be your joy, when your brother is free to offer you the gift of sight God gave to him for you! Your brother has no need but this; that you allow him freedom to complete the task God gave to him. Remembering but this; that what he does you do, along with him. And as you see your brother, so do you define the function he will have for you, until you see him differently and let him be what God appointed that he be to you.

In your brother you see the picture of your own belief in what the Will of God must be for you. In your forgiveness will you understand His Love for you; through your attack you believe He hates you, thinking Heaven must be hell. Look once again upon your brother, not without the understanding that he is the way to Heaven or to hell, as you perceive him. But forget not this; the role you give to him is given you, and you will walk the way you pointed out to him because it is your judgment on yourself.

25.6. The Special Function

The grace of God rests gently on forgiving eyes, and everything they look on speaks of God to the beholder. He who sees with forgiving eyes can see no evil; nothing in the world to fear, and no one who is different from himself. And as he who sees with forgiving eyes loves them, so he looks upon himself with love and gentleness. He would no more condemn himself for his mistakes, than damn another. He who sees with forgiving eyes is not an arbiter of vengeance, nor a punisher of sin. The kindness of his sight rests on himself with all the tenderness it offers others. For he who sees with forgiving eyes would only heal and only bless.

Eyes become used to darkness, and the light of brilliant day seems painful to the eyes grown long accustomed to the dim effects perceived at twilight. And they turn away from sunlight and the clarity it brings to what they look upon. Dimness seems better; easier to see, and better recognized. Somehow the vague and more obscure seems easier to look upon; less painful to the eyes than what is wholly clear and unambiguous. Yet this is not what eyes are for, and who can say that he prefers the darkness and maintain he wants to see?

The wish to see calls down the grace of God upon your eyes, and brings the gift of light that makes sight possible. Would you behold your brother? God is glad to have you look on him. Let your brother no more be lonely, for the lonely ones are those who see no function in the world for them to fill; no place where they are needed, and no aim which only they can perfectly fulfill.

Such is the Holy Spirit's kind perception of specialness; His use of what you made, to heal instead of harm. To each He gives a special function in salvation he alone can fill; a part for only him. Nor is the plan complete until he finds his special function, and fulfills the part assigned to him, to make himself complete within a world where incompletion rules.

Here, where the laws of God do not prevail in perfect form, can he yet do one perfect thing and make one perfect choice. And by this act of special faithfulness to one perceived as other than himself, he learns the gift was given to himself, and so they must be one. Forgiveness is the only function meaningful in time. It is the means the Holy Spirit uses to translate specialness from sin into salvation. Forgiveness is for all. But when it rests on all it is complete, and every function of this world completed with it. Then is time no more. Yet while in time, there is still much to do. And each must do what is allotted him, for on his part does all the plan depend. He has a special part in time for so he chose, and choosing it, he made it for himself. His wish was not denied but changed in form, to let it serve his brother and himself, and thus become a means to save instead of lose.

25.7. The Rock of Salvation

The Holy Spirit has the power to change the whole foundation of the world you see to something else; a basis not insane, on which a sane perception can be based, another world perceived. And one in which nothing is contradicted that would lead the Son of God to sanity and joy. In this real world nothing attests to death and cruelty; to separation and to differences. For here is everything perceived as one, and no one loses that each one may gain.

What is dependable except God's Love? And where does sanity abide except in Him? The One Who speaks for Him can show you this, in the alternative He chose especially for you. It is God's Will that you remember that you abide in God's Love, and so emerge from deepest mourning into perfect joy. Accept the function that has been assigned to you in God's Own plan to show His Son that hell and Heaven are different, not the same. And that in Heaven They are all the same, without the differences which would have made a hell of Heaven and a heaven of hell, had such insanity been possible.

Salvation is rebirth of the idea no one can lose for anyone to gain. Here is sanity restored. And on this single rock of truth can faith in God's eternal saneness rest in perfect confidence and perfect peace. Reason is satisfied, for all insane beliefs can be corrected here. And sin must be impossible, if this is true. This is the rock on which salvation rests, the vantage point from which the Holy Spirit gives meaning and direction to the plan in which your special function has a part. For here your special function is made whole, because it shares the function of the whole.

25.8. Justice Returned to Love

The Holy Spirit can use all that you give to Him for your salvation. But He cannot use what you withhold, for He cannot take it from you without your willingness.

There is a kind of justice in salvation of which the world knows nothing. To the world, justice and vengeance are the same, for sinners see justice only as their punishment, perhaps sustained by someone else, but not escaped. The laws of sin demand a victim. Who it may be makes little difference. But death must be the cost and must be paid. This is not justice, but insanity. Yet how could justice be defined without insanity where love means hate, and death is seen as victory and triumph over eternity and timelessness and life?

It is extremely hard for those who still believe sin meaningful to understand the Holy Spirit's justice. They must believe He shares their own confusion, and cannot avoid the vengeance that their own belief in justice must entail. And so they fear the Holy Spirit, and perceive the "wrath" of God in Him. Nor can they trust Him not to strike them dead with lightning bolts torn from the "fires" of Heaven by God's Own angry Hand. They do believe that Heaven is hell, and are afraid of love. And deep suspicion and the chill of fear comes over them when they are told that they have never sinned. Their world depends on sin's stability.

So do they think the loss of sin a curse. And flee the Holy Spirit as if He were a messenger from hell, sent from above, in treachery and guile, to work God's vengeance on them in the guise of a deliverer and friend. What could He be to them except a devil, dressed to deceive within an angel's cloak. And what escape has He for them except a door to hell that seems to look like Heaven's gate?

Yet justice cannot punish those who ask for punishment, but have a Judge Who knows that they are wholly innocent in truth. In justice, He is bound to set them free, and give them all the honor they deserve and have denied themselves because they are not fair, and cannot understand that they are innocent. Love is not understandable to sinners because they think that justice is split off from love, and stands for something else. And thus is love perceived as weak, and vengeance strong.

You have the right to all the universe; to perfect peace, complete deliverance from all effects of sin, and to the life eternal, joyous and complete in every way, as God appointed for His holy Son. This is the only justice Heaven knows, and all the Holy Spirit brings to earth. Your special function, of seeing the Christ in another, shows you nothing else but perfect justice can prevail for you. And you are safe from vengeance in all forms. The world deceives, but it cannot replace God's justice with a version of its own. For only love is just, and can perceive what justice must accord the Son of God. Let love decide, and never fear that you, in your unfairness, will deprive yourself of what God's justice has allotted you.

25.9. The Justice of Heaven

What can it be but arrogance to think your little errors cannot be undone by Heaven's justice? And what could this mean except that they are sins and not mistakes, forever uncorrectable, and to be met with vengeance, not with justice? Are you willing to be released from all effects of sin? You cannot answer this until you see all that the answer must entail. For if you answer "yes" it means you will forego all values of this world in favor of the peace of Heaven. Not one sin would you retain. And not one doubt that this is possible will you hold dear that sin be kept in place. You mean that truth has greater value now than all illusions. And you recognize that truth must be revealed to you, because you know not what it is.

To give reluctantly is not to gain the gift, because you are reluctant to accept it. It is saved for you until reluctance to receive it disappears, and you are willing it be given you. God's justice warrants gratitude, not fear. Nothing you give is lost to you or anyone, but cherished and preserved in Heaven, where all of the treasures given to God's Son are kept for him, and offered anyone who but holds out his hand in willingness they be received. Nor is the treasure less as it is given out. Each gift but adds to the supply. For God is fair. He does not fight against His Son's reluctance to perceive salvation as a gift from Him. Yet would His justice not be satisfied until it is received by everyone.

The sight of innocence makes punishment impossible, and justice sure. The Holy Spirit's perception leaves no ground for an attack. Only a loss could justify attack, and loss of any kind He cannot see. The world solves problems in another way. It sees a resolution as a state in which it is decided who shall win and who shall lose; how much the one shall take, and how much can the loser still defend. Yet does the problem still remain unsolved, for only justice can set up a state in which there is no loser; no one left unfairly treated and deprived.

Salvation cannot seek to help God's Son be more unfair than he has sought to be. If miracles, the Holy Spirit's gift, were given specially to an elect and special group, and kept apart from others as less deserving, then is He ally to specialness. Everyone is equally entitled to His gift of healing and deliverance and peace. To give a problem to the Holy Spirit to solve for you means that you want it solved. To keep it for yourself to solve without His help is to decide it should remain unsettled, unresolved, and lasting in its power of injustice and attack. No one can be unjust to you, unless you have decided first to be unjust. And then must problems rise to block your way, and peace be scattered by the winds of hate.

The little problems that you keep and hide become your secret sins, because you did not choose to let them be removed for you. And so they gather dust and grow, until they cover everything that you perceive and leave you fair to no one. The unforgiven have no mercy to bestow upon another. That is why your sole responsibility must be to take forgiveness for yourself.

The miracle that you receive, you give. Each one becomes an illustration of the law on which salvation rests; that justice must be done to all, if anyone is to be healed. No one can lose, and everyone must benefit. Each miracle is an example of what justice can accomplish when it is offered to everyone alike. It is received and given equally. It is awareness that giving and receiving are the same. Because it does not make the same unlike, it sees no differences where none exists. And thus it is the same for everyone, because it sees no differences in them. Its offering is universal, and it teaches but one message:

What is God's belongs to everyone, and is his due.

Chapter 26

The Transition

26.1. The "Sacrifice" of Oneness

The world you see is based on "sacrifice" of oneness. It is a picture of complete disunity and total lack of joining. Around each entity is built a wall so seeming solid that it looks as if what is inside can never reach without, and what is out can never reach and join with what is locked away within the wall. Each part must sacrifice the other part, to keep itself complete. For if they joined each one would lose its own identity, and by their separation are their selves maintained.

The little that the body fences off becomes the self, preserved through sacrifice of all the rest of oneness. And all the rest must lose this little part, remaining incomplete to keep its own identity intact. In this perception of yourself the body's loss would be a sacrifice indeed. And for this little to belong to you are limits placed on everything outside, just as they are on everything you think is yours.

And while you see your brother as a body, apart from you and separate in his cell, you are demanding sacrifice of him and you. What greater sacrifice could be demanded than that God's Son perceive himself without his Father? And his Father be without His Son? Yet every sacrifice demands that they be separate and without the other. What witness to the Wholeness of God's Son is seen within a world of separate bodies?

Those who would see the witnesses to truth instead of illusion, merely ask that they might see a purpose in the world that gives it sense and makes it meaningful. Without your special function, this world has no meaning for you. Yet, it can become a treasure house, as rich and limitless as Heaven itself. No *instant* passes here in which your brother's holiness cannot be seen.

CHAPTER 26

Make not his holiness a sacrifice to your belief in sin. You sacrifice your innocence with his, and die each time you see in him a sin deserving death.

Yet every instant can you be reborn, and given life again. In Heaven, God's Son is not imprisoned in a body, nor is sacrificed in solitude to sin. And as he is in Heaven, so must he be eternally and everywhere. He is the same forever. Born again each instant, untouched by time, and far beyond the reach of any sacrifice of life or death.

God's justice rests in gentleness upon His Son, and keeps him safe from all injustice the world would lay upon him. Condemn him not by seeing him within the rotting prison where he sees himself. It is your special function to ensure the door be opened, that he may come forth to shine on you, and give you back the gift of freedom by receiving it of you.

26.2. Many Forms; One Correction

The Holy Spirit offers you release from every problem that you think you have. One mistake is not more difficult for Him to bring to truth than is another. For there is but one mistake; the whole idea that loss is possible, and could result in gain for anyone. If this were true, then God would be unfair; sin would be possible, attack be justified and vengeance fair.

This one mistake, in any form, has one correction. There is no loss; to think there is, is a mistake. You have no problems, though you think you have.

If God is just, then can there be no problems that justice cannot solve. But you believe that some injustices are fair and good, and necessary to preserve yourself. It is these problems that you think are great and cannot be resolved. For there are those you want to suffer loss, and no one whom you wish to be preserved from sacrifice entirely. Consider once again your special function. One is given you to see in your brother his perfect sinlessness. And you will ask no sacrifice of him because you could not will he suffer loss. The miracle of justice you call forth will rest on you as surely as on him. Nor will the Holy Spirit be content until it is received by everyone. For what you give to Him is everyone's, and by your giving it, can He ensure that everyone receives it equally.

God cannot be remembered until justice is loved instead of feared. He cannot be unjust to anyone or anything, because He knows that everything that is belongs to Him, and will forever be as He created it. Nothing He loves but must be sinless and beyond attack. Your special function opens wide the door beyond which is the memory of His Love kept perfectly intact and undefiled. And all you need to do is but to wish that Heaven be given you instead of hell, and every bolt and barrier that seems to hold the door securely barred and locked will merely fall away and disappear. For it is not your Father's Will that you should offer or receive less than He gave, when He created you in perfect love.

26.3. The Borderland

There is a borderland of thought that stands between this world and Heaven. It is not a place, and when you reach it is apart from time. Here is the meeting place where thoughts are brought together; where conflicting values meet and all illusions are laid down beside the truth, where they are judged to be untrue. This borderland is just beyond the gate of Heaven. Here is every thought made pure and wholly simple.

We have referred to it as the real world. And yet there is a contradiction here, in that the words imply a limited reality, a partial truth, a segment of the universe made true. This is because knowledge makes no attack upon perception. Both knowledge and perception are brought together, and only one, knowledge continues past the gate where Oneness is. Salvation is a borderland where place and time and choice have meaning still, and yet it can be seen that place and time and choice are temporary, out of place.

Salvation stops just short of Heaven, for only perception needs salvation. Heaven was never lost, and so cannot be saved. Yet who can make a choice between the wish for Heaven and the wish for hell unless he recognizes they are not the same? This difference that Heaven and hell are not the same is the learning goal this course has set. It will not go beyond this aim. Its only purpose is to teach what is the same and what is different, leaving room to make the only choice that can be made, which is the choice for truth.

26.4. Where Sin Has Left

Nothing in boundless love could need forgiveness. No one forgives unless he has believed in sin, and still believes that he has much to be forgiven. Forgiveness thus becomes the means by which he learns he has done nothing to forgive. Forgiveness always rests upon the one who offers it, until he sees himself as needing it no more. And thus is he returned to his real function of creating, which his forgiveness offers him again.

Forgiveness turns the world of sin into a world of glory, wonderful to see. Each flower shines in light, and every bird sings of the joy of Heaven. There is no sadness and there is no parting here, for everything is totally forgiven. And what has been forgiven must join, for nothing stands between to keep them separate and apart.

What is Heaven but a song of gratitude and love and praise by everything created to the Source of its creation?

Here the Son of God Himself comes to receive each gift that brings him nearer to his home. Not one is lost, and none is cherished more than any other. Each reminds him of his Father's Love as surely as the rest. What but a miracle could change his mind, so that he understands that love cannot be feared? What other miracle is there but this? And what else need there be to make the space between you disappear?

Where sin once was perceived will rise a world that will become an altar to the truth, and you will join the lights of Heaven there, and sing their song of gratitude and praise. And each one joins the singing at the altar that was raised within the tiny spot that sin proclaimed to be its own. And what was tiny then has soared into a magnitude of song in which the universe has joined with but a single voice.

This tiny spot of sin that stands between you and your brother still is holding back the happy opening of Heaven's gate. How little is the hindrance that withholds the wealth of Heaven from you. And how great will be the joy in Heaven when you join the mighty chorus to the Love of God!

26.5. The Little Hindrance

All learning is a help or hindrance to the gate of Heaven. Nothing in between is possible. There are two teachers only, who point in different ways. And you will go along the way your chosen teacher leads. There are but two directions you can take, while time remains and choice is meaningful. For never will another road be made except the way to Heaven. You but choose whether to go toward Heaven, or away to nowhere. There is nothing else to choose.

Nothing is ever lost but time, which in the end is meaningless. For time is but a little hindrance to eternity, quite meaningless to the real Teacher of the world. Yet since you do believe in time, why should you waste it going nowhere, when time can be used to reach a goal as high as learning can achieve? Think not the way to Heaven's gate is difficult at all. Nothing you undertake with certain purpose and high resolve and happy confidence, holding your brother's hand and keeping step to Heaven's song, is difficult to do. But it is hard indeed if you choose to wander off, alone and miserable, down a road that leads to nothing and that has no purpose.

God gave His Teacher to replace the teacher you made, not to conflict with it. And what He would replace has been replaced. You cannot lose your way because there is no way but Gods way, and nowhere can you go except to Him.

Let the dead and gone be peacefully forgotten. Resurrection has come to take death's place. And now you are a part of resurrection, not of death. No past illusions have the power to keep you in a place of death, a vault God's Son entered an instant, to be instantly restored unto his Father's perfect Love. And how can he be kept in chains long since removed and gone forever from his mind?

Now you are shifting back and forth between the past and present. Sometimes the past seems real, as if it were the present. Voices from the past are heard and then are doubted. You are like to one who still hallucinates, but lacks conviction in what he perceives. This is the borderland between the worlds, the bridge between the past and present. Here the shadow of the past remains, but still a present light is dimly recognized. Once it is seen, this light can never be forgotten. It must draw you from the past into the present, where you really are.

Forgive the past and let it go, for it is gone. You stand no longer on the ground that lies between the worlds of past and present. You have gone on, and reached the world that lies at Heaven's gate. There is no hindrance to the Will of God, nor any need that you repeat again a journey that was over long ago. Look gently on your brother, and behold the world in which perception of your hate has been transformed into a world of love.

26.6. The Appointed Friend

Anything in this world that you believe is good and valuable and worth striving for can hurt you, and will do so. Not because it has the power to hurt, but just because you have denied it is but an illusion, and made it real. All belief in sin, in power of attack, in hurt and harm, in sacrifice and death, has come to you. For no one can make one illusion real, and still escape the rest.

Lead not your little life in solitude, with one illusion as your only friend. This is no friendship worthy of God's Son, nor one with which he could remain content. Yet God has given him a better Friend, in Whom all power in earth and Heaven rests. The one illusion that you think is friend obscures His grace and majesty from you, and keeps His friendship and forgiveness from your welcoming embrace. Without Him you are friendless. Seek not another illusionary friend to take His place. There is no other friend. What God appointed has no substitute, for what illusion can replace the truth?

Who dwells with shadows is alone indeed, and loneliness is not the Will of God. Make no illusion friend, for if you do, it can but take the place of Him Whom God has called your Friend. And it is He Who is your only Friend in truth. He brings you gifts that are not of this world, and only He to Whom they have been given can make sure that you receive them.

26.7. The Laws of Healing

All sickness comes from separation.

Guilt asks for punishment, and its request is granted. Not in truth, but in the world of shadows and illusions built on sin. The Son of God perceived what he would see because perception is a wish fulfilled.

Ideas are of the mind. What is projected out, and seems to be external to the mind, is not outside at all, but an effect of what is in, and has not left its source.

No illusion has any truth in it. Yet it can appear some are more true than others, although this clearly makes no sense at all. All that a hierarchy of illusions can show is preference, not reality. What relevance has preference to the truth? Illusions are illusions and are false. Your preference gives them no reality.

Forgiveness is the only function here, and serves to bring the joy this world denies to every aspect of God's Son where sin was thought to rule. Perhaps you do not see the role forgiveness plays in ending death and all beliefs that rise from mists of guilt. Sins are beliefs that you impose between your brother and yourself. This separating off is symbolized, in your perception, by a body which is clearly separate and a thing apart. Yet what this symbol represents is but your wish to be apart and separate.

Forgiveness takes away what stands between your brother and yourself. It is the wish that you be joined with him, and not apart. We call it "wish" because it still conceives of other choices, and has not yet reached beyond the world of choice entirely. Although it falls far short of giving you your full inheritance, it does remove the obstacles that you have placed between the Heaven where you are, and recognition of where and what you are.

What is the Will of God? He wills His Son have everything. This is the miracle by which creation became your function, sharing it with God. It is not understood apart from Him, and therefore has no meaning in this world.

Effects are seen as separate from their source, and seem to be beyond you to control or to prevent. What is thus kept apart can never join.

Cause and effect are one, not separate.

The miracle is possible when cause and effect are brought together, not kept separate. God's Son could never be content with less than full salvation and escape from guilt. For otherwise he still demands that he must make some sacrifice, and thus denies that everything is his, unlimited by loss of any kind. A tiny sacrifice is just the same in its effects as is the whole idea of sacrifice. If loss in any form is possible, then is God's Son made incomplete and not himself.

In every miracle all healing lies, for God gave answer to them all as one. And what is one to Him must be the same. If you believe what is the same is different you but deceive yourself. What God calls One will be forever One, not separate. His Kingdom is united.

Forgiveness is the answer to attack of any kind. So is attack deprived of its effects, and hate is answered in the name of love. To you to whom it has been given to save the Son of God from crucifixion and from hell and death, all glory be forever. For you have power to save the Son of God because his Father willed that it be so. And in your hands does all salvation lie, to be both offered and received as one.

Abide in peace, where God would have you be. And be the means whereby your brother finds the peace in which your wishes are fulfilled. For what can save each one of us can save us all. There is no difference among the Sons of God. The unity that specialness denies will save them all, for what is one can have no specialness. And everything belongs to each of them. No wishes lie between a brother and his own. To get from one is to deprive them all. And yet to bless but one gives blessing to them all as one.

26.8. The Immediacy of Salvation

The one remaining problem that you have is that you see an interval between the time when you forgive, and will receive the benefits of trusting in your brother. This but reflects the little you would keep between you and your brother, that you and he might be a little separate.

There is a distance you would keep apart from your brother, and this space you perceive as time because you still believe you are external to him. This makes trust impossible. From this perception, you cannot conceive of gaining what forgiveness offers now. The interval you think lies in between the giving and receiving of the gift seems to be one in which you sacrifice and suffer loss.

Yet space between you and your brother is apparent only in the present, now, and cannot be perceived in future time. No more can it be overlooked except within the present. Future loss is not your fear. But present joining is your dread. Who can feel desolation except now? A future cause as yet has no effects. And therefore must it be that if you fear, there is a present cause. And it is this that needs correction, not a future state.

Only here and now its cause must be, if its effects already have been judged as fearful. And in overlooking this, is it protected and kept separate from healing. For a miracle is now, it stands already here, in present grace.

Be not content with future happiness. It has no meaning, and is not your just reward. For you have cause for freedom now. Look not to time, but to the little space between you still, to be delivered from.

26.9. For They Have Come

Think but how holy you must be from whom the Voice for God calls lovingly unto your brother, that you may awake in him the Voice that answers to your call! And think how holy he must be when in him sleeps your own salvation, with his freedom joined! However much you wish he be condemned, God is in him. And never will you know He is in you as well while you attack His chosen home, and battle with His host. Regard your brother gently. Look with loving eyes on him who carries Christ within him, that you may behold his glory and rejoice that Heaven is not separate from you.

Forget not that a shadow held between your brother and yourself obscures the face of Christ and memory of God.

Chapter 26

The blood of hatred fades to let the grass grow green again, and let the flowers be all white and sparkling in the summer sun. What was a place of death has now become a living temple in a world of light. Because of the face of Christ and memory of God. It is Their Presence which has lifted holiness again to take its ancient place upon an ancient throne. Because of Them have miracles sprung up as grass and flowers on the barren ground that hate had scorched and rendered desolate. What hate has wrought have They undone. And now you stand on ground so holy Heaven leans to join with it, and make it like itself. The shadow of an ancient hate has gone, and all the blight and withering have passed forever from the land where They have come.

Around you angels hover lovingly, to keep away all darkened thoughts of sin, and keep the light where it has entered in. Your footprints lighten up the world, for where you walk forgiveness gladly goes with you. No one on earth but offers thanks to one who has restored his home, and sheltered him from bitter winter and the freezing cold. And shall the Lord of Heaven and His Son give less in gratitude for so much more?

Now is the temple of the living God rebuilt as host again to Him by Whom it was created. Where He dwells, His Son dwells with Him, never separate. In gentle gratitude do God the Father and the Son return to what is Theirs, and will forever be. Now is the Holy Spirit's purpose done. For They have come! For They have come at last!

26.10. The End of Injustice

Confused perception will block knowledge.

What does it mean if you perceive attack in certain forms to be unfair to you? It means that there must be some forms in which you think it fair. For otherwise, how could some be evaluated as unfair? Some, then, are given meaning and perceived as sensible. And only some are seen as meaningless. And this denies the fact that all are senseless, equally without a cause or consequence, and cannot have effects of any kind. God and His Son's Presence is obscured by any veil that stands between Their shining innocence, and your awareness that it is your own and equally belongs to every living thing along with you. God limits not. And what is limited cannot be Heaven. So it must be hell.

Unfairness and attack are one mistake, so firmly joined that where one is perceived, the other must be seen. You cannot be unfairly treated. The belief you are is but another form of the idea you are deprived by someone not yourself. You have no enemy except yourself, and you are enemy indeed to your brother because you do not know him as yourself. What could be more unjust than that he be deprived of what he is, denied the right to be himself, and asked to sacrifice his Father's Love and yours as not his due?

Beware of the temptation to perceive yourself unfairly treated. In this view, you seek to find an innocence that is not God and God's Son but yours alone, and at the cost of someone else's guilt. Can innocence be purchased by the giving of your guilt to someone else? And is it innocence that your attack on your brother attempts to get? Is it not retribution for your own attack upon the Son of God you seek? Is it not safer to believe that you are innocent of this, and victimized despite your innocence? Whatever way the game of guilt is played, there must be loss. Someone must lose his innocence that someone else can take it from him, making it his own.

The Holy Spirit's purpose is to let the Presence of your holy Guests be known to you. And to this purpose nothing can be added, for the world is purposeless except for this. To add or take away from this one goal is but to take away all purpose from the world and from yourself. And each unfairness that the world appears to lay upon you, you have laid on it by rendering it purposeless, without the function that the Holy Spirit sees. And simple justice has been thus denied to every living thing upon the earth.

The world is fair because the Holy Spirit has brought injustice to the light within, and there has all unfairness been resolved and been replaced with justice and with love. If you perceive injustice anywhere, you need but say:

> *By this do I deny the Presence of the Father and the Son.*
> *And I would rather know of Them than see injustice, which Their Presence shines away.*

CHAPTER 27

THE HEALING OF THE DREAM

27.1. The Picture of Crucifixion

You cannot crucify yourself alone. And if you are unfairly treated, your brother must suffer the unfairness that you see. In your release from sacrifice is his made manifest, in his innocence you find your own.

Whenever you consent to suffer pain, to be deprived, unfairly treated or in need of anything, you but accuse your brother of attack upon God's Son. You hold a picture of your crucifixion before his eyes.

Now in the hands made gentle by the Holy Spirit's touch, He lays a picture of a different you. It is a picture of a body still, for what you really are cannot be seen nor pictured. Yet this different picture of you has not been used for purpose of attack, and therefore never suffered pain at all. It witnesses to the eternal truth that you cannot be hurt, and points beyond itself to both your innocence and your brothers. Show this unto your brother, who will see that every scar is healed, and every tear is wiped away in laughter and in love. And your brother will look on his forgiveness there in this different picture, and with healed eyes will look beyond this picture to the innocence that he beholds in you. Here is the proof that your brother has never sinned; that nothing which his madness bid him do was ever done, or ever had effects of any kind. That no reproach that your brother laid upon his heart was ever justified, and no attack can ever touch him with the poisoned and relentless sting of fear.

Concerns about the body demonstrate how frail and vulnerable is your life; how easily destroyed is what you love. Depression speaks of death, and vanity of real concern with anything at all. What pleasures could there be that will endure?

Chapter 27

The Holy Spirit's picture changes not the body into something it is not. It only takes away from it all signs of accusation and of blamefulness. Pictured without a purpose, the body is seen as neither sick nor well, nor bad nor good. No grounds are offered that it may be judged in any way at all. The body has no life, but neither is it dead. It stands apart from all experience of love or fear. For now it witnesses to nothing yet, its purpose being open, and the mind made free again to choose what the body is for. Now is the body not condemned, but waiting for a purpose to be given, that it may fulfill the function that it will receive.

Into this empty space, from which the goal of sin has been removed, is Heaven free to be remembered. Here its peace can come, and perfect healing take the place of death. Let it have healing as its purpose. Then will it send forth the message it received, and by its health and loveliness proclaim the truth and value that it represents. Let it receive the power to represent an endless life, forever unattacked. And to your brother let its message be, "Behold me, brother, at your hand I live."

27.2. The Fear of Healing

No one can forgive a sin that he believes is real. And what has consequences must be real, because what sin has done is there to see. Forgiveness is not pity, which but seeks to pardon what the forgiver thinks to be the truth. Who can say and mean, "My brother, you have injured me, and yet, because I am the better of the two, I pardon you my hurt." His pardon and your hurt cannot exist together. One denies the other and must make the other false.

To witness sin and yet forgive it is a paradox that reason cannot see. For it maintains what has been done to you deserves no pardon. And by giving sin pardon, you grant your brother mercy but retain the proof he is not really innocent. The sick remain accusers. They cannot forgive their brothers and themselves as well. For no one in whom true forgiveness rests can suffer. He who truly pardons holds not the proof of sin before his brother's eyes. And thus he must have overlooked it and removed it from his own. Forgiveness cannot be for one and not the other. Who forgives is healed. And in his healing lies the proof that he has truly pardoned, and retains no trace of condemnation that he still would hold against himself or any living thing.

Forgiveness is not real unless it brings a healing to your brother and yourself. You must attest his sins have no effect on you to demonstrate they are not real. How else could he be guiltless? And how could his innocence be justified unless his sins have no effect to warrant guilt? In their undoing lies the proof that sins are merely errors. Let yourself be healed that you may be forgiving, offering salvation to your brother and yourself.

How just are miracles! For they bestow an equal gift of full deliverance from guilt upon your brother and yourself. Your healing saves him pain as well as you, and you are healed because you wished him well. This is the law the miracle obeys; that healing sees no specialness at all. It does not come from pity but from love. And love would prove all suffering is but a vain imagining, a foolish wish with no effects. Your health is a result of your desire to see your brother with no blood upon his hands, nor guilt upon his heart made heavy with the proof of sin. And what you wish is given you to see.

27.3. Beyond All Symbols

Symbols which but represent ideas that cannot be, must stand for empty space and nothingness. An empty space that is not seen as filled becomes a silent invitation to the truth to enter, and the truth to make itself at home. For what you leave as vacant, God will fill, and where He is, there must the truth abide. Unweakened power, with no opposite, is what creation is. For truth there are no symbols. Nothing points beyond the truth, for what can stand for more than everything?

As nothingness cannot be pictured, so there is no symbol for totality. Reality is ultimately known without a form, unpictured and unseen. Forgiveness is not yet a power known as wholly free of limits. Yet forgiveness sets no limits you have chosen to impose. Forgiveness is the means by which the truth is represented temporarily. It lets the Holy Spirit make exchange of pictures possible, until the time when "aids" are meaningless and learning done. No learning aid has use when its aim has been accomplished; it is functionless.

Forgiveness vanishes and symbols fade, and nothing that the eyes have ever seen or ears have heard remains to be perceived. A power wholly limitless has come, not to destroy, but to receive its own. Give welcome to the power beyond forgiveness, and beyond the world of symbols and of limitations. God would merely be, and so God merely is.

27.4. The Quiet Answer

In quietness are all things answered, and is every problem quietly resolved. In conflict there can be no answer and no resolution, for conflicts purpose is to make no resolution possible, and to ensure no answer will be plain. A problem set in conflict has no answer, for it is seen in different ways. And what would be an answer from one point of view is not an answer in another light. You are in conflict.

It must also be that, in your state of mind, solution is impossible. Therefore, God must have given you a way of reaching to another *state* of mind in which the answer is already there. Such is the *holy instant*. It is here, in the holy instant that all your problems should be brought and left. Here they belong, for here their answer is. And where the problem's answer is, a problem must be simple and be easily resolved. It must be pointless to attempt to solve a problem where the answer cannot be. Yet just as surely the problem must be resolved, if it is brought to where the answer is.

Attempt to solve no problems but within the holy instant's surety. For there the problem will be answered and resolved. Outside there will be no solution, for there is no answer there that could be found.

An honest question is a learning tool that asks for something that you do not know. It does not set conditions for response, but merely asks what the response should be. But no one in a conflict state is free to ask this question, for he does not want an honest answer where the conflict ends.

Only within the holy instant can an honest question honestly be asked. And from the meaning of the question does the meaningfulness of the answer come. Here is it possible to separate your wishes from the answer, so it can be given you and also be received. The answer is provided everywhere. Yet it is only here it can be heard. The holy instant is the interval in which the mind is still enough to hear an answer that is not entailed within the question asked. It offers something new and different from the question.

In the holy instant, you can bring the question to the answer, and receive the answer that was made for you.

27.5. The Healing Example

The only way to heal is to be healed. Accept the miracle of healing, and it will go forth because of what it is. No one can ask another to be healed. But he can let himself be healed, and thus offer the other what he has received. The Holy Spirit speaks to you. He does not speak to someone else. Yet by your listening His Voice extends, because you have accepted what He says.

If you are afraid of healing, then it cannot come through you. The only thing that is required for a healing is a lack of fear. The fearful are not healed, and cannot heal. This does not mean the conflict must be gone forever from your mind to heal. For if it were, there were no need for healing then. But it does mean, if only for an instant, you love without attack. An instant is sufficient. Miracles wait not on time.

The *holy instant* is the miracle's abiding place. From there, each one is born into this world as witness to a state of mind that has transcended conflict, and has reached to peace. It carries comfort from the place of peace into the battleground, and demonstrates that war has no effects. For all the hurt that war has sought to bring, the broken bodies and the shattered limbs, the screaming dying and the silent dead, are gently lifted up and comforted.

There is no sadness where a miracle has come to heal. What stands apart from you when you accept the blessing that the holy instant brings? Be not afraid of blessing, for the One Who blesses you loves all the world, and leaves nothing within the world that could be feared.

Come to the holy instant and be healed, for nothing that is received there is left behind on your returning to the world. And being blessed you will bring blessing. Life is given you to give the dying world. And suffering eyes no longer will accuse, but shine in thanks to you who blessing gave. The holy instant's radiance will light your eyes, and give them sight to see beyond all suffering and see Christ's face instead. Healing replaces suffering.

Peace be to you to whom is healing offered. And you will learn that peace is given you when you accept the healing for yourself. What occurred within the instant that love entered in without attack will stay with you forever. Your healing will be one of its effects, as will your brother's. Everywhere you go, will you behold its multiplied effects. God thanks you for your healing, for He knows it is a gift of love unto His Son, and therefore is it given unto Him.

27.6. The Witnesses to Sin

Pain demonstrates the body must be real. It is a loud, obscuring voice whose shrieks would silence what the Holy Spirit says, and keep His words from your awareness. Pain compels attention, drawing it away from Him and focusing upon itself. Its purpose is the same as pleasure, for they both are means to make the body real. What shares a common purpose is the same. This is the law of purpose, which unites all those who share in it within itself. Pleasure and pain are equally unreal, because their purpose cannot be achieved. Thus are they means for nothing, for they have a goal without a meaning.

Sin shifts from pain to pleasure, and again to pain. For either witness is the same, and carries but one message: "You are here, within this body, and you can be hurt. You can have pleasure, too, but only at the cost of pain."

The Holy Spirit Who brings the miracle perceives sin's witnesses all as one, and called by the name of fear. As fear is witness unto death, so is the miracle the witness unto life. It is a witness no one can deny, for it is the effects of life it brings. The dying live, the dead arise, and pain has vanished. Yet a miracle speaks not but for itself, but what it represents.

Be you then witness to the miracle, and not the laws of sin. There is no need to suffer any more. But there is need that you be healed, because the suffering and sorrow of the world have made it deaf to its salvation and deliverance.

The resurrection of the world awaits your healing and your happiness, that you may demonstrate the healing of the world. The holy instant will replace all sin if you but carry its effects with you. And no one will elect to suffer more. What better function could you serve than this?

CHAPTER 27

27.7. The Dreamer of the Dream

Suffering is an emphasis upon all that the world has done to injure you. Here is the world's demented version of salvation clearly shown. Like to a dream of punishment, in which the dreamer is unconscious of what brought on the attack against himself, he sees himself attacked unjustly and by something not himself. He is the victim of this "something else," a thing outside himself, for which he has no reason to be held responsible. He must be innocent because he knows not what he does, but what is done to him. Yet is his own attack upon himself apparent still, for it is he who bears the suffering. And he cannot escape because its source is seen outside himself.

Now you are being shown you can escape. All that is needed is you look upon the problem as it is, and not the way that you have set it up. How could there be another way to solve a problem that is very simple, but has been obscured by heavy clouds of complication, which were made to keep the problem unresolved? Without the clouds the problem will emerge in all its primitive simplicity. The choice will not be difficult, because the problem is absurd when clearly seen. No one has difficulty making up his mind to let a simple problem be resolved if it is seen as hurting him, and also very easily removed.

The "reasoning" by which the world is made is simply this: "You, my brother, are the cause of what I do. Your presence justifies my wrath, and you exist and think apart from me. While you attack I must be innocent. And what I suffer from is your attack." No one who looks upon this "reasoning" exactly as it is could fail to see it does not follow and it makes no sense. Yet it seems sensible, because it looks as if the world were hurting you. And so it seems as if there is no need to go beyond the obvious in terms of cause.

There is indeed a need. The world's escape from condemnation is a need which those within the world are joined in sharing. Yet they do not recognize their common need. Vengeance must have a focus. Otherwise is the avenger's knife in his own hand, and pointed to himself. And he must see it in another's hand, if he would be a victim of attack he did not choose. And thus he suffers from the wounds a knife he does not hold has made upon himself

The part you play in salvaging the world from condemnation is your own escape. Forget not that the witness to the world of evil cannot speak except for what has seen a need for evil in the world. And this need for evil is where your guilt was first beheld. In separation from your brother was the first attack upon yourself begun.

Once you were unaware of what the cause of everything the world appeared to thrust upon you, uninvited and unasked, must really be. This is how all illusions came about. The one who makes illusions does not see himself as making them, and their reality does not depend on him. Whatever cause they have is something quite apart from him, and what he sees is separate from his mind. He cannot doubt his dreams' reality, because he does not see the part he plays in making them and making them seem real.

No one can waken from a dream the world is dreaming for him. He becomes a part of someone else's dream. He cannot choose to waken from a dream he did not make. Helpless he stands, a victim to a dream conceived and cherished by a separate mind. Careless indeed of him this mind must be, as thoughtless of his peace and happiness as is the weather or the time of day. It loves him not, but casts him as it will in any role that satisfies its dream. So little is his worth that he is but a dancing shadow, leaping up and down according to a senseless plot conceived within the idle dreaming of the world.

This world dream is the only picture you can see; the one alternative that you can choose, the other possibility of cause, if you be not the dreamer of your dreams. And this is what you choose if you deny the cause of suffering is in your mind. Be glad indeed it is, for thus are you the one decider of your destiny in time. The choice is yours to make between a sleeping death and dreams of evil or a happy wakening and joy of life.

Awaken and forget all thoughts of death, and you will find you have the peace of God. Yet if the choice is really given you, then you must see the causes of the things you choose between exactly as they are and where they are.

You are the dreamer of the world of dreams. No other cause it has, nor ever will. Nothing more fearful than an idle dream has terrified God's Son, and made him think that he has lost his innocence, denied his Father, and made war upon himself.

Accept the dream He gave instead of yours. It is not difficult to change a dream when once the dreamer has been recognized. Rest in the Holy Spirit, and allow His gentle dreams to take the place of those you dreamed in terror and in fear of death. He brings forgiving dreams, in which the choice is not who is the murderer and who shall be the victim. In the dreams He brings there is no murder and there is no death. The dream of guilt is fading from your sight, although your eyes are closed. A smile has come to lighten up your sleeping face. The sleep is peaceful now, for these are happy dreams.

Dream softly of your sinless brother, who unites with you in holy innocence. And from this dream the Lord of Heaven will Himself awaken His beloved Son. Dream of your brother's kindnesses instead of dwelling in your dreams on his mistakes. Select his thoughtfulness to dream about instead of counting up the hurts he gave. Forgive him his illusions, and give thanks to him for all the helpfulness he gave. And do not brush aside his many gifts because he is not perfect in your dreams.

27.8. The "Hero" of the Dream

The body is the central figure in the dreaming of the world. There is no dream without it, nor does it exist without the dream in which it acts as if it were a person to be seen and be believed. It takes the central place in every dream, which tells the story of how it was made by other bodies, born into the world outside the body, lives a little while and dies, to be united in the dust with other bodies dying like itself. In the brief time allotted it to live, it seeks for other bodies as its friends and enemies. Its safety is its main concern. Its comfort is its guiding rule. It tries to look for pleasure, and avoid the things that would be hurtful. Above all, it tries to teach itself its pains and joys are different and can be told apart.

The body's serial adventures, from the time of birth to dying, are the theme of every dream the world has ever had. The "hero" of this dream will never change, nor will its purpose. Though the dream itself takes many forms, and seems to show a great variety of places and events wherein its "hero" finds itself, the dream has but one purpose, taught in many ways. This single lesson does it try to teach again, and still again, and yet once more; that it is cause and not effect. And you are its effect, and cannot be its cause.

Thus are you not the dreamer, but the dream. And so, you wander idly in and out of places and events that the dream contrives. That this is all the body does is true, for it is but a figure in a dream. But who reacts to figures in a dream unless he sees them as if they were real? The instant that he sees them as they are they have no more effects on him, because he understands he gave them their effects by causing them and making them seem real.

No one asleep and dreaming in the world remembers his attack upon himself. No one believes there really was a time when he knew nothing of a body, and could never have conceived this world as real. He would have seen at once that these ideas are one illusion, too ridiculous for anything but to be laughed away. How serious they now appear to be!

The world you see depicts exactly what you thought you did. Except that now you think that what you did is being done to you. The guilt for what you thought is being placed outside yourself, and on a guilty world that dreams your dreams and thinks your thoughts instead of you. It brings its vengeance, not your own. It keeps you narrowly confined within a body, which it punishes because of all the sinful things the body does within its dream. You have no power to make the body stop its evil deeds because you did not make it, and cannot control its actions, nor its purpose, nor its fate.

The world but demonstrates an ancient truth; you will believe that others do to you exactly what you think you did to them. But once deluded into blaming them you will not see the cause of what they do, because you want the guilt to rest on them. How childish is the petulant device to keep your innocence by pushing guilt outside yourself, but never letting go! It is not easy to perceive the jest, when all around you do your eyes behold its heavy consequences.

In gentle laughter does the Holy Spirit perceive the cause, and looks not to effects. He bids you bring each terrible effect to Him that you may look together on its foolish cause and laugh with Him a while. You judge effects, but He has judged their cause. And by His judgment are effects removed. Perhaps you come in tears. But hear Him say, "My brother, holy Son of God, behold your idle dream, in which this could occur." And you will leave the holy instant with your laughter and your brother's joined with His.

The secret of salvation is but this: that you are doing this unto yourself. No matter what the form of the attack, this still is true. Whoever takes the role of enemy and of attacker, still is this the truth. Whatever seems to be the cause of any pain and suffering you feel, this is still true. For you would not react at all to figures in a dream you knew that you were dreaming. Let them be as hateful and as vicious as they may, they could have no effect on you unless you failed to recognize it is your dream.

This single lesson learned will set you free from suffering, whatever form it takes. The Holy Spirit will repeat this one inclusive lesson of deliverance until it has been learned, regardless of the form of suffering that brings you pain. Whatever hurt you bring to Him He will make answer with this very simple truth. For this one answer takes away the cause of every *form* of sorrow and of pain. And you will understand that miracles reflect the simple statement, "I have done this thing, and it is this I would undo."

Bring, then, all forms of suffering to Him Who knows that every one is like the rest. He sees no differences where none exists, and He will teach you how each one is caused. None has a different cause from all the rest, and all of them are easily undone by but a single lesson truly learned. Salvation is a secret you have kept but from yourself. The universe proclaims it so. Yet to its witnesses you pay no heed at all. For they attest the thing you do not want to know. They seem to keep it secret from you. Yet you need but learn, you chose but not to listen, not to see.

How differently will you perceive the world when this is recognized! When you forgive the world your guilt, you will be free of it.

Chapter 28

The Undoing of Fear

28.1. The Present Memory

The miracle does nothing. All it does is to undo. And thus it cancels out the interference to what has been done. It does not add, but merely takes away. The miracle but shows the past is gone, and what has truly gone has no effects.

All the effects of guilt are here no more. For guilt is over. In its passing went its consequences, left without a cause. Why would you cling to it in memory if you did not desire its effects? Remembering is as selective as perception, being its past tense. It is perception of the past as if it were occurring now, and still were there to see. Memory, like perception, is a skill made up by you to take the place of what God gave in your creation. And like all the things you made, it can be used to serve another purpose, and to be the means for something else. It can be used to heal and not to hurt, if you so wish it be.

The Holy Spirit can indeed make use of memory, for God Himself is there. There is no link of memory to the past. If you would have past there, then there it is. But only your desire made the link to the past, and only you have held memory to a part of *time*.

The Holy Spirit's use of memory is quite apart from time. He does not seek to use it as a means to keep the past, but rather as a way to let it go. And if it seems to serve to cherish ancient hate, and gives you pictures of injustices and hurts that you were saving, then this is what you asked its message be, and that it is. Committed to its vaults, the history of all the body's past is hidden there. All of the strange associations made to keep the past alive, the present dead, are stored within it, waiting your command that they be brought to you, and lived again.

Yet time is but another phase of what does nothing. It works hand in hand with all the other attributes with which you seek to keep concealed the truth about yourself. Time neither takes away nor can restore. And yet you make strange use of it, as if the past had

Chapter 28

caused the present, which is but a consequence in which no change can be made possible because its cause has gone. No change can be made in the present if its cause is past. Only the past is held in memory as you make use of it, and so it is a way to hold the past against the now.

And who would keep a senseless lesson in his mind, when he can learn and can preserve a better one? When ancient memories of hate appear, remember that their cause is gone. And so you cannot understand what they are for. Let not the cause that you would give them now be what it was that made them what they were, or seemed to be. Be glad that it is gone, for this is what you would be pardoned from.

How instantly the memory of God arises in the mind that has no fear to keep the memory away! There is no past to keep its fearful image in the way of glad awakening to present peace.

What better way to close the little gap between illusions and reality than to allow the memory of God to flow across it, making it a bridge an instant will suffice to reach beyond? For God has closed it with Himself. His memory has not gone by, and left a stranded Son forever on a shore where he can glimpse another shore that he can never reach. His Father wills that he be lifted up and gently carried over. He has built the bridge, and it is He Who will transport His Son across it. Have no fear that He will fail in what He wills. Nor that you be excluded from the Will that is for you.

28.2. Reversing Effect and Cause

An empty storehouse, with an open door, holds all your shreds of memories and dreams. Yet if you are the dreamer, you perceive this much at least: that you have caused the dream, and can accept another dream as well. But for this change in *content* of the dream, it must be realized that it is you who dreamed the dreaming that you do not like. It is but an effect that you have caused.

In forgiving dreams is no one asked to be the victim and the sufferer. These are the happy dreams the miracle exchanges for your own.

The dreamer of a dream is not awake, but does not know he sleeps. He sees illusions of himself as sick or well, depressed or happy, but without a stable cause with guaranteed effects. The miracle establishes you dream a dream, and that its content is not true. This is a crucial step in dealing with illusions. No one is afraid of them when he perceives he made them up. The fear was held in place because he did not see that he was author of the dream, and not a figure in the dream.

Like every lesson that the Holy Spirit requests you learn, the miracle is clear. It demonstrates what He would have you learn, and shows you its effects are what you want. In His forgiving dreams are the effects of yours undone, and hated enemies perceived as friends with merciful intent. Their enmity is seen as causeless now, because they did not make it. And you can accept the role of maker of their hate, because you see that it has no effects. Now are you freed from this much of the dream; the world is neutral, and the bodies that still seem to move about as separate things need not be feared.

This world is full of miracles. They stand in shining silence next to every dream of pain and suffering, of sin and guilt. They are the dream's alternative, the choice to be the dreamer, rather than deny the active role in making up the dream. The body is released because the mind acknowledges "this is not done to me, but I am doing this." And thus the mind is free to make another choice instead.

28.3. The Agreement to Join

What waits in perfect certainty beyond salvation is not our concern. The miracle alone is your concern at present. Here is where we must begin. When you accept a miracle, you do not add your dream of fear to one that is already being dreamed. Without support, the dream will fade away without effects. For it is your support that strengthens it.

The end of dreaming is the end of fear. The gap is little, yet it was made to keep you separated, in a body which you see as if it were the cause of pain.

The cause of pain is separation, not the body, which is only its effect. Yet, separation is but empty space, enclosing nothing, doing nothing, and as unsubstantial as the empty place between the ripples that a ship has made in passing by. And covered just as fast, as water rushes in to close the gap, and as the waves in joining cover it. Where is the gap between the waves when they have joined, and covered up the space which seemed to keep them separate for a little while? Where are the grounds for sickness when the minds have joined to close the little gap between them, where the seeds of sickness seemed to grow?

God builds the bridge, but only in the space left clean and vacant by the miracle. The seeds of sickness and the shame of guilt He cannot bridge, for He cannot destroy the alien will that He created not. Let its effects be gone and clutch them not with eager hands, to keep them for yourself. The miracle will brush them all aside, and thus make room for Him Who wills to come and bridge His Son's returning to Himself.

Be not afraid, my child, but let your world be gently lit by miracles. And where the little gap was seen to stand between you and your brother, join him there. And so sickness will now be seen without a cause. The dream of healing in forgiveness lies, and gently shows you that you never sinned. The miracle would leave no proof of guilt to bring you witness to what never was. And in your storehouse it will make a place of welcome for your Father and your Self. The door is open, that all those may come who would no longer starve, and would enjoy the feast of plenty set before them there.

28.4. The Greater Joining

There is a way of finding certainty right here and now. Refuse to be a part of fearful dreams whatever form they take, for you will lose identity in them. You find yourself by not accepting fearful dreams as causing you, and giving you effects. You stand apart from the fearful dream, but not apart from him who dreams them. Thus you separate the dreamer from the dream, and join in one, but let the other go. The dream is but illusion in the mind. And with the mind you would unite, but never with the dream. It is the dream you fear, and not the mind. You see them as the same, because you think that you are but a dream. And what is real and what is but illusion in yourself you do not know and cannot tell apart.

Like you, your brother thinks he is a dream. Think, rather, of him as a mind in which illusions still persist. His body and his dreams but seem to make a little gap, where yours have joined with his.

The Holy Spirit is in both your minds, and He is One, because there is no gap that separates His Oneness from Itself. The gap between your bodies matters not, for what is joined in Him is always One.

The Holy Spirit's function is to take the broken picture of the Son of God and put the pieces into place again. This holy picture, healed entirely, does He hold out to every separate piece that thinks it is a picture in itself. To each He offers his Identity, which the whole picture represents, instead of just a little, broken bit that he insisted was himself. And when he sees this picture he will recognize himself. If you share not your brother's evil dream, this is the picture that the miracle will place within the little gap, left clean of all the seeds of sickness and of sin. And here the Father will receive His Son, because His Son was gracious to himself.

I thank You, Father, knowing You will come to close each little gap that lies between the broken pieces of Your holy Son. Your Holiness, complete and perfect, lies in every one of them. And they are joined because what is in one is in them all. How holy is the smallest grain of sand, when it is recognized as being part of the completed picture of God's Son! The forms the broken pieces seem to take mean nothing. For the whole is in each one. And every aspect of the Son of God is just the same as every other part.

28.5. The Alternate to Dreams of Fear

You share no evil dreams if you forgive the dreamer, and perceive that he is not the dream he made. And so he cannot be a part of yours, from which you both are free. Forgiveness separates the dreamer from the evil dream, and thus releases him. Remember if you share an evil dream, you will believe you are the dream you share. And fearing it, you will not want to know your own Identity, because you think that It is fearful. And you will deny your Self, and walk upon an alien ground which your Creator did not make, and where you seem to be a something you are not. You will make war upon your Self, which seems to be your enemy; and will attack your brother, as a part of what you hate. There is no compromise. You are your Self or an illusion.

Let not your eyes behold a dream; your ears bear witness to illusion. For eyes and ears are senses without sense, and what they see and hear they but report. It is not they that hear and see, but you, who put together every jagged piece, each senseless scrap and shred of evidence, and make a witness to the world you want. Let not the body's ears and eyes perceive these countless fragments seen within the gap that you imagined, and let them persuade their maker his imaginings are real.

You who believe there is a little gap between you and your brother, do you not see that it is here you are as prisoners, in a world perceived to be existing here. The world you see does not exist, because the place where you perceive it is not real. The gap is carefully concealed in fog, and misty pictures rise to cover it with vague uncertain forms and changing shapes, forever unsubstantial and unsure. Yet, in the gap is nothing. Look at the little gap, and you behold the innocence and emptiness of sin when you have lost the fear of recognizing love.

28.6. The Secret Vows

The body behaves in ways you want. It takes no sides and judges not the road it travels. The body perceives no gap, because it does not hate. It can be used for hate, but it cannot be hateful.

The thing you hate and fear and loathe and want, the body does not know. You send it forth to seek for separation and be separate. And then you hate it, not for what it is, but for the uses you have made of it. You shrink from what it sees and what it hears, and hate its frailty and littleness. And you despise its acts, but not your own. It sees and acts for you. It hears your voice. And it is frail and little by your wish. It seems to punish you, and thus deserve your hatred for the limitations that it brings to you. Yet you have made of it a symbol for the limitations that you want your mind to have and see and keep.

The body represents the gap between the little bit of mind you call your own and all the rest of what is really yours. You hate it, yet you think it is your Self, and that, without it, would your Self be lost. This is the secret vow that you have made with every brother who would walk apart. This is the secret oath you take again, whenever you perceive yourself attacked. No one can suffer if he does not see himself attacked, and losing by attack. Unstated and unheard in consciousness is every pledge to sickness. Yet it is a promise to another to be hurt by him, and to attack him in return.

Whoever says, "There is no gap between my mind and yours" has kept God's promise, not his tiny oath to be forever faithful unto death. And by his healing is his brother healed.

28.7. The Ark of Safety

God asks for nothing, and His Son, like Him, need ask for nothing. For there is no lack in him. An empty space, a little gap, would be a lack. And it is only there that he could want for something he has not. A space where God is not, a gap between the Father and the Son is not the Will of Either, Who have promised to be One. God's promise is a promise to Himself, and there is no one who could be untrue to what He wills as part of what He is.

Either there is a gap between you and your brother, or you are as one. There is no in between, no other choice, and no allegiance to be split between the two. A split allegiance is but faithlessness to both, and merely sets you spinning round, to grasp uncertainly at any straw that seems to hold some promise of relief. Yet who can build his home upon a straw, and count on it as shelter from the wind? The body can be made a home like this, because it lacks foundation in the truth. And yet, because it does, it can be seen as not your home, but merely as an aid to help you reach the home where God abides.

What is the sense in seeking to be safe in what was made for danger and for fear? Why burden it with further locks and chains and heavy anchors, when its weakness lies, not in itself, but in the frailty of the little gap of nothingness whereon it stands? What can be safe that rests upon a shadow? Would you build your home upon what will collapse beneath a feather's weight?

Your home is built upon your brother's health, upon his happiness, his sinlessness, and everything his Father promised him. No secret promise you have made instead has shaken the foundation of his home. The winds will blow upon it and the rain will beat against it, but with no effect. The world will wash away and yet this house will stand forever, for its strength lies not within itself alone. It is an ark of safety, resting on God's promise that His Son is safe forever in Himself.

Chapter 29

The Awakening

29.1. The Closing of the Gap

There is no time, no place, no *state* where God is absent. There is nothing to be feared. There is no way in which a gap could be conceived of in the Wholeness that is His. The compromise the littlest gap would represent in His eternal Love is quite impossible. For it would mean His Love could harbor just a hint of hate, His gentleness turn sometimes to attack, and His eternal patience sometimes fail. All this do you believe, when you perceive a gap between your brother and yourself. How could you trust Him, then? For He must be deceptive in His Love.

Here is the fear of God most plainly seen. For love is treacherous to those who fear, since fear and hate can never be apart. He fears to love and loves to hate, and so he thinks that love is fearful; hate is love. This is the consequence the little gap must bring to those who cherish it, and think that the gap is their salvation and their hope.

The fear of God! The greatest obstacle that peace must flow across has not yet gone. This one still remains to block your path, and make the way to light seem dark and fearful, perilous and bleak. You had decided that your brother is your enemy.

It is not love that asks a sacrifice. But fear demands the sacrifice of love, for in love's presence fear cannot abide. For hate to be maintained, love must be feared; and only sometimes present, sometimes gone. Thus is love seen as treacherous, because it seems to come and go uncertainly, and offer no stability to you. You do not see how limited and weak is your allegiance, and how frequently you have demanded that love go away, and leave you quietly alone in "peace."

There is a shock that comes to those who learn their savior is their enemy no more. There is a wariness that is aroused by learning that the body is not real. And there are overtones of seeming fear around the happy message, "God is Love."

Chapter 29

Yet all that happens when the gap is gone is peace eternal. Nothing more than that, and nothing less. Without the fear of God, what could induce you to abandon Him? What toys or trinkets in the gap could serve to hold you back an instant from His Love? Would you allow the body to say "no" to Heaven's calling, were you not afraid to find a loss of self in finding God? Yet can your self be lost by being found?

29.2. The Coming of the Guest

Why does an easy path, so clearly marked that it is impossible to lose the way, seem thorny, rough and far too difficult for you to follow? Until you realize you give up nothing, until you understand there is no loss, you will have some regrets about the path that you have chosen. And you will not see the many gains your choice has offered you. Yet though you do not see the gains, they are there. Their cause has been effected, and they must be present where their cause has entered in.

It has been hopeless to attempt to find the hope of peace upon a battleground. It has been futile to demand escape from sin and pain of what was made to serve the function of retaining sin and pain. For pain and sin are one illusion, as are hate and fear, attack and guilt but one. You are free of pain and sickness, misery and loss, and all effects of hatred and attack. No more is pain your friend and guilt your god, and you should welcome the effects of love.

Your Guest has come. You asked Him, and He came. You did not hear Him enter, for you did not wholly welcome Him. And yet His gifts came with Him. He has laid them at your feet, and asks you now that you will look on them and take them for your own. He needs your help in giving them to all who walk apart, believing they are separate and alone. They will be healed when you accept your gifts, because your Guest will welcome everyone whose feet have touched the holy ground whereon you stand, and where His gifts for them are laid.

You cannot see your Guest, but you can see the gifts He brought. And when you look on them, you will believe His Presence must be there. For what you now can do, could not be done, without the love and grace His Presence holds.

29.3. God's Witnesses

Within the dream of bodies and of death is yet one theme of truth; no more, perhaps, than just a tiny spark, a space of light created in the dark, where God still shines. You cannot wake yourself. Yet you can let yourself be wakened. You can overlook your brother's dreams. So perfectly can you forgive him his illusions he becomes your savior from your dreams. And as you see him shining in the space of light where God abides within the darkness, you will see that God Himself is where your brother's body is. Before this light the body disappears, as heavy shadows must give way to light. The darkness cannot choose that it remain. The coming of the light means it is gone. In glory will you see your brother then, and understand what really fills the gap so long perceived as keeping you apart. There, in its place, God's witness has set forth the gentle way of kindness to God's Son. Whom you forgive is given power to forgive you your illusions. By your gift of freedom is it given unto you.

Make way for love, which you did not create, but which you can extend. On earth this means forgive your brother, that the darkness may be lifted from your mind. When light has come to him through your forgiveness, he will not forget his savior, leaving him unsaved. For it was in your face he saw the light that he would keep beside him, as he walks through darkness to the everlasting light.

How holy are you, that the Son of God can be your savior in the midst of dreams of desolation and disaster. See how eagerly your brother comes, and steps aside from heavy shadows that have hidden him, and shines on you in gratitude and love. He is himself, but not himself alone. And now the light in you must be as bright as shines in him. This is the spark that shines within the dream; that you can help him waken, and be sure his waking eyes will rest on you. And in his glad salvation you are saved.

29.4. Dream Roles

Depression or assault must be the theme of every dream, for they are made of fear. The thin disguise of pleasure and of joy in which depression and assault may be wrapped but slightly veils the heavy lump of fear that is their core. And it is this fear the miracle perceives, and not the wrappings in which it is bound.

The core of dreams the Holy Spirit gives is never one of fear.

29.5. The Changeless Dwelling Place

There is a place in you where this whole world has been forgotten; where no memory of sin and of illusion lingers still. There is a place in you which time has left, and echoes of eternity are heard.

The still infinity of endless peace surrounds you gently in its soft embrace, so strong and quiet, tranquil in the might of its Creator, nothing can intrude upon the sacred Son of God within.

Here is the role the Holy Spirit gives to you who wait upon the Son of God, and would behold him waken and be glad. He is a part of you and you of him, because he is his Father's Son, and not for any purpose you may see in him. Nothing is asked of you but to accept the changeless and eternal that abide in him, for your Identity is there. The peace in you can but be found in him. And every thought of love you offer your brother but brings you nearer to your wakening to peace eternal and to endless joy.

CHAPTER 29

This sacred Son of God is like yourself; the mirror of his Father's Love for you, the soft reminder of his Father's Love by which the Sonship was created and which still abides in him as it abides in you. Be very still and hear God's Voice in your brother, and let It tell you what his function is.

A dream is given you in which your brother is your savior, not your enemy in hate. A dream is given you in which you have forgiven him for all his dreams of death; a dream of hope you share with him, instead of dreaming evil separate dreams of hate.

Forgiving dreams are means to step aside from dreaming of a world outside yourself. And leading finally beyond all dreams, unto the peace of everlasting life.

29.6. Forgiveness and the End of Time

How willing are you to forgive your brother? How much do you desire peace instead of endless strife and misery and pain? These questions are the same, in different form. Forgiveness is your peace, for herein lies the end of separation and the dream of danger and destruction, sin and death; of madness and of murder, grief and loss. This is the "sacrifice" salvation asks, and gladly offers peace instead of this.

You were not born to die. Your function has been fixed by God. Goals are set in time and change, that time might be preserved. Forgiveness does not aim at keeping time, but at its ending, when it has no use. Its purpose ended, it is gone. And where it once held seeming sway is now restored the function God established for His Son in full awareness. Time can set no end to its fulfillment. There is no death because the living share the function their Creator gave to them. Life's function cannot be to die. It must be life's extension, that it be as one forever and forever, without end.

This world will bind your feet and tie your hands and kill your body only if you think that it was made to crucify God's Son. For even though it was a dream of death, you need not let it stand for this to you.

How lovely is the world whose purpose is forgiveness of God's Son! How free from fear, how filled with blessing and with happiness! And what a joyous thing it is to dwell a little while in such a happy place! Nor can it be forgot, in such a world, it is a little while till timelessness comes quietly to take the place of time.

29.7. Seek Not Outside Yourself

Seek not outside yourself. For it will fail, and you will weep each time an idol falls. Heaven cannot be found where it is not, and there can be no peace excepting there. Each idol that you worship when God calls will never answer in His place. There is no other answer you can substitute, and find the happiness His answer brings. Seek not outside yourself. For all your pain comes simply from a futile search for what you want, insisting where it must be found. What if it is not there? Do you prefer that you be right or happy? Be you glad that you are told where happiness abides, and seek no longer elsewhere.

No one who comes to outside idols but must still have hope, some lingering illusion, or some dream that there is something outside of himself that will bring happiness and peace to him. If everything is in him this cannot be so. This is the purpose he bestows upon the body; that it seek for what he lacks, and give him what would make himself complete. And thus he wanders aimlessly about, in search of something that he cannot find, believing that he is what he is not.

Whenever you attempt to reach a goal in which the body's betterment is cast as major beneficiary, you try to bring about your death. For you believe that you can suffer lack, and lack is death. To sacrifice is to give up, and thus to be without and to have suffered loss. And by this giving up is life renounced. Seek not outside yourself. The search implies you are not whole within and fear to look upon your devastation, but prefer to seek outside yourself for what you are.

Idols must fall because they have no life, and what is lifeless is a sign of death. You came to die, and what would you expect but to perceive the signs of death you seek? No sadness and no suffering proclaim a message other than an idol found that represents a parody of life which, in its lifelessness, is really death, conceived as real and given living form. Yet each must fail and crumble and decay, because a form of death cannot be life, and what is sacrificed cannot be whole.

All idols of this world were made to keep the truth within from being known to you, and to maintain allegiance to the dream that you must find what is outside yourself to be complete and happy. It is vain to worship idols in the hope of peace. God dwells within, and your completion lies in Him. No idol takes His place.

Let us forget the purpose of the world the past has given it. For otherwise, the future will be like the past, and but a series of depressing dreams, in which all idols fail you, one by one, and you see death and disappointment everywhere.

You choose your dreams, for they are what you wish, perceived as if it had been given you. Your idols do what you would have them do, and have the power you ascribe to them. And you pursue them vainly in the dream, because you want their power as your own.

Yet where are dreams but in a mind asleep? And can a dream succeed in making real the picture it projects outside itself? Save time, my brother; learn what time is for. Your holy mind is altar unto God, and where He is no idols can abide. The fear of God is but the fear of loss of idols. It is not the fear of loss of your reality. But you have made of your reality an idol, which you must protect against the light of truth. And all the world becomes the means by which this idol can be saved. Salvation thus appears to threaten life and offer death.

It is not so. Salvation seeks to prove there is no death, and only life exists. The sacrifice of death is nothing lost. An idol cannot take the place of God. Let Him remind you of His Love for you, and do not seek to drown His Voice in chants of deep despair to idols of yourself. Seek not outside your Father for your hope. For hope of happiness is not despair.

29.8. The Anti-Christ

What is an idol? Do you think you know? For idols are unrecognized as such, and never seen for what they really are. That is the only power that they have. Their purpose is obscure, and idols are feared and worshiped, both, because you do not know what they are for, and why they have been made. An idol is an image of your brother that you would value more than what he is. Idols are made that he may be replaced, no matter what their form. And it is this replacement of your brother's value that never is perceived and recognized. Be it a body or a thing, a place, a situation or a circumstance, an object owned or wanted, or a right demanded or achieved, the idol is the same.

Let not the idol's form deceive you. Idols are but substitutes for your reality. In some way, you believe they will complete your little self, for safety in a world perceived as dangerous, with forces massed against your confidence and peace of mind. They have the power to supply your lacks, and add the value that you do not have. No one believes in idols who has not enslaved himself to littleness and loss. And thus must seek beyond his little self for strength to raise his head, and stand apart from all the misery the world reflects.

An idol is a false impression, or a false belief; some form of anti-Christ, that constitutes a gap between the Christ and what you see. An idol is a wish, made tangible and given form, and thus perceived as real and seen outside the mind. Yet it is still a thought, and cannot leave the mind that is its source. Nor is its form apart from the idea it represents. All forms of anti-Christ oppose the Christ. And fall before His face like a dark veil that seems to shut you off from Him, alone in darkness. Yet the light is there. A cloud does not put out the sun. No more a veil can banish what it seems to separate, nor darken by one speck the light itself.

This world of idols is a veil across the face of Christ, because its purpose is to separate your brother from yourself. A dark and fearful purpose, yet a thought without the power to change one blade of grass from something living to a sign of death. Its form is nowhere, for its source abides within your mind where God abideth not.

What is an idol? Nothing! It must be believed before it seems to come to life, and given power that it may be feared. Its life and power are its believer's gift, and this is what the miracle restores to what has life and power worthy of the gift of Heaven and eternal peace.

The miracle does not restore the truth, it merely lifts the veil, and lets the truth shine unencumbered.

An idol is established by belief, and when it is withdrawn the idol "dies." This is the anti-Christ; the strange idea there is a power past omnipotence, a place beyond the infinite, a time transcending the eternal. Here the world of idols has been set by the idea this power and place and time are given form, and shape the world where the impossible has happened. Here the deathless come to die, the all-encompassing to suffer loss, the timeless to be made the slaves of time. Here does the changeless change; the peace of God, forever given to all living things, give way to chaos. And the Son of God, as perfect, sinless and as loving as his Father, come to hate a little while; to suffer pain and finally to die.

Nothing and nowhere must an idol be, while God is everything and everywhere.

What purpose has an idol, then? What is it for? This is the only question that has many answers, each depending on the one of whom the question has been asked. The world believes in idols. Each worshipper of idols harbors hope his special deities will give him more than other men possess. It must be more. It does not really matter more of what; more beauty, more intelligence, more wealth, or even more affliction and more pain. But more of something, is an idol for. And when one fails another takes its place, with hope of finding more of something else. Be not deceived by forms the "something" takes.

If Heaven is within, why would you seek for idols that would make of Heaven less, to give you more than God bestowed upon your brother and on you, as one with Him? God gave you all there is. And to be sure you could not lose it, did He also give the same to every living thing as well. And thus is every living thing a part of you, as of Himself. No idol can establish you as more than God.

29.9. The Forgiving Dream

There can be no salvation in the dream as you are dreaming it. For idols must be part of it, to save you from what you believe you have accomplished, and have done to make you sinful, and put out the light within you. Little child, the light is there. You do but dream, and idols are the toys you dream you play with. Who has need of toys but children? They pretend they rule the world, and give their toys the power to move about, and talk and think and feel and speak for them. Yet everything their toys appear to do is in the minds of those who play with them. But they are eager to forget that they made up the dream in which their toys are real, nor recognize their wishes are their own.

Nightmares are childish dreams. The toys have turned against the child who thought he made them real. Yet can a dream attack? Or can a toy grow large and dangerous and fierce and wild? This does the child believe, because he fears his thoughts and gives them to the

Chapter 29

toys instead. And their reality becomes his own, because they seem to save him from his thoughts. Yet do they keep his thoughts alive and real, but seen outside himself, where they can turn against him for his treachery to them. He thinks he needs them that he may escape his thoughts, because he thinks the thoughts are real.

There is a time when childhood should be passed and gone forever. Seek not to retain the toys of children. Put them all away, for you have need of them no more.

Forgiving dreams remind you that you live in safety and have not attacked yourself. So do your childish terrors melt away, and dreams become a sign that you have made a new beginning, not another try to worship idols and to keep attack. Forgiving dreams are kind to everyone who figures in the dream. And so they bring the dreamer full release from dreams of fear.

Chapter 30

The New Beginning

Introduction

The new beginning now becomes the focus of the curriculum. The goal is clear, but now you need specific methods for attaining it. The speed by which it can be reached depends on this one thing alone; your willingness.

30.1. Rules for Decision

Decisions are continuous. You do not always know when you are making them. Think about the kind of day you want, and tell yourself there is a way in which this very day can happen.

You can begin a happy day with the determination not to make decisions by yourself. This seems to be a real decision in itself. And yet, you cannot make decisions by yourself. The only question really is with what you choose to make them. For they are made with idols or with God. And you ask help of anti-Christ or Christ, and which you choose will join with you and tell you what to do.

Your day is not at random. It is set by what you choose to live it with, and how the "friend" whose counsel you have sought perceives your happiness. You always ask advice before you can decide on anything. You and your adviser must agree on what you want before it can occur. It is but this agreement that permits all things to happen. Nothing can be caused without some form of union, be it with a dream of judgment or the Voice for God.

Decisions cause results because they are not made in isolation. They are made by you and your "adviser", for yourself and for the world as well. The day you want, you offer to the world, for it will be what you have asked for, and will reinforce the *rule* of your adviser in the world. Whose kingdom is the world for you today? What kind of day will you decide to have?

30.2. Freedom of Will

Do you not understand that to oppose the Holy Spirit is to fight yourself? He tells you but your *will*; He speaks for you. In His Divinity is but your own. God is no enemy to you.

How wonderful it is to do your will! For that is freedom. Unless you do your will you are not free. God would not have His Son made prisoner to what he does not want. He joins with you in willing you be free. And to oppose Him is to make a choice against yourself, and choose that you be bound.

Look once again upon your enemy, the one you chose to hate instead of love. For thus was hatred born into the world, and thus the rule of fear established there. Now hear God speak to you, through Him Who is His Voice and yours as well, reminding you that it is not your will to hate and be a prisoner to fear, a slave to death, a little creature with a little life. Your will is boundless; it is not your will that it be bound.

What cause have you for anger in a world that merely waits your blessing to be free? If you be prisoner, then God Himself could not be free. This world awaits the freedom you will give when you have recognized that you are free. But you will not forgive the world until you have forgiven Him Who gave your will to you. For it is by your will the world is given freedom. Nor can you be free apart from Him Whose holy Will you share.

God turns to you to ask the world be saved, for by your own salvation is it healed. And no one walks upon the earth but must depend on your decision, that your brother learn death has no power over him, because he shares your freedom as he shares your will. It is your will to heal him, and because you have decided with him, he is healed. And now is God forgiven, for you chose to look upon your brother as a friend.

30.3. Beyond All Idols

Idols are quite specific. But your will is universal, being limitless. And so it has no form, nor is content for its expression in the terms of form. Idols are limits. They are the belief that there are forms that will bring happiness, and that, by limiting, is all attained. It is as if you said, "I have no need of everything. This little thing I want, and it will be as everything to me". And this must fail to satisfy, because it is your will that everything be yours. Decide for idols and you ask for loss. Decide for truth and everything is yours.

It is not form you seek. What form can be a substitute for God the Father's Love? What form can take the place of all the love in the Divinity of God the Son? What idol can make two of what is one? And can the limitless be limited? You do not want an idol. It is not your will to have one. It will not bestow on you the gift you seek. When you decide upon the form of what you want, you lose the understanding of its purpose. So you see your will within the idol, thus reducing it to a specific form. Yet this could never be your will, because what shares in all creation cannot be content with small ideas and little things.

Behind the search for every idol lies the yearning for completion. Wholeness has no form because it is unlimited. To seek a special person or a thing to add to you to make yourself complete, can only mean that you believe some form is missing. And by finding this, you will achieve completion in a form you like. This is the purpose of an idol; that you will not look beyond it, to the source of the belief that you are incomplete. Only if you had sinned could this be so. For sin is the idea you are alone and separated off from what is whole. And thus it would be necessary for the search for wholeness to be made beyond the boundaries of limits on yourself.

It never is the idol that you want. But what you think it offers you, you want indeed, and have the right to ask for. Nor could it be possible it be denied. Your will to be complete is but God's Will, and this is given you by being His. God knows not form. He cannot answer you in terms that have no meaning. And your will could not be satisfied with empty forms, made but to fill a gap that is not there. It is not this you want. Creation gives no separate person and no separate thing the power to complete the Son of God. What idol can be called upon to give the Son of God what he already has?

Beyond all idols is the Thought God holds of you. Completely unaffected by the turmoil and the terror of the world, the dreams of birth and death that here are dreamed, the myriad of forms that fear can take; quite undisturbed, the Thought God holds of you remains exactly as it always was. Surrounded by a stillness so complete no sound of battle comes remotely near, it rests in certainty and perfect peace.

30.4. The Truth behind Illusions

You will attack what does not satisfy, and thus you will not see you made it up. You always fight illusions. For the truth behind them is so lovely and so still in loving gentleness, were you aware of it you would forget defensiveness entirely, and rush to its embrace. The truth could never be attacked. And this you knew when you made idols. They were made that this might be forgotten. You attack but false ideas, and never truthful ones. All idols are the false ideas you made to fill the gap you think arose between yourself and what is true. And you attack them for the things you think they represent. What lies beyond them cannot be attacked.

Appearances deceive because they are appearances, and not reality. Dwell not on them in any form. Appearances but obscure reality, and they bring fear because they hide the truth.

Appearances can but deceive the mind that wants to be deceived. And you can make a simple choice that will forever place you far beyond deception. You need not concern yourself with how this will be done, for this you cannot understand. But you will understand that mighty changes have been quickly brought about, when you decide one very simple thing; you do not want whatever you believe an idol gives. For thus the Son of God declares that he is free of idols. And thus is he free.

Here does the dream of separation start to fade and disappear. For here the gap that is not there begins to be perceived without the toys of terror that you made. No more than this is asked. Be glad indeed salvation asks so little, not so much. It asks for nothing in reality. And even in illusions salvation but asks forgiveness be the substitute for fear. Such is the rule for happy dreams. The gap is emptied of the toys of fear, and then the gap's unreality is plain. Dreams are for nothing. And the Son of God can have no need of them. Dreams offer him no single thing that he could ever want. He is delivered from illusions by his will, and but restored to what he is.

30.5. The Only Purpose

The real world is the state of mind in which the only purpose of the world is seen to be forgiveness. Fear is not its goal, for the escape from guilt becomes its aim. The value of forgiveness is perceived and takes the place of idols, which are sought no longer, for their "gifts" are not held dear. No rules are idly set, and no demands are made of anyone or anything to twist and fit into the dream of fear. Instead, there is a wish to understand all things created as they really are. And it is recognized that all things must be first forgiven, and then understood.

Here, in the dream, it is thought that understanding is acquired by attack. There, in the real world, it is clear that by attack is understanding lost. The folly of pursuing guilt as goal is fully recognized. And idols are not wanted there, for guilt is understood as the sole cause of pain in any form. No one is tempted by its vain appeal, for suffering and death have been perceived as things not wanted and not striven for. The possibility of freedom has been grasped and welcomed, and the means by which it can be gained can now be understood. The world becomes a place of hope, because its only purpose is to be a place where hope of happiness can be fulfilled.

How light and easy is the step across the narrow boundaries of the world of fear when you have recognized Whose hand you hold! Within your hand is everything you need to walk with perfect confidence away from fear forever, and to go straight on, and quickly reach the gate of Heaven itself. For He Whose hand you hold was waiting but for you to join Him. Now that you have come, would He delay in showing you the way that He must walk with you?

An ancient hate is passing from the world. And with it goes all hatred and all fear. Look back no longer, for what lies ahead is all you ever wanted in your heart. Give up the world! But not to sacrifice. You never wanted it. What "happiness" have you sought here, that did not bring you pain? Joy has no cost. It is your sacred right, and what you pay for joy, is not happiness.

30.6. The Justification for Forgiveness

Anger is never justified. Attack has no foundation. It is here escape from fear begins, and will be made complete. Here is the real world given in exchange for dreams of terror. For it is on this forgiveness rests, and is but natural.

No one who sees himself as guilty can avoid the fear of God. But he is saved from this dilemma if he can forgive. The mind must think of its Creator as it looks upon itself. If you can see your brother merits pardon, you have learned forgiveness is your right as much as his. Nor will you think that God intends for you a fearful judgment that your brother does not merit. For it is the truth that you can merit neither more nor less than he.

You must forgive God's Son entirely. Or you will keep an image of yourself that is not whole, and will remain afraid to look within and find escape from every idol there. Salvation rests on faith, there cannot be some forms of guilt that you cannot forgive. And so there cannot be appearances that have replaced the truth about God's Son.

God's Son is perfect, or he cannot be God's Son. Nor will you know him, if you think he does not merit the escape from guilt in all its consequences and its forms. There is no way to think of him but this, if you would know the truth about yourself.

I thank You, Father, for Your perfect Son, and in his glory will I see my own.

Here is the joyful statement that there are no forms of evil that can overcome the Will of God; the glad acknowledgment that guilt has not succeeded by your wish to make illusions real.

Look on your brother with this hope in you, and you will understand he could not make an error that could change the truth in him. It is not difficult to overlook mistakes that have been given no effects.

30.7. The New Interpretation

Would God have left the meaning of the world to your interpretation? If He had, it has no meaning. For it cannot be that meaning changes constantly, and yet is true. The Holy Spirit looks upon the world as with one purpose, *changelessly* established.

A common purpose is the only means whereby perception can be stabilized, and one interpretation given to the world and all experiences here. In this shared purpose is one judgment shared by everyone and everything you see. You do not have to judge, for you have learned one meaning has been given everything, and you are glad to see it everywhere. It cannot change because you would perceive it everywhere, unchanged by circumstance. And so you offer it to all events, and let them offer you stability.

Escape from judgment simply lies in this; all things have but one shared purpose, which you share with all the world. And nothing in the world can be opposed to one purpose, for it belongs to everything, as it belongs to you. In single purpose is the end of all ideas of sacrifice, which must assume a different purpose for the one who gains and him who loses. There could be no thought of sacrifice apart from this idea. And it is this idea of different goals that makes perception shift and meaning change. In one united goal does this become impossible, for your agreement makes interpretation stabilize and last.

How can communication really be established while the symbols that are used mean different things? The Holy Spirit's goal gives one interpretation, meaningful to you and to your brother. Thus can you communicate with him, and he with you. In symbols that you both can understand the sacrifice of meaning is undone. Look not to separate dreams for meaning. Only dreams of pardon can be shared. They mean the same to both of you.

We have one Interpreter. And through His use of symbols are we joined, so that symbols mean the same to all of us. Our common language lets us speak to all our brothers, and to understand with our brothers that forgiveness has been given to us all.

30.8. Changeless Reality

Appearances deceive, but can be changed. Reality is changeless. It does not deceive at all, and if you fail to see beyond appearances you are deceived. For everything you see will change, and yet you thought it real before, and now you think it real again. Reality is thus reduced to form, and capable of change. Reality is changeless. It is this that makes it real, and keeps it separate from all appearances. It must transcend all form to be itself. It cannot change.

Because reality is changeless, is a miracle already there to heal all things that change, and offer them to you to see in happy form, devoid of fear. It will be given you to look upon your brother thus. But not while you would have it otherwise in some respects. For this but means you would not have him healed and whole. The Christ in your brother is perfect. Is it this that you would look upon? Then let there be no dreams about him that you would prefer to seeing this. And you will see the Christ in him because you let Him come to you. And when He has appeared to you, you will be certain you are like Him, for He is the changeless in your brother and in you.

This will you look upon when you decide there is not one appearance you would hold in place of what your brother really is. Let no temptation to prefer a dream allow uncertainty to enter here. Be not made guilty and afraid when you are tempted by a dream of what your brother is. But do not give it power to replace the changeless Christ in your brother in your sight of him. There is no false appearance but will fade, if you request a miracle instead. There is no pain from which your brother is not free, if you would have him be but what he is. Why should you fear to see the Christ in him? You but behold yourself in what you see. As your brother is healed are you made free of guilt, for his appearance is your own to you.

Chapter 31

The Final Vision

31.1. The Simplicity of Salvation

The egoic lessons you have taught yourself have been so over learned and fixed that they rise like heavy curtains to obscure the simple and the obvious. The world began with one strange egoic lesson, powerful enough to render God forgotten, and His Son an alien to himself, in exile from the home where God Himself established him. You who have taught yourself the Son of God is guilty!

Yet you will learn the Voice of truth's lessons, for their learning is the only purpose for your learning skill the Holy Spirit sees in all the world. His simple lessons in forgiveness have a power mightier than yours, because they call from God and from your Self, the Christ, to you.

The lessons to be learned are only two. You are either guilty or guiltless. Each has its outcome in a different world. And each world follows surely from its source.

> [1] The outcome of the lesson that *God's Son is guilty* is the world you see. It is a world of terror and despair. Nor is there hope of happiness in it. There is no plan for safety you can make that ever will succeed. There is no joy that you can seek for here, and hope to find.

Yet this is not the only outcome which your learning can produce. However much you may have over learned your chosen task, the lesson that reflects the Love of God is stronger still. And you will learn God's Son is innocent, and see another world.

> [2] The outcome of the lesson that *God's Son is guiltless* is a world in which there is no fear, and everything is lit with hope and sparkles with a gentle friendliness. Nothing but calls to you in soft appeal to be your friend, and let it join with you. And never does a call remain unheard, misunderstood, nor left unanswered in the selfsame tongue in which the call was made. And you will understand it was this call

Chapter 31

that everyone and everything within the world has always made, but you had not perceived it as it was. And now you see you were mistaken. You had been deceived by *forms* the call was hidden in. And so you did not hear it, and had lost a friend who always wanted to be part of you. The soft eternal calling of each part of God's creation to the whole is heard throughout the world this second lesson brings.

The Christ in you remembers God with all the certainty with which the Christ knows God's Love. But only if His Son is innocent can He be Love. For God were fear indeed if His Son whom God created innocent could be a slave to guilt. God's perfect Son remembers his creation. But in guilt he has forgotten what he really is.

The fear of God results as surely from the lesson that His Son is guilty as God's Love must be remembered when he learns his innocence.

What is temptation but a wish to make the wrong decision on what you would learn, and have an outcome that you do not want? It is the recognition that it is a state of mind unwanted that becomes the means whereby the choice is reassessed; another outcome seen to be preferred. You are deceived if you believe you want disaster and disunity and pain. Hear not the call for this within yourself. But listen, rather, to the deeper call beyond it that appeals for peace and joy. And all the world will give you joy and peace. For as you hear, you answer. And behold! Your answer is the proof of what you learned. Its outcome is the world you look upon.

Let us be still an instant, and forget all things we ever learned, all thoughts we had, and every preconception that we hold of what things mean and what their purpose is. Let us remember not our own ideas of what the world is for. We do not know. Let every image held of everyone be loosened from our minds and swept away.

Be innocent of judgment, unaware of any thoughts of evil or of good that ever crossed your mind of anyone. Now do you know your brother not. But you are free to learn of him, and learn of him anew. Now is he born again to you, and you are born again to him, without the past that sentenced him to die, and you with him. Now is your brother free to live as you are free, because an ancient learning passed away, and left a place for truth to be reborn.

31.2. Walking with Christ

Let us review again what seems to stand between you and the truth of what you are.

The leader and the follower emerge as separate roles, each seeming to possess advantages you would not want to lose. So in their fusion there appears to be the hope of satisfaction and of peace. You see yourself divided into both these roles, forever split between the two. And every friend or enemy becomes a means to help you save yourself from this.

You hate the brother you gave the leader's role when you would have it, and you hate as well his not assuming it at times you want to let the follower in you arise, and give away the role of leadership. And this "role playing" is what you made your brother for, and learned to think that this his purpose is. Unless he serves it, he has not fulfilled the function that was given him by you. And thus he merits death, because he has no purpose and no usefulness to you.

And what of your brother? What does he want of you? What could he want, but what you want of him? Herein is life as easily as death, for what you choose you choose as well for him. Two calls, death or life, you make to him, as he to you. Between these two is choice, because from them there is a different outcome. If he calls for death or calls for life, for hate or for forgiveness, is not the same in outcome. Hear the choice for death, and you are separate from him and are lost. But hear the choice for life, and you join with him and in your answer is salvation found. The voice you hear in him is but your own. What does he ask you for? And listen well! For he is asking what will come to you, because you see an image of yourself and hear your voice requesting what you want.

Before you answer, pause to think of this:

The answer that I give my brother is what I am asking for,
and what I learn of him is what I learn about myself.

Then let us wait an instant and be still, forgetting everything we thought we heard; remembering how much we do not know. This brother neither leads nor follows us, but walks beside us on the selfsame road. He is like us, as near or far away from what we want as we will let him be. We make no gains he does not make with us, and we fall back if he does not advance. Take not his hand in anger but in love, for in his progress do you count your own.

Together is your joint inheritance remembered and accepted by you both. Alone it is denied to both of you. Is it not clear that while you still insist on leading or on following, you think you walk alone, with no one by your side? This is the road to nowhere, for the light cannot be given while you walk alone, and so you cannot see which way you go. And thus there is confusion, and a sense of endless doubting as you stagger back and forward in the darkness and alone.

31.3. The Self-Accused

Only the self-accused condemn. As you prepare to make a choice that will result in different outcomes, there is first one thing that must be overlearned. It must become a habit of response so typical of everything you do that it becomes your first response to all temptation, and to every situation that occurs. Learn that only the self-accused condemn, and learn it well, for it is here delay of happiness is shortened by a span of time you cannot

Chapter 31

realize: *You never hate your brother for his sins, but only for your own.* Whatever form his sins appear to take, it but obscures the fact that you believe them to be yours, and therefore meriting a "just" attack.

Why should your brother's sins be sins, if you did not believe they could not be forgiven in you? Why are they real in him, if you did not believe that they are your reality? And why do you attack your brother's sins everywhere, except that you must hate yourself? Are you a sin? You answer "yes" whenever you attack, for by attack do you assert that you are guilty, and must give as you deserve. And what can you deserve but what you are? If you did not believe that you deserved attack, it never would occur to you to give attack to anyone at all. Why should you? What would be the gain to you? What could the outcome be that you would want?

Sins are in bodies. They are not perceived in minds. They are not seen as purposes, but actions. Bodies act, and minds do not. And therefore must the body be at fault for what it does. The body is not seen to be a passive thing, obeying your commands, and doing nothing of itself at all. If you are sin you are a body, for the mind acts not. And purpose must be in the body, not the mind. The body must act on its own, and motivate itself. If you are sin you lock the mind within the body, and you give the mind's purpose to its prison house, which acts instead of it. A jailer does not follow orders, but enforces orders on the prisoner.

Yet is the body prisoner, and not the mind? The body thinks no thoughts. It has no power to learn, to pardon, nor enslave. It gives no orders that the mind need serve, nor sets conditions that it must obey. The body holds in prison but the willing mind that would abide in it. The body sickens at the bidding of the mind that would become its prisoner. And it grows old and dies, because that mind is sick within itself. Learning is all that causes change. And so the body, where no learning can occur, could never change unless the mind preferred the body change in its appearances, to suit the purpose given by the mind. For mind can learn, and there is all change made.

The mind that thinks it is a sin has but one purpose; that the body be the source of sin, to keep the mind in the prison house of the body, the mind chose and guards and holds itself at bay, a sleeping prisoner to the snarling dogs of hate and evil, sickness and attack; of pain and age, of grief and suffering. Here are the thoughts of sacrifice preserved, for here guilt rules, and orders that the world be like itself; a place where nothing can find mercy, nor survive the ravages of fear except in murder and in death. For here are you made sin, and sin cannot abide the joyous and the free, for they are enemies which sin must kill. In death is sin preserved, and those who think that they are sin must die for what they think they are.

Let us be glad that you will see what you believe, and that it has been given you to change what you believe.

31.4. The Real Alternative

Real choice is no illusion. But the world has no real choice to offer. All the world's roads but lead to disappointment, nothingness and death. There is no choice in its alternatives. Seek not escape from problems here. The world was made that problems could not be escaped. Be not deceived by all the different names the world's roads are given. They have but one end. And each is but the means to gain that end, for it is here that all its roads will lead to disappointment, however differently they seem to start; however differently they seem to go. The end of the world's roads is certain, for there is no choice among them. All of them will lead to death. On some you travel gaily for a while, before the bleakness enters. And on some the thorns are felt at once. The choice is not what will the ending be, but when it comes.

There is no choice where every end is sure. Perhaps you would prefer to try them all, before you really learn they are but one. The roads this world can offer seem to be quite large in number, but the time must come when everyone begins to see how alike they are to one another. All must reach this point, and go beyond it. It is true indeed there is no choice at all within the world. But this is not the lesson in itself. The lesson has a purpose, and in this you come to understand what it is for.

Learn now, without despair, there is no hope of answer in the world. But do not judge the lesson that is but begun with this. Seek not another signpost in the world that seems to point to still another road.

Who would be willing to be turned away from all the roadways of the world, unless he understood their real futility? Is it not needful that he should begin with this, to seek another way instead? For while he sees a choice where there is none, what power of decision can he use? The great release of power must begin with learning where it really has a use. And what decision has power if it be applied in situations without choice?

The learning that -the world can offer but one choice, no matter what its form may be- is the beginning of acceptance that there is a real alternative instead. To fight against this step is to defeat your purpose here. You did not come to learn to find a road the world does not contain. The search for different pathways in the world is but the search for different forms of truth. And this would keep the truth from being reached.

He has not left His Thoughts! But you forgot His Presence and remembered not His Love. No pathway in the world can lead to Him, nor any worldly goal be one with His. What road in all the world will lead within, when every road was made to separate the journey from the purpose it must have, unless it be but futile wandering? All roads that lead away from *what* you are will lead you to confusion and despair.

There is no road that leads away from Him. A journey from yourself does not exist.

Forgive yourself your madness, and forget all senseless journeys and all goal-less aims. They have no meaning. You can not escape from what you are. For God is merciful, and did not let His Son abandon Him. For what He is be thankful, for in that is your escape from madness and from death. Nowhere but where He is can you be found. There is no path that does not lead to Him.

31.5. Self-Concept versus Self

A concept of the self is made by you. It bears no likeness to your Self at all. It is an idol, made to take the place of your reality as Son of God. The concept of the self, the world would teach, is not the thing that it appears to be. Every day a hundred little things make small assaults upon its innocence, provoking it to irritation, and at last to open insult and abuse. On this conception of the self the world smiles with approval, for it guarantees the pathways of the treacherous world are safely kept, and those who walk on them will not escape.

Concepts are learned. They are not natural. Apart from learning they do not exist. They are not given, so they must be made. Not one concept of the world is true, and many come from feverish imaginations, hot with hatred and distortions born of fear. What is a concept but a thought to which its maker gives a meaning of his own? Concepts maintain the world. But they can not be used to demonstrate the world is real. For all of them are made within the world, born in its shadow, growing in its ways and finally "maturing" in its thought. They are ideas of idols, painted with the brushes of the world, which cannot make a single picture representing truth.

A concept of the self is meaningless, for no one here can see what it is for, and therefore cannot picture what it is. Yet is all learning that the world directs begun and ended with the single aim of teaching you this concept of yourself, that you will choose to follow this world's laws, and never seek to go beyond its roads nor realize the way you see yourself. Now must the Holy Spirit find a way to help you see this concept of the self must be undone, if any peace of mind is to be given you.

The concept of the self has always been the great preoccupation of the world. And everyone believes that he must find the answer to the riddle of himself. Salvation can be seen as nothing more than the escape from concepts. It does not concern itself with content of the mind, but with the simple statement that it thinks. And what can think has choice, and can be shown that different thoughts have different consequence. So it can learn that everything it thinks reflects the deep confusion that it feels about how it was made and what it is. And vaguely does the concept of the self appear to answer what it does not know.

Seek not your Self in symbols. There can be no concept that can stand for what you are. What matters it which concept you accept while you perceive a self that interacts with *evil*, and reacts to *wicked* things? Your concept of yourself will still remain quite meaningless. And you will not perceive that you can interact but with yourself. To see a guilty world is but the sign your learning has been guided by the world, and you behold it as you see yourself. The concept of the self embraces all you look upon, and nothing is outside of this perception. If you can be hurt by anything, you see a picture of your secret wishes. Nothing more than this.

You will make many concepts of the self as learning goes along. Each one will show the changes in your own relationships, as your perception of yourself is changed. There will be some confusion every time there is a shift, but be you thankful that the learning of the world is loosening its grasp upon your mind. And be you sure and happy in the confidence that it will go at last, and leave your mind at peace. The role of the accuser will appear in many places and in many forms. And each will seem to be accusing you. Yet have no fear it will not be undone.

The world can teach no images of you unless you want to learn them. There will come a time when images have all gone by, and you will see you know not what you are. It is to this unsealed and open mind that truth returns, unhindered and unbound. Where concepts of the self have been laid by is truth revealed exactly as it is. When every concept has been raised to doubt and question, and been recognized as made on no assumptions that would stand the light, then is the truth left free to enter in its sanctuary, clean and free of guilt. There is no statement that the world is more afraid to hear than this:

> *I do not know the thing I am, and therefore do not know what I am doing,*
> *where I am, or how to look upon the world or on myself.*
> *Yet in this learning is salvation born.*
> *And What you are will tell you of Itself.*

31.6. Recognizing the Spirit

You see the flesh or recognize the spirit. There is no compromise between the two. What you decide in this determines all you see and think is real and hold as true. On this one choice does all your world depend, for here have you established what you are, as flesh or spirit in your own belief. If you choose flesh, you never will escape the body as your own reality, for you have chosen that you want it so. But choose the spirit, and all Heaven bends to touch your eyes and bless your holy sight, that you may see the world of flesh no more except to heal and comfort and to bless.

CHAPTER 31

Salvation is undoing. If you choose to see the body, you behold a world of separation, unrelated things, and happenings that make no sense at all. This one appears and disappears in death; that one is doomed to suffering and loss. And no one is exactly as he was an instant previous, nor will he be the same as he is now an instant hence. Who could have trust where so much change is seen, for who is worthy if he be but dust? Salvation is undoing of all this. For constancy arises in the sight of those whose eyes salvation has released from looking at the cost of keeping guilt, because they chose to let it go instead.

Salvation does not ask that you behold the spirit and perceive the body not. It merely asks that this should be your choice. For you can see the body without help, but do not understand how to behold a world apart from the body. It is your world salvation will undo, and let you see another world your eyes could never find.

Are you invulnerable? Then the world is harmless in your sight. Do you forgive? Then is the world forgiving, for you have forgiven it its trespasses, and so it looks on you with eyes that see as yours. Are you a body? So is all the world perceived as treacherous, and out to kill. Are you a spirit, deathless, and without the promise of corruption and the stain of sin upon you? So the world is seen as stable, fully worthy of your trust; a happy place to rest in for a while, where nothing need be feared, but only loved. Who is unwelcome to the kind in heart? And what could hurt the truly innocent?

31.7. The Savior's Vision

Learning is change. Salvation does not seek to use a means as yet too alien to your thinking to be helpful, nor to make the kinds of change you could not recognize. Concepts are needed while perception lasts, and changing concepts is salvation's task. For concepts must deal in contrasts, not in truth, which has no opposite and cannot change. In this world's concepts are the guilty "bad"; the "good" are innocent. And no one here but holds a concept of himself in which he counts the "good" to pardon him the "bad." Nor does he trust the "good" in anyone, believing that the "bad" must lurk behind. This concept emphasizes treachery, and trust becomes impossible. Nor could it change while you perceive the "bad" in you.

You could not recognize your "evil" thoughts as long as you see value in attack. You will perceive them sometimes, but will not see them as meaningless. And so they come in fearful form, with content still concealed, to shake your sorry concept of yourself and blacken it with still another "crime." You cannot give yourself your innocence, for you are too confused about yourself. But should one brother dawn upon your sight as wholly worthy of forgiveness, then your concept of yourself is wholly changed. Your "evil" thoughts have been forgiven with this brother, because you let them all affect you not. No longer do you choose that you should be the sign of evil and of guilt in him. And as you give your trust to what is good in this brother, you give it to the good in you.

By focusing upon the good in him, the body grows decreasingly persistent in your sight, and will at length be seen as little more than just a shadow circling round the good. And this will be your concept of yourself, when you have reached the world beyond the sight your eyes alone can offer you to see. For you will not interpret what you see without the Aid that God has given you. And in His sight there is another world.

Have faith in your brother who walks with you, so that your fearful concept of yourself may change. And look upon the good in him, that you may not be frightened by your "evil" thoughts because they do not cloud your view of him. And all this shift requires is that you be willing that this happy change occur. No more than this is asked. On its behalf, remember what the concept of yourself that now you hold has brought you in its wake, and welcome the glad contrast offered you. Hold out your hand, that you may have the gift of kind forgiveness which you offer one whose need for it is just the same as yours. And let the cruel concept of yourself be changed to one that brings the peace of God.

The concept of yourself that *now* you hold would guarantee your function here remain forever unaccomplished and undone. And thus it dooms you to a bitter sense of deep depression and futility. Yet it need not be fixed, unless you choose to hold it past the hope of change, and keep it static and concealed within your mind. Give it instead to Him Who understands the changes that it needs to let it serve the function given you to bring you peace. Alternatives are in your mind to use, and you can see yourself another way. Would you not rather look upon yourself as needed for salvation of the world, instead of as salvation's enemy?

The concept of the self stands like a shield, a silent barricade before the truth, and hides it from your sight. All things you see are images, because you look on them as through a barrier that dims your sight and warps your vision, so that you behold nothing with clarity. The light is kept from everything you see. At most, you glimpse a shadow of what lies beyond. At least, you merely look on darkness, and perceive the terrified imaginings that come from guilty thoughts and concepts born of fear. And what you see is hell, for fear is hell. All that is given you is for release; the sight, the vision and the inner Guide all lead you out of hell with those you love beside you, and the universe with them.

Behold your role as savior within the universe! To every part of true creation has the Lord of Love and life entrusted all salvation from the misery of hell. And to each one has He allowed the grace to be a savior to the holy ones especially entrusted to his care. And this he learns when first he looks upon one brother as he looks upon himself, and sees the mirror of himself in him. Thus is the concept of himself laid by, for nothing stands between his sight and what he looks upon, to judge what he beholds. And in this single vision does he see the face of Christ, and understands he looks on everyone as he beholds this one. For there is light where darkness was before, and now the veil is lifted from his sight.

CHAPTER 31

The veil across the face of Christ (the fear of God and of salvation, and the love of guilt and death) they all are different names for just one error; that there is a space between you and your brother, kept apart by an illusion of yourself that holds him off from you, and you away from him. The sword of judgment is the weapon that you give to the illusion of yourself, that it may fight to keep the space that holds your brother off unoccupied by love. Yet while you hold this sword, you must perceive the body as yourself, for you are bound to separation from the sight of him who holds the mirror to another view of what he is, and thus what you must be.

The savior's vision is as innocent of what your brother is as it is free of any judgment made upon yourself. It sees no past in anyone at all. And thus it serves a wholly open mind, unclouded by old concepts, and prepared to look on only what the present holds. It cannot judge because it does not know. And recognizing this, it merely asks, "What is the meaning of what I behold?" Then is the answer given. And the door held open for the face of Christ to shine upon the one who asks, in innocence, to see beyond the veil of old ideas and ancient concepts held so long and dear against the vision of the Christ in you.

Be vigilant against temptation, then, remembering that it is but a wish, insane and meaningless, to make yourself a thing that you are not. And think as well upon the thing that you would be instead. Temptation is a thing of madness, pain and death; a thing of treachery and black despair, of failing dreams and no remaining hope except to die, and end the dream of fear. This is temptation; nothing more than this. Can this be difficult to choose against? Consider what temptation is, and see the real alternatives you choose between. There are but two. Be not deceived by what appears as many choices. There is hell or Heaven, and of these you choose but one.

Let not the world's light, given unto you, be hidden from the world. It needs the light, for it is dark indeed, and men despair because the savior's vision is withheld and what they see is death. Their savior stands, unknowing and unknown, beholding them with eyes unopened. And they cannot see until he looks on them with seeing eyes, and offers them forgiveness with his own. Can you to whom God says, "Release My Son!" be tempted not to listen, when you learn that it is you for whom He asks release? And what but this is what this course would teach? And what but this is there for you to learn?

31.8. Choose Once Again

Choose once again if you would take your place among the saviors of the world, or would remain in hell, and hold your brothers there.

You always choose between your weakness and the strength of Christ in you. And what you choose is what you think is real. Simply by never using weakness to direct your actions, you have given it no power. And the light of Christ in you is given charge of everything you do. For you have brought your weakness unto Him, and He has given you His strength instead.

Trials are but lessons that you failed to learn presented once again, so where you made a faulty choice before you now can make a better one, and thus escape all pain that what you chose before has brought to you. In every difficulty, all distress, and each perplexity Christ calls to you and gently says, "My brother, choose again." He would not leave one source of pain unhealed, nor any image left to veil the truth. He would not leave you comfortless, alone in dreams of hell, but would release your mind from everything that hides His face from you. His Holiness is yours because He is the only power that is real in you. His strength is yours because He is the Self that God created as His only Son.

The images you make cannot prevail against what God Himself would have you be. Be never fearful of temptation, then, but see it as it is; another chance to choose again, and let Christ's strength prevail in every circumstance and every place you raised an image of yourself before. For what appears to hide the face of Christ is powerless before His majesty, and disappears before His holy sight. The saviors of the world, who see like Him, are merely those who choose His strength instead of their own weakness, seen apart from Him. They will redeem the world, for they are joined in all the power of the Will of God. And what they will is only what He wills.

Learn, then, the happy habit of response to all temptation to perceive yourself as weak and miserable with these words:

> *I am as God created me.*
> *His Son can suffer nothing.*
> *And I am His Son.*

Thus is Christ's strength invited to prevail, replacing all your weakness with the strength that comes from God and that can never fail. And thus are miracles as natural as fear and agony appeared to be before the choice for holiness was made. For in that choice are false distinctions gone, illusory alternatives laid by, and nothing left to interfere with truth.

You are as God created you, and so is every living thing you look upon, regardless of the images you see. What you behold as sickness and as pain, as weakness and as suffering and loss, is but temptation to perceive yourself defenseless and in hell. Yield not to this, and you will see all pain, in every form, wherever it occurs, but disappear as mists before the sun. A miracle has come to heal God's Son, and close the door upon his dreams of weakness, opening the way to his salvation and release. Choose once again what you would have God's Son be, remembering that every choice you make establishes your own identity as you will see it and believe it is.

Deny me not the little gift I ask, when in exchange I lay before your feet the peace of God, and power to bring this peace to everyone who wanders in the world uncertain, lonely, and in constant fear. For it is given you to join with your brother, and through the Christ in you unveil his eyes, and let him look upon the Christ in him.

Chapter 31

My brothers in salvation, do not fail to hear my voice and listen to my words. I ask for nothing but your own release. There is no place for hell within a world whose loveliness can yet be so intense and so inclusive it is but a step from there to Heaven. To your tired eyes I bring a vision of a different world, so new and clean and fresh you will forget the pain and sorrow that you saw before. Yet this is a vision which you must share with everyone you see, for otherwise you will behold it not. To give this gift is how to make it yours. And God ordained, in loving kindness, that it be for you.

Let us be glad that we can walk the world, and find so many chances to perceive another situation where God's gift can once again be recognized as ours! And thus will all the vestiges of hell, the secret sins and hidden hates be gone. And all the loveliness which they concealed appear like lawns of Heaven to our sight, to lift us high above the thorny roads we traveled on before the Christ appeared. Hear me, my brothers, hear and join with me. God has ordained I cannot call in vain, and in His certainty I rest content. For you will hear, and you will choose again. And in this choice is everyone made free.

And now we say "Amen." For Christ has come to dwell in the abode You set for Him before time was, in calm eternity. The journey closes, ending at the place where it began. No trace of it remains. Not one illusion is accorded faith, and not one spot of darkness still remains to hide the face of Christ from anyone. Thy Will is done, complete and perfectly, and all creation recognizes You, and knows You as the only Source it has. Clear in Your likeness does the light shine forth from everything that lives and moves in You. For we have reached where all of us are one, and we are home, where You would have us be.

Glossary

[Note: The definitions are not meant for doctrinal purposes, as doctrine can create rigidity and exclusivity, and cause distractions. The definitions are offered in order to provide a language context so that anyone can recognize and apply the universal wisdom this Course has to offer, regardless of one's religion or spiritual practice.]

altar	A place in the mind that chooses what we are devoted to. It is a place where one chooses between God and the ego.
Atonement	Rectifying the false belief in the separation of God and human by accepting the Truth that we are One with God. The release from guilt by complete acceptance through forgiveness; the knowledge that we are all joined together and not separate.
attack	The expression of anger toward others. It is an attempt to justify our own guilt by projecting it out unto others.
awaken	A shift in consciousness. An aperception of true reality which had been previously unrealized. The continuance of such realizations brings us to the recognition of our oneness with all of existence.
body	A physical instrument (device) our mind uses to communicate with the outer world. The body is neutral and has no opinions or influence of its own. Only the mind assigns meaning to things.
Christ	Our shared Identity of Oneness. The *Self* that God created by the extension of His Spirit. Our spiritual Identity.
Christ vision	Spiritual sight; seeing beyond the body and the ego. Interpreting others behaviors as (1) an act of love or (2) a calling out for love. *Seeing* both as no reason for defense or attack, and every reason for extending love. The ability to mentally *see* beyond all worldly interference and *see* the light of holiness in everything.
content and form	All things in this world have two aspects, the *form* and the *content*. *Form* refers to "the things" in the world while *content* is the meaning behind those things. We must realize that what will bring lasting change in us is not the change of form, but a change in how we perceive the meaning (content) of things.

create (self-mind)	The power of the mind "to make" something in this physical world.
create (Self-Mind)	The act of extending God's love "outward" by acceptance and forgiveness; extending God's Kingdom.
Creation	The Oneness of God's Kingdom.
crucifixion	The crucifixion is the symbol of the ego, whereas the resurrection is the symbol of awakening. Each day, each hour and minute, we are deciding between the crucifixion and the resurrection; between the ego and God. The ego is the choice for guilt, and God is the choice for guiltlessness.
darkness	Thoughts of illusions and separation, denial of eternal Reality.
death	The expiration of the physical device called a body. Death is the superficial proof of the misguided concept that we are not eternal, thus supposedly confirming our separation from the undying God. In this viewpoint, we are not eternal because we can die and God cannot.
devil	An egoic projection that shifts the blame of calamity and suffering onto a powerful external entity, making it the responsible source. This fear-based thinking augments our feeling of separation from our Creator, thereby causing suffering.
dream	Living in illusions; living in time and space.
ego	The ego is a part of the mind (a set of beliefs) that promotes fear and separation. It tenaciously seeks for validation and fulfillment in the material world. Conditions in the material world are the results of projections, perceptions, and actions involving our emotions, thoughts, and attitudes. The ego habitually involves itself in various dramas and struggles, aggrandizing the little self and its story in order to distract us from our real purpose of knowing God and His Creations. The process of *waking up* and getting beyond the ego's deceptions is the pathway to salvation, and finding peace, joy, and contentment in this world.
error	A wrong decision, mistake, or mis-creation of the mind. Only the mind is capable of errors and they are expressed through the body. Something we perceive as punishable and irreversible, which can cause great anxiety. Errors are corrected through forgiveness.

error (original)	The thought system based on the separation from God, followed by the fear of God. The feeling of being cast out of heaven.
extension (self)	The thoughts of the self-mind expressed outward causing "worldly effects".
extension (Self)	The inner radiance of God given out to others. Extending love, forgiveness, and healing to others. The ability of our spirit to express forgiveness and experience oneness.
faithlessness	Faith in the little self of illusions, lacking faith in God. Belief in separation.
fear	A sensation of vulnerability, despair, doubt, confusion, and anxiety. The emotion created by the belief we are separated from the Divine.
forgiveness	Seeing ourselves and others with the vision of Christ which shifts our perception away from blame, resentment, judgment, punishment, and differences. Being able to take ownership of our thoughts and actions without fear. In this way, we can view wrongness as a projection of separation, and understand that forgiveness is the plan for salvation.
free will	The freedom of choice in the world of time and space. It is a free choice as to which voice to listen to, the ego or the Holy Spirit. The freedom to choose a thought of separation or a thought of oneness.
God	The infinite and eternal Source of all that exists. The One Who has no gender, no form, and no ego. One Who is pure Love, without any anger or attack.
guilt	The negative emotion experienced when we believe we have committed an offense or wrongdoing, causing us to feel separated from God and others. Fear arises because we mistakenly think God will punish us for our misconduct, which in turn continues the cycle of feeling guilty and afraid.
guiltlessness	The removal of the concept of guilt as being something wrong and punishable. The children of God are not guilty, but rather in a state of growth and awakening – the evolution of shifting our worldly perceptions into an internal knowing of the Christ within. It is the truth about who we are as His Creations.

heal	To heal is to correct the perception that we are separate from God and others. It is the mending of the mind's thought system that believes that the self is comprised only of a body that suffers. Healing is releasing the illusion of fear that we are vulnerable and can be victims of the world. Our bodies experience physical sickness, but our true Identity is Spirit, not a body. Healing occurs when we let go of the attachment to the body and embrace the unity with God and others.
Heaven	It is a state of mind in which we see the world as a place of union, peace, joy and serenity, without the veil of fear upon it. It is an awareness of perfect unity, and the knowledge that there is nothing else; nothing outside this unity. Heaven can be experienced in the world through the channel of unified relationships; which is accomplished through the extending and receiving of love and acceptance.
hell	It is a state of mind in which we seem to be separate, vulnerable, deficient, unfulfilled, and mistreated. A feeling that someone or something is trying to control or harm us, and we have to fight or flee to be safe. It is the pursuit of the egoic thought system which lead us to selfish and destructive behaviors that are rooted in fear and guilt; which cause pain and suffering to us and others.
holy instant	Any moment when we still our minds and become centered and present. In this stillness, we have no sense of fear, and nothing stands in the way of our connection to God's acceptance. We are illuminated with true oneness and freedom. The holy instant is a learning device that can be used to teach and share love's meaning, a moment we can experience the feeling of peace, joy, and love; a release from past and future; alignment with unity and oneness. It is an opportunity to receive guidance, and identify with what we are. Ultimately, our goal is to make every instant a holy instant.
holy relationship	A relationship of forgiveness and truth. The process of personal growth, through Christ's vision where one's perceptions change the experience of separation to embracing oneness.
Holy Spirit	The communication link from God to us, the Voice for God, the Internal Teacher. The Holy Spirit's function is (1) to translate the fear we see in the world into the knowledge that fear is a false perception (2) to show us that separation is error and how to express love's unity through forgiveness (3) to teach us the joy of *what we are*.

host to God	Observing God within ourselves.
hostage to the ego	Listening to the confused and limited split (ego) mind. Choosing to think thoughts of separation.
idol	The allegiance to an external thing, body, place, substance, possession, relationship, idea, or achievement that we believe holds our escape from pain and the answer to pleasure. A belief that those effects will bring us to completion as a substitution for what God has to offer.
illusion	Something that deceives by producing a false or misleading impression of reality.
insanity	The state of believing in the ego's system of control and manipulation which create repetitive and destructive thoughts and emotions that maintain the feelings of isolation and separation. The thought that we can control our life while defending against things trying to take control of it.
Jesus	One of God's Sons, and brother to us all. Jesus serves as our role model in the awakening unto Christ consciousness.
judgment	The mental process of deciding and selecting as to what to accept or reject. When wrongly used, it promotes the reality of separation and specialness. The correct use of judgment is to judge the ego's voice as insane and replace it with the sanity of God's Voice.
justice	The principle which gives love and forgiveness to everyone with complete impartiality and without limit.
Kingdom of God	Oneness with God.
lack	The belief that we are not enough, or that we do not have enough. This belief is founded on the misguided principle that there is not enough to go around, and we try to fill that lack by acquiring "things". We imagine that those things will at last make us feel safe, accepted, and satisfied.
love	The essence of *being*; which contains the emotions of acceptance, peace and joy. Love is already within each of us, and as the blocks to love's awareness are removed (such as; guilt, shame, etc.), we become mindful that love always has and always will encircle us and everything.

GLOSSARY

mind	The expression of the self that includes awareness, choice, thought, and emotion. Mind is non-physical, not to be confused with the brain.
Mind of God	The promoter of the Spirit delivering creative energy as an extension of God's Oneness.
miracle	A divine healing of human perception; a change of mind that shifts perception from guilt and fear to love and forgiveness. The undoing of delusions and illusion through divine revelation. It is an awakening that heals the mind from pain and suffering.
mis-create	The act of projection, rejection, fear, and separation.
murder	Thoughts of blame, anger, revenge, and vengeance toward ourselves or another. What is not love, is murder.
perception	The manner in which we process our understanding of the world around us, which we inherently see as entirely separate from ourselves. Perceptions define how we see the world; some perceptions are right-minded some are wrong-minded. Both influence our thoughts, beliefs, actions, and feelings. Miracles change distorted perceptions into perceptions that foster love.
projection	The act of deflecting our own internal conflicts and suffering onto others, making it appear as though other people are the ones that carry these damages and not ourselves. It is a method of separatism that demonstrates internal guilt and anguish over our perceived sins, and extends this guilt onto others at the same time.
right-minded	The part of our mind that contains the Holy Spirit which allows us to see the "real world" through Christ's Vision. The state of mind in which the escape from fear is possible.
sacrifice	A belief in the ego's thought system that someone must lose if another is to gain. A perception that we must pay a price to receive God's Love. It is the ego, not God, that demands sacrifice.
salvation	Correction to the thoughts of separation. The undoing of the belief in sin and guilt; a change of mind, through the power of miracles.
sickness	It is the part of the mind that believes in separation. Confusion and wrong-mindedness that does not allow us to recognize the Oneness of all creation. It is the expression of fear and vulnerability. **Regardless of the conditions that our bodies experience, our true Identity is Spirit, not a body.**

sin	A mistake, error, wrong decision, or imagining against God's laws or goodness. It is the lack of love. The belief that we are separated from God and this causes us to withdraw from Him into a state of folly. We think God demands punishment and the ego's goal is to make sin a permanent reality. Yet, to God, sin is simply an error and therefore easily forgiven and healed.
Son of God	We are all the One Son of God. Mankind is not separate from the universal Self Who encompasses all beings.
Sonship	The sum of all that God created.
specialness	The idea of being superior to others, which requires others to be inferior. Specialness always makes comparisons and judgments, thereby becoming the source of separation. We crave it because we think that specialness is the opposite of rejection. It is a feeble attempt to get what we feel God has withheld. In truth, God's love is indiscriminate and thus makes specialness irrelevant.
special function	The function of extending forgiveness, acceptance, and love. Our assignment in His plan for the salvation of the world.
special relationship	A relationship with someone that we think will contribute to our specialness and save us from the perceived lack we feel within ourselves. This love is not real and will sooner or later end in disappointment. God's answer to this mistaken endeavor is to create holy relationships joined together by His Love. Refer to holy relationship.
spirit	The very essence of God and creation. The energy of Oneness. The core of our true nature which is nonphysical, eternal, formless, changeless, holy and perfect.
split-mind	A mind divided among two parts; the "right mind" or home of God, and the "wrong mind" or home of the ego. The right mind embraces love, acceptance, and peace, while the wrong mind promulgates fear, sin, and guilt. In this divided state, the mind can become confused and short-circuits, cutting off our ability to create and communicate with God and others.
teacher of God	The process of examining the thoughts about "what we believe we are" for the purpose of undoing the sense of separation from God. Sorting out truth from illusion to advance to higher perceptions that get expressed out in the world of time and space.

temptation	It is an attraction to make a wrong decision, which would lead to an outcome you do not want. Temptation is an assertion that some things have a powerful appeal - making them harder to resist. It is the perception that they can bring us satisfaction as a substitute for God's Love. Temptation feeds on the internal feeling of lack – lack of things, love, or specialness.
time and space	The "physical world" which is home to illusions of separation, where the body and mind are acting out in a linear progression. The "place" where love and fear, joy and pain, forgiveness and judgment, peace and attack, birth and death occur. It is where past, present, and future compete for our attention, with past and future dominating our thoughts, distracting us from the reality of the present. To the struggling-self, it is a prison; to the awakening-Self, it is classroom.
vision	"Seeing" through the eyes of Christ rather than seeing through the eyes of the body. Seeing beyond the body to the spirit which leads to true perception.
wrong-minded	The part of our separated mind entangled with the ego's thought system, which creates and stockpiles false perceptions.

Glossary resources:

Glossary-Index for *A Course in Miracles* (6th edition) by Kenneth Wapnick

Glossary of Terms from *A Course in Miracles* (2nd edition) by Robert Perry

A Course in Miracles Textbook by Helen Schucman

Google

THE FOUNDATION FOR INNER PEACE

To learn more about *A Course in Miracles*, I recommend you visit the website of the authorized publisher and copyright holder of the Course, the Foundation for Inner Peace: **www.acim.org**. While there are many excellent organizations supporting study of *A Course in Miracles*, this is the original one with the greatest variety and depth of Course-related materials, including biographies and photos of the scribes, DVDs, free access to daily Lessons, audio recordings, information about the many languages into which the Course has been translated, and electronic versions of the Course, including mobile device apps.

The Foundation for Inner Peace is a non-profit organization dedicated to uplifting humanity through *A Course in Miracles*. The organization depends on donations and is currently immersed in translating the Course into many languages (26 to date). The Foundation also donates thousands of copies of the Course. If you would like to support more people to benefit from *A Course in Miracles*, donating to the Foundation for Inner Peace or one of the many other fine Course-related organizations would be a worthy endeavor. A portion of the proceeds from this book will be donated to the Foundation for Inner Peace and other organizations proliferating the message of *A Course in Miracles*.

Book Recommendations

A Course in Miracles Combined Volume	Helen Schucman
The Bhagavad Gita A New Translation	Stephen Mitchell
The Upanishads: A Classic of Indian Spirituality	Eknath Easwaran
Tao Te Ching	Lao Tzu
The Heart of the Buddha's Teaching	Thich Nhat Hanh
The Power of Now	Eckhart Tolle
A New Earth	Eckhart Tolle
A Return to Love	Marianne Williamson
From Futility to Happiness	Kenneth Wapnick
The Way of Mastery	Shanti Christo Foundation
Resurrecting Jesus	Adyashanti
The Four Agreements	Don Miguel Ruiz
Mindfulness for Beginners	Jon Kabat-Zinn
Excuses Begone	Wayne Dyer
From Plagues to Miracles	Robert S. Rosenthal
Is God a Mathematician	Mario Livio
The Power of Awareness	Neville Goddard
Take me to Truth	Nouk Sanchez / Tomas Vieira
Three Magic Words	Uell S. Andersen
Living a Course in Miracles	Jon Mundy
A Gradual Awakening	Stephen Levine
Jesus the Son of Man	Kahlil Gibran
I Don't Believe in Atheists	Chris Hedges
The Presence Process	Michael Brown
Ask and it is Given	Esther and Jerry Hicks
Path of Light	Robert Perry
Journey Without Distance	Robert Skutch
The ACIM Mentor Articles: Answers for Students of ACIM	Elizabeth Cronkhite
A Course in Miracles for Dummies Volume I & II	Thomas Wakechild
The Bible	

Made in the USA
Coppell, TX
21 February 2022